SEX WORK & Sex Workers

Sexuality & Culture   Volume 2

Sexuality & Culture

EDITOR-IN-CHIEF
Barry M. Dank
(Sociology)
California State University, Long Beach

MANAGING EDITOR
Roberto Refinetti
(Psychology)
Birmingham, Alabama

FILM REVIEW EDITOR
Warren Farrell *(Gender Psychology)*, Encinitas, California

ASSOCIATE EDITORS
Klaus de Albuquerque *(Sociology)*, College of Charleston
Priscilla Alexander *(Sex Research)*, North American Task Force on Prostitution
Elizabeth Rice Allgeier *(Psychology)*, Bowling Green State University
Ferrel Christensen *(Philosophy)*, University of Alberta
John Fekete *(Cultural Studies)*, Trent University
Martin Fiebert *(Psychology)*, California State University, Long Beach
Joseph S. Fulda *(Philosophy)*, New York City
John J. Furedy *(Psychology)*, University of Toronto
Valerie Jenness *(Sociology)*, University of California, Irvine
Rhoda Estep Macdonald *(Sociology)*, California State University, Stanislaus
Louis Marinoff *(Philosophy)*, City College of New York
Michael E. Mills *(Psychology)*, Loyola Marymount University
Daphne Patai *(Spanish & Portuguese)*, University of Massachusetts, Amherst
Roberto Hugh Potter *(Criminology)*, Morehead State University
Eugene Volokh *(Law)*, University of California, Los Angeles
Cathy Young *(Journalism)*, Cato Institute

CONSULTING EDITORS
Grant Brown *(Management)*, University of Lethbridge
Vern L. Bullough *(History and Sociology)*, State University of New York
Leslie Cole *(Sociology)*, University of Southern California
James P. Dillard *(Communication)*, University of Wisconsin, Madison
James Elias *(Sex Research)*, California State University, Northridge
David F. Greenberg *(Sociology)*, New York University
Marvin B. Krims *(Psychoanalysis)*, Harvard Medical School
Robert P. Maccubbin *(Literature)*, College of William & Mary
Kevin Macdonald *(Psychology)*, California State University, Long Beach
Wolfgang Hirczy de Miño *(Political Science)*, Oklahoma State University
John K. Noyes *(Theory of Literature)*, University of Cape Town, South Africa
Sakire Pogun *(Physiology)*, Ege University, Turkey
Pepper Schwartz *(Sociology)*, University of Washington
Laurence Senelick *(Performance)*, Tufts University
Richard W. Smith *(Psychology)*, California State University, Northridge
Gerard Sullivan *(Behavioral Sciences)*, University of Sydney, Australia
Donald Symons *(Evolutionary Psychology)*, University of California, Santa Barbara

Barry M. Dank, Editor-in-Chief
Roberto Refinetti, Managing Editor

SEX WORK & Sex Workers

Sexuality & Culture   Volume 2

Transaction Publishers
New Brunswick (U.S.A.) and London (U.K.)

This book is printed on acid-free paper that meets the American National Standard for Permanence of Paper for Printed Library Materials.

ISSN: 1095-5143
ISBN: 0-7658-0491-3
Printed in the United States of America

Sexuality & Culture

Volume 2   1998

THEMATIC ISSUE: SEX WORK AND SEX WORKERS

SEX WORK, SEX WORKERS, AND BEYOND

Barry M. Dank
Editor-in-Chief

This issue of *Sexuality & Culture* is dedicated to a central theme: Sex Work and Sex Workers. The concepts of sex work and sex workers embrace myriad forms of commercialized sexuality: prostitution, pornography, erotic dancing, phone sex, dominatrixes, and more. Each form of sex work is itself extremely diverse. For example, falling under the rubric of prostitution are drug addicted street hustlers, teenage Thai girls sold by their parents to brothel owners, and high-priced career call girls working as independent entrepreneurs or for escort agencies and mainstream corporations. Similarly, pornography embraces myriad forms of diverse sexualities.

Cross-cutting these diverse forms of sex work are legal definitions. Contemporarily, prostitution flourishes in diverse jurisdictions regardless of whether it is deemed legal or illegal. Such is also the situation with regard to nude erotic dancing and pornography. Given the widespread availability of commercial sexual services, it is not surprising that persons working in this field are often referred to as being part of the sex industry.

Film-studies professor Linda Williams has observed that pornography has traditionally been off-scene, but now it has become highly visible and on-scene. This is the case for just about all forms of sex work. Such accessibility has been technology-driven. Explicit sexual imageries effectively became on-scene in the United States in the 1980s with the introduction of the VCR into American homes. Very quickly, sexually explicit videos became a vitally important product for the retail video business. In the 1990s, access to such videos increased via the pay-per-view TV

1

Spice Channel, and it skyrocketed as the modem, the telephone, and the computer became linked allowing a vast array of sexually related materials to be brought into the home. These materials have included not only pornographic images, but actual access to prostitution (via escort services), to dominatrixes, and to a wide variety of sexual aids that are available for purchase.

Efforts to stop the growth of the sex industries have failed. The 1997 Supreme Court decision declaring the Community Decency Act unconstitutional aborted governmental efforts to control accessibility on the Internet. Web search engines have come into being that totally focus on sexual materials; one such search engine, Persian Kitty Adult Links, has approximately 240,000 hits per day. Efforts to make many forms of pornography illegal under the rubric of sex discrimination in the United States have failed, but even in Canada, where such laws have been found to be constitutional, erotic materials of all sorts are highly available. Similarly, in reference to commercialized nude dancing, the 1991 U.S. Supreme Court decision, *Barnes v. Glen Theatre,* held that "public" nudity offered in commercial clubs not in view of persons outside of the club could be banned since the public's "moral disapproval" of nudity was held to outweigh the first amendment's protection of free expression. *Barnes v. Glen Theatre* has had little practical effect on the availability of nude dancing establishments. Such is also the case for prostitution in the United States, which remains illegal in most jurisdictions but which is still highly available in most cities.

Irrespective of the availability of commercialized sexual services and the impotence of the laws regulating said services, public disavowal and stigmatization of sex workers remain predominant. Playing a major role in the affirmation of this stigma and the associated stereotypical imageries of the sex worker has been an anti-sexual feminism that has been essentially university-based. Women's studies articles and texts have often promoted a purity feminism that has been victim-oriented. Sex workers have been held to lack sexual agency, and the state's intrusion into this area is seen as benefiting sex workers who have been held to be victimized by pimps, panderers, and predators. At the core of both the feminist and traditional religious condemnation of sex workers is the concept that women cannot freely choose sex work since this is at odds with what it means to be a woman. Consequently, protection becomes paramount. Such was the rhetoric of the advocates of the white slave trade mythology at the beginning of this century and such is the rhetoric of much of contemporary feminism.

A feminist victim-imagery of sex workers has not been without its critics. Pro-sex feminists and feminist sex workers and performance artists have come forward and articulated a dissenting form of feminism. Porn-star and now porn-producer Candida Royalle, who has emerged as a vocal critic of purity feminism, was instrumental in the establishment of Feminists for Free Expression. Kat Sunlove, owner of the *Spectator Magazine*—which is a guide to the sex scene in San Francisco—and a retired dominatrix, is well known for her lobbying activities in Sacramento, where she formally represents the Free Speech Coalition. Performance artist and ex-prostitute Annie Sprinkle is a committed advocate for a pro-sex feminism that is also embraced by pro-feminist writers such as Carol Queen, Susie Bright, Sallie Tisdale, Lacey Sloan, Wendy McElroy, and Shannon Bell.

Feminist imageries of sex workers as helpless victims are at odds with the reality of sex workers who have taken the initiative in organizing work/labor associations for sex workers. For example, exotic dancers Johanna Breyer and Dawn Passar organized the Exotic Dancer's Alliance in San Francisco; veteran porn star Sharon Mitchell has engaged in HIV prevention work for porn performers in Los Angeles; and porn-star Johnni Black and her husband David Johnson founded the Erotic Entertainers Guild. In 1998, sex worker activist Carol Leigh symbolically affirmed sex workers' affiliation with all laboring men and women by designating May 1 as Sex Worker's Solidarity Day in San Francisco.

The involvement of sex workers in labor activism is not limited to the United States. Wendy Chapkis in her book, *Live Sex Acts: Women Performing Erotic Labor*, which is reviewed in the current volume by Leslie Cole, provides evidence that a labor activism by sex workers transcends national borders. In this book,

Chapkis profiles sex work activist Jo Doezema, who has been an activist sex worker in both the Netherlands and the United Kingdom.

The global nature of sex work and sex worker's activism was highlighted by a conference of sex workers from throughout Asia, which was held in Calcutta in 1998 and was sponsored by the India-based Women Coordination Association. Conference attendees demanded legalization of prostitution and better working conditions to help prevent the spread of disease. In this volume, Bronwen Lichtenstein profiles sex-work activism in her article, "Reframing 'Eve' in the AIDS Era: The Pursuit of Legitimacy by New Zealand Sex Workers."

Of course, there have been a number of academic sex researchers and cultural critics who have never embraced the purity feminist framework of sex workers as helpless victims. Until recently, academic sex researchers almost always saw themselves as studying sex workers and not as working with them in their quest for knowledge. However, in 1997, historian Vern Bullough and sociologist Jim Elias—both professors at California State University, Northridge—joined forces with prostitute and prostitution-rights activist Norma Jean Almodovar, who is also the head of the Los Angeles chapter of COYOTE, in sponsoring the first International Conference on Prostitution (ICOP). ICOP represented a major breakthrough, as academics and sex workers worked together in presenting a professional scholarly conference for the benefit of both. I was personally in attendance at this conference, and it was as a result of this attendance that a commitment was made to devote this volume of *Sexuality & Culture* to the theme of sex work and sex workers. Such a commitment also embraced the goal of seeking contributions that would represent the diversity of those involved in sex work as well as contributions that would give greater insight into sex work issues, particularly issues relating to power and empowerment.

Many of the people who were in attendance at this conference have functioned as either editors or contributors to this volume. British sex worker and activist Jo Doezema reviews *Trafficking in Women, Forced Labour and Slavery-Like Practices in Mar-*

riage; porn star Nina Hartley reviews *Three in Love*; Valerie Jenness, a prostitution-rights scholar and associate editor of *Sexuality & Culture*, deals with core pro-sex feminist issues in her review of *Feminist Accused of Sexual Harassment*; and Carol Queen, who played a major organizational role at ICOP and is both a sex worker and a leading cultural critic of the contemporary sexual scene, has her 1997 book, *Real Live Nude Girl,* reviewed by Daphne Patai. Priscilla Alexander, one of the leading authorities on prostitution, was in attendance at ICOP and has functioned as associate editor; and both Jim Elias and Vern Bullough are consulting editors for *Sexuality & Culture*.

A number of articles in this volume deal with feminist imageries of the sex worker. Melanie Simmons ("Theorizing Prostitution: The Question of Agency") focuses on the various feminist conceptions of prostitutes and how such conceptions impact on agency issues. Kari Lerum ("Twelve-Step Feminism Makes Sex Workers Sick: How the State and the Recovery Movement Turn Radical Women into 'Useless Citizens'") reveals how dominant ideologies, including feminism, function to pathologize and victimize sex workers. Jody Norton ("Invisible Man: A Queer Critique of Feminist Anti-Pornography Theory") focuses on pornography and argues that feminist anti-pornography theory embraces an essentialist framework that functions to deny the ambiguities in pornographic representations of gender and power relations. Roberto Hugh Potter ("Long-Term Consumption of 'X-Rated' Materials and Attitudes toward Women among Australian Consumers of X-Rated Videos") finds, in a survey of Australian pornography consumers, that exposure to pornography does not impact on attitudes toward women. Merri Lisa Johnson ("Pole Work: Autoethnography of a Strip Club") deals with the complexity of her own experiences as a nude dancer, a complexity and richness that is often omitted in analyses by "outsiders." And, finally, Klaus de Albuquerque ("Sex, Beach Boys, and Female Tourists in the Caribbean") describes the negotiated sexual encounters between Barbados beach boys and female tourists and presents an overview of sex tourism in the Caribbean.

Needless to say, the articles and reviews in this issue of *Sexuality & Culture* are but a small contribution to the understanding of the sociology, psychology, and philosophy of sex work. Nevertheless, the material presented here constitutes a significant addition to the literature on the commercialization of sexuality. It contributes significantly to the analysis of the interaction of sexuality and culture.

TWELVE-STEP FEMINISM MAKES SEX WORKERS SICK: HOW THE STATE AND THE RECOVERY MOVEMENT TURN RADICAL WOMEN INTO "USELESS CITIZENS"

Kari Lerum
Department of Sociology, University of Washington
Seattle, WA 98195

Within the contemporary United States, sex work is typically viewed in terms of a disease, meaning that sex workers are seen as "sick." This medical understanding is due to the widespread jurisdiction of science, but other factors are at work as well: the "fit" with the bureaucratic nation-state, the ascendancy of the twelve-step recovery movement, the process of institutionalizing knowledge, and a climate of increased tolerance for "victims." Within these political, cultural, and institutional frames, experts—regardless of sympathetic or feminist intentions—often view sex workers condecendingly. Furthermore, the study of sex work has achieved social and scientific legitimacy at the price of dehumanizing sex workers. This dehumanization may not be intended, but it is a requirement for the production of contemporary institutionalized knowledge.

Introduction

In 1993, just prior to completing my master's thesis on sex work, I presented my findings for the first time to an eager, standing-room-only group of feminist scholars at the University of Washington. Though I knew my presentation would be controversial, nothing in my training as a sociologist had prepared me for the political uproar I was about to create. Throughout my talk, entitled, "Is it Exploitative if I Like it?: Sex Workers Compare Notes with Feminists and the Social Problems Industry," I was

7

aware that I was holding my audience in rapt attention. I noticed people both nodding and frowning, but more than anything I noticed that they cared about what I was saying. I described my interviews with women incarcerated for prostitution, compared these interviews with those I held with non-incarcerated sex workers, and pointed out that *all* of these women spoke of their sex work in complex, nuanced ways. None of them, even the most down-and-out, spoke of sex work in purely negative terms. None of them, even the most culturally privileged (who were more likely to "love" their work), portrayed sex work as unproblematic. I argued that experts rarely acknowledge sex work as a complicated experience; rather, experts hear what validates their position and disregard the rest—and this happens whether it is a feminist position, a social work position, or even a pro-sex work position. I argued that a better way to do research, and a method long advocated by prominent feminist theorists like Dorothy Smith (1979), is to take seriously the words of women and build those words into our theories about women. I proposed that the argument over whether sex work is *either* exploitative *or* liberating is a ridiculous one that produces ridiculous conclusions, and that this debate had little relevance to the complex, contradictory, and widely varied experiences of sex workers. I finished my talk with breathless enthusiasm and hope, and was met with polite, if enthusiastic, applause.

Little did I know, sitting to my immediate left was a prominent scholar of prostitution. Not a moment of post-applause calm had settled before the scholar turned to me, right index finger pointing, and began her stormy reprimand. She accused me of being an irresponsible researcher, of denying the vast amount of evidence that proves that most sex workers have been sexually abused, of trivializing the pain of sex workers, of being swept up with glamorized visions of prostitution. I responded with my feminist armor up, saying I was just following Dorothy Smith's lead— and if the women I interviewed claimed that they liked certain aspects about sex work, then I will report that. The scholar responded that if my interviewees claimed they liked their work, they only said that to impress me (the authority) or to maintain some pride under extremely humiliating circumstances. She also pointed out (and I think this is valid) that the unequal power dynamic between researcher and subject makes it virtually impossible for subjects to tell the "truth." And yet she did not offer a solution to this problem (such as give up some of our power as researchers) other than to suggest that I educate myself about which statements are untruthful and become aware that "they're not going to *admit* they're victims." The exchange went round and round; others chimed in to both our defenses, though no professors came to mine. I continued to reiterate that sex work is *not* completely liberating for anyone, and that many sex workers, especially street-level prostitutes, *do* experience great physical and emotional pain. But the stage was set, and I was cast as a traitor. The whole exchange not only left me with an enormous headache, but also a fresh commitment to understanding not only sex work, but the politics of its meaning.

Throughout history, humans have been fascinated with sex workers. Whether this fascination comes in the form of condemnation, titillation, pity, or celebration, it's clear that as an activity it captures the attention of many. The reason lies in considering why *anyone* or *anything* is fascinating; we are fascinated by people or things when we see them as unusual and exotic, as complex, as possessing some power we do not fully understand, and as symbolically relevant to our own lives and identities. If none of these features are present, the person or action is ignored, dismissed, and forgotten. With sex workers, this has never been the case. We do not ignore sex workers, we pay attention to them, and we pay attention because we have a personal stake in the matter. While there is tremendous variation in the economic and social *position* of our stakes, in the following pages I will discuss how most expert views of sex work are framed by a few dominant institutions, institutions that inevitably make sex workers "sick." I conclude by arguing that the study of sex work has achieved social and scientific legitimacy at the expense of dehumanizing sex workers, and that this dehumanization is not an unfortunate coincidence, but a *requirement* for the production of contemporary institutionalized knowledge.

Sex Work and the Business of Morals and Truth

Throughout written history, there are many examples of people attempting to make their own interpretation of sex work into a culturally hegemonic one—and as with any issue, the people with the most social pull "win" the right to legislate truth and morality (e.g., Marx, 1864/1996; Becker, 1963). Although in pre-Biblical times "temple prostitutes" were apparently considered honorable and holy (Walker, 1983), religious authorities later claimed that sex, especially for women, may only occur with a marriage mate sanctioned by the church (and state). But as religious authority began to weaken (corresponding with the rise of "scientific" authorities and a growing middle class), secular authorities began overtaking the business of morals and truth—including the truths about sex work. In the United States, secular authorities (e.g., politicians, police officers, social scientists, social workers, health officials, and feminist scholars) have linked commercial sex work with organized crime, sexually transmitted disease, substance abuse, sexual abuse, violence, and a generally unpleasant social climate. Their rationales for opposing sex work differ, but the overlap is vast. *Overall*, authorities still agree that sex work is a problem.

And so the official story about sex work is still that there is something inherently wrong with it, but the reasons have changed. Official accounts of sex work no longer describe the phenomenon as a "sin," and sex workers are no longer officially seen as the conduits of sin. Within the increasingly secularized climates of nineteenth-century Britain and North America, groups of new experts began asserting that prostitutes should be pitied rather than condemned, "taken in" rather than ostracized, and seen as "in trouble" rather than as trouble makers. These new experts were the women social reformers of the late nineteenth century—the same group of women we might retrospectively lump into the "first wave of feminism." The following is Kristin Luker's (1996) description of nineteenth-century women reformers in the United States:

> Women reformers, mobilizing for the first time as women, engineered a new way of talking and thinking about "women in trouble." Whether prostitutes, abandoned mistresses, or unmarried mothers, such "unfortunates"

were now defined as victims of social and economic circumstance rather than as moral pariahs. The reformers, who came out of a rich evangelical tradition, were armed with an implicit (and at times explicit) critique of gender relations. Most centrally, they saw themselves as not so different from the women they wished to help: anyone, they argued, could fall prey to sin and to the devil in the person of men. (Luker, 1996, p. 20)

These women reformers' approach created more sympathy for female sexual deviants, which reduced the sting of religious condemnation. However, the notion of "sin" did not immediately disappear: instead, evil became incarnate in promiscuous men rather than promiscuous women. In those times, sexual double standards were criticized, but the solution was seen as holding men to women's "naturally" chaste standards. Rather than arguing for increased female sexual freedoms, promiscuity was universally condemned, and men were at fault for all sex outside of marriage. During this transitional time, notions of sin remained, but the agents of temptation switched genders.

For contemporary western feminists, this religious framing of sex work seems distracting and irrelevant, since the task now is not to curtail the devil's manifestation in men, but to equalize societal entitlements. And yet, this integration of old (religious) and new (feminist) ideas is how all knowledge is made: new ideas are only "seen" if they can fit within an existing cultural frame. In that case, the frame was a religious one.

Feminism, religion, science, or any other philosophy, does not exist as a closed system. In the past century, people from all of these fields have influenced the official story about sex work, but their stories are also affected by their cultural contexts and institutional positions. Therefore, to better grasp the current approaches to sex work, it is helpful to consider the following three questions: 1) Which institutions dominate our contemporary theoretical frames?, 2) How do people get their ideas institutionalized, and what happens to an idea once it is institutionalized? and 3) What are the gaps between sex worker and expert accounts, and how concerned should we as social scientists be about such gaps? Answering these questions makes it easier to make sense of the politics of sex work, as well as to better evaluate any proposed "solutions."

Cultural and Institutional Frames

From Anger about Sexism to Concern about "Fixing" Women

Since the late 1800s and early 1900s, women's increasing activism began influencing expert attitudes about many issues affecting women, including sex work. As a result of this activism, there is today more official sympathy toward the "plight" of sex workers. However, an irony of this increased sympathy lies in how it has become fused with an *individualized* understanding of all social problems: so that a concern for people in troublesome circumstances becomes a concern for troubled people, a focus on fixing unfair social conditions becomes a focus on fixing people, and radical, structural critiques of gender inequality transform into worries about "fixing" women. How did this happen? Examples from history again give us clues.

In her informative book, *Prostitution in Victorian Society: Women, Class, and the State*, Judith Walkowitz (1980) traces the history of how a well-meaning radical women's group, the "Ladies National Association" (LNA), organized around the issue of sex work. The group formed in Britain during the 1860s in response to Britain's "Contagious Diseases Acts," which required any unescorted woman to submit to official genital examinations—a measure which made sex workers targets for harassment, and institutionalized sexual double standards for everyone. For a brief time, the women of the LNA were able to summon public indignation over these Acts. However, due to their lack of cultural and legislative power, LNA members failed in their attempt to discard these Acts, as well as their goal of requiring men to emulate women's "superior" (i.e., chaste) sexual standards. Furthermore, instead of halting men's sexual licentiousness, the anger of the LNA "was easily co-opted and rechanneled into repressive anti-vice campaigns" leading to a "rise of social-purity crusades and...police crackdowns on streetwalkers and brothel keepers" (Walkowitz, 1980, p. 7). These state-sponsored crusades created a fearful and punitive climate for female sex workers, where they (but not their clients) were stigmatized, isolated, and driven away from networks of community support—all of which certainly brought these women distress and increased their reliance on (male) organized criminals.

Thus, the mixture of nineteenth-century religious and feminist ideas with the British legal system seems to have hurt sex workers more than it helped them. Sex workers became marked as an official "problem," and what began as feminist and religious indignation over state-sponsored sexism resulted in even *more* state-sponsored harassment of specific women—those identified as prostitutes. This result should not be explained away as an anomalous, unintended coincidence; once the eye of the state rests upon a group spotlighted as "troublesome," that group becomes an easy target of interrogation, scrutiny, and control. At first, well-meaning people may merely place their ideological spotlights on specific groups who are "in trouble," but eventually those spotlighted people may beseen as the *source* of trouble.

The Frame of Disease and Recovery

While religious and feminist views helped focus the British (and U.S.) state's attention on sex work around the turn of the twentieth century, this was also a growing time for a new cultural authority: science. In the United States, science began overtaking religious authority in the mid- to late 1800s, and its influence and authority continues to spread throughout American culture. Scientific trends have certainly come and gone (such as the popularity of social Darwinism and "scientific management"), but what remains is people's tendency to see science as the arbiter of truth. Particularly compelling has been the concept of "disease," which we understand as something that can and should be studied, isolated, and cured. And we not only see disease in the biological sense; since "disease" is something everyone avoids, the word also works as a strong metaphor, as Suzanne Pharr (1988) uses it when she calls homophobia a "societal disease." So, due to the cultural authority of science, "disease" has replaced "sin" as the legitimate explanation for why bad things happen to people.

In 1935, Bill Wilson and Dr. Robert Holbrook Smith, the founders of Alcoholics Anonymous, utilized this culturally compelling metaphor when they began referring to alcoholism as a disease. The metaphor worked, and thus began the onset of an enormous Twelve-Step empire. Scientifically speaking, alcoholism has never "really" been a disease (Fingarette, 1988; Rapping, 1996), but the prevalence of this metaphorical slogan is so vast that whether it is "true" or not has not mattered.

In *The Culture of Recovery*, Elayne Rapping (1996) argues that the hegemony of the Twelve-Step movement has created widespread faith in a disease-based understanding of behavior, so that not just alcoholism but *all* social problems are understood in terms of disease and recovery. The disease explanation of personal troubles is now so foundational that, when alternatives are proposed, people get confused and even frantic. For example, Rapping reports that on a talk show discussing eating disorders, "an audience member suggested that eating disorders were different from cancer, a biological disease which one did in fact 'just get'…rather than a form of behavior we learn." This proposal allegedly made audience members furious:

> "How can you question this woman's suffering?" said many participants, in one way or another. As though the idea that eating was not an addiction or disease somehow was a way of "blaming the victim" for her pain. "Of course she has a disease," said one and all in support of the distressed guest. (Rapping, 1996, p. 43)

Since the audience member was not blaming women for their eating disorders but was simply suggesting that this behavior was the result of social rather than biological processes, Rapping concludes that "the dominance of addiction theory thus works as an automatic censoring mechanism, making it difficult for any other way of thinking—even a feminist counter-agenda—to be credited" (p. 43).

This example comes from popular culture, but the disease model is also prevalent amongst experts outside the media lens—including those experts concerned with the "problem" of sex work. Here the story is often identical to that of talk shows: "Person X" (insert here person who: throws up his/her food, drinks too much, or sells sex) has no "choice," no power over his/her behavior, and therefore needs "treatment." What is distinctive about the treatment of sex workers, however, is that they are far more likely to be diagnosed as drug addicts or sexual abuse victims than as sexual deviants. One could imagine a situation in which sex workers are diagnosed as being "addicted" to selling sex, but instead of *directly* pathologizing sex work or sex workers, experts focus on the addictions and diseases that must be forcing people into such (pathological) behavior.

In my interviews and conversations with officials in the legal system and the "helping professions" (whether they be jail officials, counselors, social workers, or police officers), drug addiction and sexual abuse are always brought up as causes of prostitution. Not symptoms or correlates, but *causes*. It is sexual abuse and drug addiction that "force" women to be whores. If we treat those causes, they will stop acting that way.

In a 1995 videotaped interview with a Seattle Vice Officer, I asked the officer if he felt any "societal changes" needed to be made to help solve what he saw as the problem of prostitution. He responded, "oh, of course.... it's plagued with drugs...bad families...." I replied that some people felt that if women just had other options, other job opportunities, then they would not be as likely to go out on the street. He quickly shot that suggestion down, saying, "no, people don't go out because of lack of jobs; they go out because step-dad's raping her at home."

Sexual abuse and drug addiction clearly bring people pain and suffering, and people in the "helping professions" do observe, and are concerned about, these troubles amongst their sex worker clients (as they should be). Furthermore, the stress, humiliation, and violence that is integral to many sex workers' experiences should never be dismissed. However, what *should* change is the monopolistic frame through which these "bad things" are seen— not only because we could be released from individualistic, medical visions, but because it will enable "helpers" to see other people as something besides patients. Since the crucial aspects of sex work are now seen as "diseased," it follows that most helpers see sex workers as "sick."

The idea that all sex workers are forced into it certainly makes it easier for outsiders to sympathize, and it is obviously a better response than stoning sexual deviants to death, as people in Biblical times did. So, in addition to crediting early women reformers for creating a more measured, sympathetic understanding of sex work, perhaps the notion of "victims," is a necessary adaptation to an increasingly secularized, anonymous, nation-state environment. By this I mean that the less anchored people are in their community and extended family, the less they can rely on unconditional help, and the more they have to either pay for it or conduct campaigns to convince people that they are worthy of help. According to "attribution theory," people are more likely to help someone when they perceive that person's trouble as being outside their control, and the response is likely to come in the form of sympathy and pity. If, however, the person's need is perceived as due to a personal flaw, then people are less likely to help and more likely to respond with anger and irritation (Schmitt, 1994, p. 76). Yet, if the person asking for help is a long-time friend or family member, there is no need to play victim; help is simply part of the reciprocal contract of love and friendship. But if the person asking for help is a stranger—or someone people prefer to keep at arms length—then the victim approach is a rational one, since it increases the likelihood of help.

And so the victim story, in all the ways that it has come about, has brought women and sex workers (and anyone else on the outskirts of power) a reprieve from condemnation and sometimes very welcome help. If someone is forced into deviant outskirt behaviors, it is not their fault, and thus they should be helped, not blamed. In the early 1900s women activists promoted this idea, pointing out that sexist social conditions steer women towards all sorts of unhappy situations and behaviors. Today this structural critique is a basic sociological tenet, and it is an important one, since it takes the heat off "deviants" and begins the process of making the people "in charge" of social conditions accountable (although usually we get no further than a vague, non-confrontational blaming of "society"). Within this frame of structural blame, sex workers are victims, but at least someone or something (like "society") is held accountable for bad things. But with our current faith in disease, *no one* is accountable. Sex workers are still victims, but disease "just happens." Social problems experts are the "doctors," but they merely "treat" existing diseases. This approach results in both personal *and* political passivity, and this, as Rapping says, is "a far cry from feminism."

Contemporary Feminist Frames

This politically passive state of affairs cannot be what Andrea Dworkin and Catharine MacKinnon intended when, in the early 1980s, they began their thunderous attack against the sex industry. In the tradition of earlier women reformers, feminists like Dworkin and MacKinnon have strongly argued that sex work is not the product of faulty individuals, but of larger forces like patriarchy and economic inequality. They claimed that sex work is incompatible with gender equality; when a man "buys" a prostitute, he has the right to objectify, exploit, and abuse her as he wishes, and this leads him to see *all* women as potential property.

Due to the success of "second wave" (i.e., 1970s) feminism, a cultural frame existed in which such articulation of male abuses could be "seen," and institutions existed in which they could settle. And for a short time (primarily in the 1980s), the Dworkin/MacKinnon camp became the predominant feminist position on sex work. Feminist scholars articulated disturbing similarities between traditional gender roles and commercial sex work (e.g., Boyer and James, 1983) and traditional marriage and sex work: "[t]raditional marriage is premised on the long-term private ownership of a woman by an individual man, whereas the institution of prostitution is built upon the short-term public ownership of women by many men" (Giobbe, 1991, p. 144). However, these anti-sex work positions were not without feminist critics, and during the 1980s an ongoing argument known as the "sex wars" ensued amongst feminists. While these "wars" were initially lopsided,[1] the bald assumptions of the Dworkin/MacKinnon camp provided easy contrasting points, which probably made it easier for others to articulate a "pro-sex work" feminist frame. This new frame critiqued (and continues to critique) the anti-sex work feminist position as patronizing, sex-negative, and disrespectful of any professional pride a sex worker espouses. Furthermore, in direct contradiction to anti-sex work feminist assumptions, many of these critiques assert that sex work can radically *disrupt* patriarchy and traditional gender roles.

However, despite increasing articulation of pro-sex work feminism (and increasing proliferation of pro-sex work publications),[2] this particular feminist position is still seen as radical, and has yet to be institutionalized in most U.S. (or even feminist) institutions. Just four years ago, when I asked a spokesperson from the Seattle branch of the National Organization for Women about her position on prostitution, I received this standard reply:

> In general, the position is that prostitution, along with pornography, is a civil rights violation of women...in general..., that it's a form of violence against women, and that it is part of...patriarchal oppression of women. That would be in a nutshell. I mean it's a fairly complex issue.... We do not look down on women who earn their living through prostitution; rather we see it as a form of cultural oppression of women and violence against them.

In addition to institutionalizing their claims in feminist realms, anti-sex work feminists have also found a home in the legal realm. In 1983 and 1984, Dworkin and MacKinnon wrote and led efforts to install anti-pornography ordinances in Minneapolis and Indianapolis.[3] In 1985 the Los Angeles County Board of Supervisors considered an ordinance similar to the original Minneapolis version (Ellis et al., pp. 29, 64, 72). Although these legal measures did not stick, the ideas behind them made their way in through the State's back door. For example, in 1993, I attended a Washington State sponsored conference "for legal and social service professionals" in which clear threads of this feminist position were prominent. The conference began with a keynote speaker who linked sex work to universal patriarchal oppressions: "My hope is to inspire you...we must fight sexism, racism, homophobia. All of these oppressions are symptoms of prostitution." For an entire state-sponsored day, this speaker, along with a folder full of anti-sex work pamphlets, produced resounding anti-sex work feminist messages. Looking back on the experience, these messages now seem remarkable to me (since I was, after all, sitting amongst more police officers than women studies professors):

> Prostitution serves men alone. Nobody ever asks if it was good for her. Every time you look at the act itself it is unwanted sex. She is forced to leave her body and endure this. (Keynote speaker)

> The prostitute-client relationship is almost always one of abuse, degradation and violence. The "sex" which the client buys turns women's bodies into an instrument for men's use. The woman becomes a commodity and the trade of which she is the object seriously damages her identity and destroys her sense of self-worth. (Tremblay, 1987)

> As I talk to you about prostitution, I am referring to this as a system of cruelty to women. This is true whether it's an escort service, street work, working at the Four Seasons, or at a strip joint. (Keynote speaker)

The fact that the state now sees sex work as a "women's issue" as well as a moral or public health issue, is reflective of a significant cultural shift; it is a sign that feminism continues to succeed in heralding women as a legitimate group with interests and concerns independent of men. With this legitimacy comes the right to elbow one's way into state-sponsored conferences, into the inner circle—the place where cultural truths are made. However, why are only anti-sex work feminist positions allowed into the state's sacred circle? And why is it that when feminist ideas get institutionalized in state and social service industries, the targets are no longer sexism, racism, economic inequality, or homophobia, but sexual abuse and drug addiction?

Disease, Institutionalized Feminism, and the State: A Nice Fit

Institutionalized feminism is soft on structural critiques and heavy on individual solutions for at least two reasons: it fits better into state and other institutions, and it makes sense within our cultural frame. After "The State" squishes the radical out of any feminist thought, one crucial essence of the feminist anti-sex work position remains, and it remains because it resonates with state-sanctioned approaches. This crucial essence is the idea that sex workers are victims with no choice.

In addition to fitting into the state welfare system, the institutionalization of anti-sex work feminism is also understandable from the perspectives of the sociology of science and social problems theory. In her study of cancer research, Joan Fujimura (1987) shows that scientific solutions are possible only when they are simplified, or "doable." Bruno Latour (1987) points out that a scientific category is an extremely condensed version of "reality." Both Fujimura and Latour envision science, facts, and knowledge as a social process that *requires* the simplification of an empirical phenomenon. Similarly, social problems theorists, such as Gusfield (1989), have shown that remedies for social problems are usually narrowly focused—not because social problem workers are dim, but because this is institutionally required: "[I]f the condition is perceived as that of individual illness or deficiency, then there can be a social technology, a form of knowledge and skill, that can be effectively learned" (p. 433). Thus, while feminists have expansive and varied visions of why sex work is a "problem," patriarchy is not a scientifically "doable" problem. State institutionalized feminism, therefore, must be far more compressed.

What *is* a doable problem? It is something that is small, simple, and contained. Radical ideas like overthrowing patriarchy do not settle very well outside of feminist camps. But the notion that women are victims and that they have no choice *does* make sense; it fits right into the larger cultural frame of disease.

This victim notion also fits right into the need for large institutions (like the state) to encourage passivity and deference in its members. Alvin Gouldner (1970), a critic of standard solutions to social problems, argues that "[i]ncreasingly, the Welfare State's strategy is to transform the sick, the deviant, and the unskilled into *'useless citizens,'* and to return them to 'society' only after periods of hospitalization, treatment, counseling, training, or retraining" (Gusfield, 1989, p. 433, emphasis mine). Why would "the state" or anyone in the helping professions want a citizen to be "useless"? As Gusfield (1989) points out, the social problems industry *requires* its clients to be dependent and weak—victims of forces outside their control. Today this is expressed in terms of "sickness": "The development of professions dedicated to benevolence, the so-called 'helping' professions, depend upon and accentuate the definition of problem populations as 'sick,' as objects of medical and quasi-medical attention" (Gusfield, 1989, p. 432).

As well as fitting into the cultural frame of disease, this scientific categorization of humans is a convenient fit with the bureaucratic state system. Max Weber pointed out that bureaucracy (in its ideal form) seeks out efficient, "rational," standardized ways of treating people. In this way, bureaucracies—ideally, anyway—are able to transcend tribalism, nepotism, and favoritism, and get on with the task at hand. The problem is that any time anyone must navigate through a bureaucracy his or her humanity begins to disintegrate. For those who encounter state agencies on a frequent basis (i.e., the poor and the "sick"), official dehumanization is a way of life (Funiciello, 1993). And this dehumanization is integral to the institutionalized, scientific measures through which we "treat" sex workers. It is one thing to take a germ out of its context, isolate it, categorize it, and then treat it. It is another thing to do this to a human. When we focus solely on sorting, categorizing, and diagnosing people, we shrink people into a label, and much of their humanity and power is excluded—even when it is done with feminist, religious, or humanitarian intentions.

In an effort to help a sex worker out of a bad situation, must we also require her to don a victim identity, like a flimsy hospital robe? Must we strip her down and examine only specific aspects of her body, while ignoring the multifaceted, interwoven, and non-biological aspects that affect her health? Within our current cultural and institutional frame (and anonymous social circumstances), it seems we must. And in so doing we degrade ourselves into making dichotomous choices. (For example, if a person is "sick," how can she or he also be healthy? If a person is a victim, how can he or she also be liberated?) For those wishing to jump out of these mutually exclusive notions, it is useful to consider how they become institutionalized as our only options.

The Social Problems Industry: How Issues Become Problems and Solutions Get Institutionalized

Social problems become institutionalized through at least three mechanisms. First, the social problem must be defined in reasonable terms; it must be mapped, framed and isolated as conquerable territory. Second, the group claiming this territory must be widely recognized as legitimate owners. Third, the group claiming ownership must have enough power and resources to build solutions within the problem's defined borders. Once this occurs, solutions can become institutionalized. This generates new jobs and new needs, and people employed by the institution are motivated to rebuff any attempts at re-framing the original problem.

Mapping and Framing the Territory

In order to understand a phenomenon, people select portions of the phenomenon, dissect those portions, and then try to explain them. With each new explanation, new labels are created; the more specialized the understanding, the more specialized the labels, leading to a language only specialists can comprehend. In his book, *Science in Action*, Bruno Latour writes, "When we use a map, we rarely compare what is written on the map with the landscape—to be capable of such a feat you would need to be yourself a well-trained topographer" (Latour, 1987, p. 254). So, unless one knows the map-maker's language, one may live in mapped territory yet not recognize the map.

This difference in how people see an issue results in a quandary when experts stop trying to *explain* people and start trying to *help* them. Since people won't seek out help if they don't recognize themselves as falling into official categories, experts must teach people how to translate their problems into expert language. For instance, at the Washington State conference on sex work, one counselor noted that "[s]ome of the women don't identify themselves as being a part of domestic violence—these women do not have the right terminology when they approach services—so they aren't helped as much as they could be."

In a personal interview, a counselor recalled for me an instance in which she had to explain to a client that she had been sexually abused: " She said that she had sex with her father and brother, but that she wasn't *abused* by them!" When I asked this same counselor if she thought her clients who work as erotic dancers thought of themselves as being "objectified," she replied: "When a person is doing it they don't see it as being objectified. It's more about learning how to demean yourself and do it well. *Until someone teaches you what that is, you don't know you're demeaning yourself."*

One element of starting a new social movement is in creating a new language for old things, as well as in making new linkages between things previously seen as unrelated. These new linkages and words are then placed within a new theoretical frame. Something I find intriguing about this process is how one phenomenon (like sex work), can wind up with completely separate frames (such as that it is either "liberating" or "exploitative"; that it is either "just a job," or "sexual slavery") with no room for variation, overlap, or considerations of social context. For example, a former sex worker now specializing in counseling sex workers defines sex work as "erotic dancing, stripping, pornography, prostitution, and phone sex; any job where a person's body, mind, or emotions are sexually exploited for purposes of money or another's gratification." According to this definition, there is no real difference between phone sex work and prostitution; there is no situation in which a sex worker might *not* be exploited, and presumably one's race and class background is not very relevant. All sex workers fit into the same frame of exploitation. In my readings and interviews, I have observed that anti-sex work proponents are far more likely to use this reductive tactic, but the "other" side does this as well. Pro-sex work activists also "close ranks" and give out only flattering information—again, in my observation, often overstepping how and why race and class can bring about significant differences in the experience of sex work. In no case would I say that this oversight is malicious; experts are simply mapping and framing the same enormous landscape that is sex work from two very different observation decks. One view is that of the State, which requires its people to be victims; the other is from the Professional point of view, which assumes that people have full control over their circumstances.

Claiming Ownership

The second stage of institutionalizing a social problem comes when people claim ownership over the territory they have mapped.

As with physical property, conflicts arise over territory boundaries, but if one group's "ownership" is generally accepted by outsiders, then others vying for a claim sometimes choose not to fight but to form coalitions—or a least to co-opt the more dominant language. For instance, when political and religious conservatives joined feminists in supporting the Indianapolis anti-pornography ordinance, their official reason for doing this was not that pornography destroys "the family," but that pornography degrades women (Ellis et al., 1992, p. 68).

Before people can claim ownership of a social problem, they must convince others of their authority. Outsiders are more convinced of a claim if a consistent argument is publicly maintained and if the argument rests on accepted truths. However, to convince non-feminists of either anti- or pro-sex work feminist arguments is difficult because many find the implications too radical and unsettling. As a result, the ideas of both anti- and pro-sex work feminists become oversimplified; the arguments become packaged and displayed in a more palatable form. Boyer and James (1983) allude to this tension between feminist theory and application when they write: "Viewing the prostitute as a victim may be a positive first step, but only if the prostitute is viewed as the victim of a contradiction in the structure of male/female relations rather than of individual psychopathology" (p. 141). And yet, in a twelve-step, bureaucratic climate, this psychopathologizing is exactly what seems to be necessary for claiming ownership over a social problem.

Building an Industry

Studies of the social problems industry (or what Joseph Gusfield calls "the troubled person's professions") have shown that movements addressing social problems eventually develop into industries with their own agendas (Gusfield, 1989; Beck, 1978). Thus, ideology can inspire individual action, but when ideology is streamlined into a social movement—especially a well-established, well-funded one—ideology is but one inspiration for action. In *Outsiders*, Howard Becker (1963) theorized that people concerned with solving social problems (whom he called "moral entrepreneurs") come in two varieties: rule makers and rule enforcers. Rule makers are often sincerely concerned about an issue and internally motivated to influence social change, but rule enforcers may be "people whose motives are less pure than those of the crusader" (p. 149). Keeping in mind that there is overlap, this distinction between rule makers and rule enforcers seems appropriate for comparing anti-sex work feminists with workers in the social problems industry.

If a social problem, as framed by rule makers, is to develop into an industry, people must learn to see the problem within that same particular frame. After ownership is established, people must be uniformly trained to diagnose and treat the specific problem. This ensures help for the problem population as well as employment for the helpers, or rule enforcers. When an issue is officially defined as a social problem, when its "causes" are isolated and simplified, and when there is an official frame or "master narrative" (as Rapping calls it) enveloping it, the issue becomes an official problem, and the problem can then be institutionalized. Also, successful (or institutionalized) social movements usually have catchy terms or tenets, such as "alcoholism is a disease," or "pornography is rape." Organizational savvy, monetary funds and influential believers all help elevate such tenets into truths. Once truths are mapped and structured, entirely new supporting structures (e.g., social work departments, twelve-step programs, specialized government departments) cushion them. Much energy is devoted to teaching others how to maintain these new structures. Meanwhile, other terms or tenets remain homeless and ignored, living on the outskirts of mainstream institutions.

There is not anything inherently wrong with favoring certain ideas over others, of paying attention to certain details while ignoring others; in fact, this process is necessary to get anything accomplished. By choosing to focus on certain issues while weeding out the rest, and doing this within a structure that supports these choices, the task at hand becomes more manageable. So the problem is not the fact that specialized knowledge exists. It is a problem, however, when alternative perspectives are systematically blocked by the skyscrapers of institutional-ized knowledge.

This systematic blocking of alternative views is what has hap-pened, and continues to happen, to sex work. Sex workers are gen-erally less organized and financially supported than experts, who have the political and economic resources to generate and dissemi-nate their truths. And the social recognition of truth is what Bruno Latour (1987) has argued is the main difference between experts and non-experts: "You may have written a paper that settles a fierce controversy once and for all, but if readers ignore it, [it] cannot be turned into a fact; it simply *cannot*" (p. 41). In other words, facts achieve their status through a social process. Like people working their way up a corporate ladder, claims do not become facts unless an authority gives them a promotion. The more powerful people supporting a claim, the harder the fact becomes, and the more likely it is that the fact becomes institutionalized.

Further, since a position needs social recognition to become a fact, and since social recognition is related to social status, the construction of facts is a class-related (as well as race- and gen-der-related) endeavor. For example, one (religiously-based) anti-pornography movement during the 1960s attempted to convince people that "pornography had the potential to become an item the consumption or support of which indicated the social status of the user or approver" (Zurcher et al., 1971, p. 222). And, in 1993, the president of the National Organization for Women, Cathy Ire-land, proposed an identical anti-pornography approach: that is, to "make the consumption of pornography seem philistine and un-enlightened, as humiliating and socially unacceptable as smok-ing has become" (Wilkerson, 1993).

Professional images—the flip side of "stigmatizing" working-class images—also enhance social recognition of knowledge. Realizing this, spokespersons in the sex industry have increas-ingly used professional words in an effort to gain more respect and legitimacy for their issue, as when sex industry executives coined the term "the sex industry" (D'Emilio & Freedman, 1989, p. 328). Similarly, by highlighting the professional aspect of pros-titution, COYOTE has been moderately successful in redefining prostitution from "sex as sin to sex as work" (Jenness, 1990). This process of "professionalization" thus allows people to climb out of "deviant" categories into the realms of legitimacy, which in turn transports them from *being* a social problem into agents in redefining the social problem (Kitsuse, 1980).

In sum, if a social problem is to be institutionalized, it must be mapped and framed, claimed, and then channeled into small-scale solutions. If the solution is well advertised, utilizes class and/or professional images, and is backed by enough money and influential people, then it can become institutionalized. An industry is created, experts are trained, their jurisdiction is set, and people take their appropriate places.

Institutional and Ideological Gaps
between Experts and Sex Workers

Convincing sex workers to see their experiences through outsider-defined frames takes some work, but this is what experts in the social problems industry do every day. While exposure to external views can be a positive experience (since it offers alternative, and perhaps more helpful, frames for seeing the world), problems arise when ideologies and remedies are administered to people "for their own good" (Ehrenreich & English, 1978). Thus far I have focused on how experts in the helping professions do this, but social researchers also participate in this unfortunate dynamic. Academic careers, like social problems careers, rely on a certain amount of "protection" from outside competitors, so that experts in each world can maintain their authority. If lay people could do the job just as well or better, experts would lose their jobs, identities, and privileged social positions. Therefore, experts generally have a vested interest in disproving the validity of non-expert positions.

One way that social science experts maintain authority is through use of standard research methodologies. For example, when administering interviews and surveys, social scientists are warned to watch for "socially desirable" (i.e., false) answers, a warning that usually comes without any concerted discussion (except in feminist methodology classes) about why anyone would "lie" in a research setting. For instance, people are probably less likely to lie to their equals or to people they see as insiders. Therefore, the risk of people lying (in either direction) is probably heightened when there is a large gap of status and trust between interviewers and interviewees.

Furthermore, if one accepts that all social researchers indirectly affect their data, then one should also accept that all researchers, regardless of their position on sex work, may intimidate respondents into saying certain things and omitting others. This is especially relevant in cases where the interviewer has influence over the respondent's future, as is the case when the respondent is incarcerated or requesting social services. This point is plainly illustrated by the following conversations, tape-recorded in jail. The first of these excerpts comes from a twenty-three-year-old white woman from a working-class background—a woman who though small in stature seemed to me tougher and more emotionally impenetrable than Clint Eastwood. Here she is responding to my question about her relationship with the jail supervisor:

> RE: I open up to her to a certain point, but when I know I'm getting too far in, you know what I'm sayin'? I cut it off.
>
> KL: Have you told her stuff you've told me?
>
> RE: No.
>
> KL: Why is it easier for you to tell me?
>
> RE: Cause you kinda...you've talked to a few prostitutes, you know how it is.... But see...she don't, she can't...she can't like, how do you say it? She don't know how it is to be a prostitute, you know what I'm sayin'? She can't...she can't fit in with...you know what I'm sayin'? *So you got to tell her, you know you can tell her little white lies, cause you don't want to tell her the truth* cause she'll look at you like (shocked face)...you know, she's kind of like, she's a square.

This second excerpt is from a twenty-five-year-old African American woman who appeared to be from a middle-class background. Here she is replying to my questions about the support groups available in jail:

> KL: What sorts of groups here do you like the best?

BE: The best group we do have here are the meetings where it's just us women, no counselors, no SDAs, nobody's patrolling us, and we can get some honest feelings. A lot of the time, the threat of someone that's an authority is that we feel that we have to say certain things. And not say others.

Apparently, the incarcerated women were more comfortable talking with me about certain issues because, unlike jail employees, I am perceived as holding little power over their lives. Therefore, just as sex workers may not admit they are victims with some interviewers (as my critic pointed out), with other interviewers sex workers may not admit enjoyment.

Most of my respondents were not familiar with either feminist terminology or the feminist debate over sex work. However, four of my twenty-one interviewees identified themselves as feminists, and all four of them demonstrated disgust for and alienation from "mainstream" (i.e., anti-sex work) feminism. One woman with years of prostitution experience and a self-described "women's libber" argued that "if a woman has got enough sense, has got enough intelligence in her to even know what a feminist is all about, she doesn't have, she could not possibly be in that situation where she would have no choice, O.K.? [She waits for me to nod in agreement.] O.K."

An erotic dancer who attended a private woman's college and grew up in a sexually liberal home argued that objectification is not confined to sex work, but a normal part of life: "I think that we all objectify people constantly in our life. The bellboy, the grocery clerk, the receptionist—we pass by these people and they have no impact on our lives. It's not necessary to go, 'Gee, I wonder what they like for breakfast.... I wonder what their political views are.' Who cares!"

And another erotic dancer justified her work as a way to play economic "catch up":

For me...as a dancer I have always struggled to place my work in a feminist context. I made on the average $25 an hour...and sex work is the only work I could get paid that amount of money for. I just felt that I was playing a very fair game of catch-up. I had a theater company for four years—my rent was $150 a month and in a good night I could make $150. So I would work a few days a month and the rest of the time I could do what I wanted...theater, travel...and I really resent the fact that people tell me that I'm a victim of patriarchy. I mean, I'm a vegetarian—and if I hadn't danced I probably would've been working in a burger joint or something. To me that would be worse.

Another woman, who had eleven years of erotic dance experience and some intermittent prostitution experiences, said she felt alienated when she went back to school and encountered what she calls the "textbook mentality":

KL: When did you start reading or knowing about feminism?

D: I took some social work courses.... I don't think I was a feminist then, but I understood empowerment. But I became disillusioned because of this textbook mentality. I thought, "you will never be able to help people like me...fuck you people."

Finally, a phone sex worker (with brief experiences in pornography and exotic dancing) who declared she was *not* a feminist, saw the anti-sex work feminist view as interfering with her freedom:

I don't think that we're buying into anything. I think that we see our power, we see what we have, and that we should damn well use it whichever way we fuckin' want to. And that's the bottom line. I think that no one, as a group or individually, should tell any woman what she should do or how she should feel about her own body, or with her own body, or with her own talent, or expertise. In any area whatsoever. I think that freedom is the thing that I'm after, the thing that I stand up for even more than anything else. I can't think of anything else. Personal freedoms, I think need to be upheld.

It is important to note that all these rebuttals to anti-sex work feminism come from women with post-high school education. Of the four explicitly feminist women, the first attended vocational-technical school, and the last three attend(ed) (and one graduated from) four-year universities. Being the educational elite of my sample, these women had more non-sex work options available to them than most, and thus were probably more likely to feel they had chosen their work. Further, their outrage at feeling patronized and at being labeled "victims" is further evidence of their class privilege. Nevertheless, it is clear that all of these women, whether incarcerated or not and despite their class or race, felt alienated from, and distrustful of, the experts. And why wouldn't they be distrustful, if the experts seem to be systematically ignoring much of what they are saying?

Conclusions

The fact that sex work is now seen as a "women's issue" is a general advance for women. However, history is full of examples of activists whose radical intentions are stymied because: 1) they rely on conventional assumptions; 2) they lack access to conventional, culturally legitimate tools; or, ironically, 3) their ideas become enveloped by those same conventional, culturally legitimate tools. In the case of women radicals attempting to define sex work, all three of these factors have inhibited truly radical approaches.

Within the contemporary United States, social problems are most commonly seen in disease terms, meaning that people in problematic circumstances are seen as "sick." This frame has developed in response to several societal factors, such as: scientific authorities taking over the jurisdiction of religious authorities, women activists campaigning for more sympathy for "deviants," the rise of individualism and the decline of community and family anchors, the rise of the bureaucratic nation-state, the hegemony of the twelve-step recovery movement, and the nature of how ideas get institutionalized within a bureaucratic, science-focused environment. Add to that a long cultural tradition of managing "problem populations" (where people on the outside of legitimized institutions are seen as both threatening and disposable), and we end up with a situation in which the people in problematic circumstances come to be seen as problem people.

For a time, women activists in the late nineteenth and early twentieth centuries were able to shift their focus from "women in trouble" to problems of sexism. Again, during the 1960s and 1970s in the United States, with the civil rights movement and the second wave of feminism, people sought out structural explanations for social problems. With much work, some of these ideas were institutionalized and, as a result, it is now far more likely that ethnic minorities and women will be afforded legal entitlements and rights. So, in cases where equal rights and entitlements are ensured, the institutionalization process is very helpful. However, an insidious process often occurs when an issue becomes institutionalized as a problem rather than an entitlement. In these cases, my concern is not just that complex issues are girdled into simplistic and individualized solutions, but that the issues are defined from a point of condescension.

Social problems experts do address some problems that concern some sex workers (such as drug abuse and sexual abuse), but there is still substantial variety between how experts and sex workers understand sex work. Experts, whether they be "rule makers" who frame the issue in broad ideological terms or "rule enforcers" who shrink this broad ideology into more doable problems, often miss central aspects of the people they are trying to explain. In part, the gap between expert and sex worker perspectives is simply due to the process of institutionalizing truths. Since sex workers have less centralized organization and fewer influential allies, many of their views are not easily promoted and thus they remain on the outskirts of institutionalized knowledge. Meanwhile, state-funded agencies, or other socially recognized authorities, have organizational, economic, and political advantages in institutionalizing their positions. Some divergence in opinions between sex workers and experts is also to be expected; it is the expert's job to point out patterns not obvious to people who are concentrating on other things. However, experts in the social problems industry also systematically *ignore* sex workers' challenges to expert ideologies.

If we accept that social problems are constructed, and that the success of social movements depends on their ability to package knowledge for general consumption, then we must realize that the social problems industry never "clearly" reflects the issues of its subjects. Knowledge is a *social* process, produced by people with specific positions that they generally want to advance or protect. Yet, rather than giving up on institutionalized solutions altogether, thinking of oneself as a *knowledge maker*[4] enables one to self-consciously strengthen connections between research and institutionalized knowledge. Rather than being controlled by ideology, we can dictate its course, or at least be more honest about our positions within the machine of institutionalized ideology. One need not choose between ideological slavery and cynicism; the view that knowledge is socially constructed does not have to exclude dreams of progressive social change. But when we see our options in only two camps—like seeing "bad things" as either true *or* false, objective *or* constructed—then we will forever be trapped in a headache of an argument. Defining something as socially constructed does not mean that its effects do not hurt.

One advantage to cultivating more complex understandings of sex work is that we could improve the social services for sex workers. However, any call for social services I make with great caution; just as there is sometimes a fine line between sexual admiration and sexual harassment, so there is sometimes a fine line between state benevolence and state oppression. But there is a difference between admiration and harassment, and benevolence and oppression, and it lies in how much social power the "gazed upon" has to alter, prohibit and/or act upon the "gazer." Furthermore, institutions, when we build them for ourselves, give us safety, predictability, and livelihood, but when we build institutions for others, we do it to contain others.

It is true that the urge to study a group often comes out of concern or sympathy, but it is also true that researchers overwhelmingly study those to whom they believe they have rightful access. In the early days of medicine, for example, medical researchers took study subjects from the poorest ranks, particularly those already contained in state institutions (Ehrenreich & English, 1978). So, unless researchers are studying their own in-group, this assumption (or exertion) of rightful access to others, is usually a disrespectful act—especially in the context of researching a social problem.

Sex workers have been contained, scrutinized, analyzed, criminalized, and disrespected long enough. In research, a halt to this treatment can be accomplished in two ways. First, by refocusing the research lens on non-sex workers; for instance, rather than asking sex workers how they "manage" the stigma of selling sex (as several sociological studies in the 1970s and 1980s did), question non-sex workers about why they use words like "slut" in a derogatory manner. Rather than study how prostitutes run from the law, ask law makers and police officers what business they think they have telling people what to do with their bodies. (Psychological diagnoses could then be utilized to explain such odd behaviors and attitudes.) A second way of improving the treatment of sex workers is by cultivating a closer relationship between researcher and subject. Namely, more sex workers should become researchers, and more researchers should become sex workers. Not only would this dramatically cut down on the level of disrespect and condescension towards sex workers, but it would increase the quality of both the scholarship and its applications. Scholars would be more personally invested in telling and institutionalizing truths that enhance, rather than degrade, the quality and integrity of sex workers' lives.

Radical ideas look different when they are contained and institutionalized because they are seen through increasingly standardized lenses. The point is not to discard institutional frames, but to recognize them, use them as tools, and create new ones that better coincide with one's visions. So, if your vision is to enhance rather than degrade the status of sex workers, wear a pair of frames that allows a sex worker to look you in the eye.

Notes

1. Gayle Rubin reflects that the term "war" deceptively invokes the "image of equally polarized sides," when in fact the pro-sex work side was merely "defending itself against attack" (Nagle, 1997, p. 14).
2. See, for example, Bell, 1987; Chapkis, 1997; Delacoste & Alexander, 1987; McElroy, 1995; Nagle, 1997; Pheterson, 1989.
3. The Minneapolis bill passed, but the mayor vetoed it on constitutional grounds. The Indianapolis bill passed in 1984 but was declared unconstitutional by the Supreme Court in 1986.
4. In a presentation at the Gender Research Roundtable at the University of Washington, Kathryn Addelson argued that scientists (and humans in general) are "knowledge makers" rather than "knowledge seekers."

References

Beck, B. (1978). The politics of speaking in the name of society. *Social Problems*, 25, 353–360.

Becker, H. S. (1963). *Outsiders*. New York: Free Press.

Bell, L. (Ed.) (1987). *Good girls/bad girls: Feminists and sex trade workers face to face*. Seattle: Seal Press.

Boyer, D. K., & James, J. (1983). Prostitutes as victims. In MacNamara, D. E. J., and Karmen, A. (Eds.), *Deviants: Victims or victimizers?* Beverly Hills: Sage.

Chapkis, W. (1997). *Live sex acts: Women performing erotic labor*. New York: Routledge.

D'Emilio, J., & Freedman, E. B. (1989). *Intimate matters: A history of sexuality in America*. New York: Harper & Row.

Delacoste, F., & Alexander, P. (1987). *Sex work: Writings by women in the sex industry*. Pittsburgh: Cleis Press.

Ehrenreich, B., & English, D. (1978). *For her own good*. New York: Bantam.

Ellis, K. et al. (1992). *Caught looking: Feminism, pornography and censorship*. East Haven: LongRiver Books.

Fingarette, H. (1988). Alcoholism: The mythical disease. *Utne Reader*, November/December, 64–69.

Fujimura, J. H. (1987). Constructing "do-able" problems in cancer research: Articulating alignment. *Social Studies of Science*, 17, 257–93.

Funiciello, T. (1993). The brutality of the bureaucracy. In Funiciello, T., *The tyranny of kindness*. New York: Atlantic Monthly Press.

Giobbe, E. (1991). Prostitution: Buying the right to rape. In Burgess, A. W. (Ed.), *Rape and sexual assault III: A research handbook*. New York: Garland Publishing.

Gouldner, A. (1970). *The coming crisis of western sociology*. New York: Basic Books.

Gusfield, J. R. (1989). Constructing the ownership of social problems: Fun and profit in the welfare state. *Social Problems*, 36, 431–441.

Jenness, V. (1990). From sex as sin to sex as work: COYOTE and the reorganization of prostitution as a social problem. *Social Problems*, 37, 403–420.

Kituse, J. I. (1980). Coming out all over: Deviants and the politics of social problems. *Social Problems*, 28, 1–13.

Latour, B. (1987). *Science in action*. Cambridge: Harvard University Press.

Luker, K. (1996). *Dubious conceptions: The politics of teenage pregnancy*. Cambridge: Harvard University Press.

Marx, K. (1864/1996). Class and the production of ideas. In Charon, J. M. (Ed.), *The meaning of sociology*. Englewood Cliffs, NJ: Prentice Hall.

McElroy, W. (1995). *A woman's right to pornography*. New York: St. Martin's Press.

Nagle, J. (Ed.) (1997). *Whores and other feminists*. New York: Routledge.

Pharr, S. (1988). *Homophobia: A weapon of sexism*. Little Rock: Chardon Press.

Pheterson, G. (1989). *A vindication of the rights of whores*. Seattle: Seal Press.

Rapping, E. (1996). *The culture of recovery: Making sense of the self-help movement in women's lives*. Boston: Beacon Press.

Schmitt, D. R. (1994). *Readings in social psychology: Perspectives on social behavior*. Needham Heights: Simon & Schuster.

Smith, D. (1979). A sociology for women. In Sherman, J. A., & Beck, E. T. (Eds.), *The prism of sex*. Madison: University of Wisconsin Press.

Tremblay, J. (1987). Prostitution is not a profession. Translated from French and reprinted in *Women's World*, No. 15.

Walkowitz, J. R. (1980). Prostitution in Victorian society: Women, class, and the state. Cambridge: Cambridge University Press.

Walker, B. (1983). *The woman's encyclopedia of myths and secrets*. New York: Harper & Row.

Wilkerson, I. (1993). Foes of pornography and bigotry join forces. *New York Times*, March 12, A–15.

Zurcher, L. A., Jr., et al. (1971). The anti-pornography campaign: A symbolic crusade. *Social Problems*, 19, 217–238.

REFRAMING "EVE" IN THE AIDS ERA: THE PURSUIT OF LEGITIMACY BY NEW ZEALAND SEX WORKERS

Bronwen Lichtenstein
Department of Sociology, University of Alabama at Birmingham Birmingham, AL 35294

In 1987, New Zealand sex workers were recruited by health department officials to form a publicly funded community organization devoted to HIV prevention. This organization, the New Zealand Prostitutes' Collective (NZPC), is credited with considerable success in preventing HIV transmission among sex workers and their clients, and in educating the wider public about AIDS. Since its inception, the NZPC has sought occupational legitimacy for sex workers by engaging in political activism, most notably in the arena of legislative reform. One aspect of this political activism has been the challenge to a long-standing "Eve" discourse that traditionally labeled prostitutes as disease-bearers and whores. This article outlines how sex workers framed their HIV prevention activities with a language of empowerment. A case study illustrates how the "Eve" discourse was challenged through NZPC research into safer sex practices in the sex industry.

Introduction

I contend that the epidemiological focus on sex workers as vectors of HIV/AIDS had its origins in the syphilis, cholera, and leprosy epidemics. This phenomenon relates to Judeo-Christian mythology about "good" and "bad" women and the corrupting influence of Eve in the garden of Eden. The ancient notion of the sexually corrupt "Eve" so powerfully shaped responses to the syphilis epidemic, for example, that women (rather than men) were framed as the vectors of sexually transmitted diseases (see Gilman, 1988). Similar notions about prostitutes emerged in New Zealand after syphilis became a public health problem in the nineteenth century, giving rise to legislation that curtailed the sexual activities of sex workers and other so-called "promiscuous" women (Fleming, 1988; Jordan, 1991; Kehoe, 1992). In New Zealand's AIDS epidemic, measures to curb HIV infection among prostitutes have taken a less discriminatory form. The formation of the New Zealand Prostitutes' Collective (NZPC), a government-funded HIV prevention group, is an example of a public health measure based on the inclusivity and health promotion principles of the Ottawa Charter, a 1986 health-promotion document supported by the World Health Organization (WHO).[1] The New Zealand government's rationale for funding the NZPC centered on the recognition that sex workers must be recruited as peer educators for HIV prevention efforts to be successful. In the course of their HIV prevention work, sex workers began to seek legitimacy, particularly through efforts to repeal the soliciting and brothel-keeping laws passed during New Zealand's syphilis epidemic. This article outlines the ways in which New Zealand sex workers organized and educated their members within the existing health promotion paradigm, and how they sought legitimacy for their activist agenda by arguing that they are both "responsible" and "safe" sexual partners in the HIV/AIDS epidemic. The Collective's strategies to change the public's attitude toward sex workers and their putative role in the HIV/AIDS epidemic has manifested through media publicity, community activism, and a pilot survey on the sexual behavior of male clients.

The present report is one component of a multi-source, multi-method analysis of local public health policy and epidemiological discourse on responses to HIV/AIDS in New Zealand. The government's response to AIDS drew on a tradition of involvement in disease prevention and health promotion, but also on the stereotypes about "promiscuous" women and gay men as the vectors of sexually transmitted disease (Lichtenstein, 1997). These stereotypes, and the belief that marginalized groups could spread HIV infection to the heterosexual community, convinced the government that it should allocate funding, logistical support, and medical expertise to community groups as a preventive health measure. A salient effect of this partnership was that HIV prevention became the realm of so-called risk groups which, coincidentally, have secured a degree of respectability in their official role in HIV prevention. The government also funded these groups for "human rights" activities. The resulting political activism meant that community AIDS organizers actively sought to challenge stereotypes about "disease-bearers," as well as the repeal of legislation relating to homosexuality and the sex industry. In the case of sex workers, funding has facilitated their desire to challenge popular discourse about prostitution in order to "undermine and expose it, render it fragile, and make it possible to thwart it" apropos Michel Foucault's politics of resistance as articulated in his 1978 book *The History of Sexuality: An Introduction* (p.95). In brief, such discourse can be used to mobilize groups or individuals to challenge hegemonic beliefs, practices, and systems (p. 96). Initially, the NZPC's primary objective was to portray sex workers as health workers ("vanguards of public health") rather than disease-bearing vectors. Thus, the sex workers' project was to "reverse" traditional discourse about the role of prostitutes as sexually corrupt disease-bearers. This article sets the NZPC's formation, goals, and progress within this political and discursive context.

Background

New Zealand is a small Pacific nation populated by people of British, Maori, and Pacific Island ancestry. New Zealand's population was approximately 3,500,000 in 1991, of whom the majority (79.1%) claimed British or European heritage (*The New Zealand Yearbook*, 1994). The nation became a British colony in 1840 and adopted Britain's style of governmental infrastructure and health policy. New Zealand's response to the syphilis epidemic in the nineteenth century thus echoed Britain's in that it was predicated on eugenics concerns, or the "racial fitness" of the European settlers (Kehoe, 1992). Official concern centered primarily on the sexual activities of "promiscuous" women, particularly the Maori women who had contracted syphilis from European traders. The moral panic of the syphilis epidemic prompted stern warnings from politicians and physicians about "the consequences of venereal disease for the race and for national efficiency" (Fleming, 1989, p. 28). These warnings culminated in the Contagious Diseases Act of 1869 and its amendments that forced prostitutes and other "promiscuous" women to undergo compulsory medical examination, followed by detention if they were found to be syphilitic. Later, the "common prostitute" category was widened to include "the casual prostitute" or "young woman at risk." Other legislation passed in the name of syphilis control included The Medical Defectives Act of 1911. This Act legalized the detention of "female degenerates and imbeciles" whose "unrestrained sexuality" was believed to result in widespread syphilis and racial degeneration (Fleming, 1989). While there were laws targeting individuals, mainly prostitutes, who "willfully or knowingly" infected others, additional laws prohibited the operation of brothels, including the so-called "one woman" brothels operating from a prostitute's home. This type of legislation demonstrated the power and particularity of the sexual double standard; all such legislation was directed at the sexual activities of women (there were no parallels for men).

New Zealand's response to the syphilis epidemic introduced proscriptive measures for a single group of citizens, i.e., "promiscuous" women, rather than the public at large. These measures were vigorously protested by feminist groups such as the Women's Christian Temperance Union (WCTU), the Country Women's Institute, and the National Council of Women on the grounds that women were unfairly targeted by the law. This social activism resulted in the repeal of the Contagious Diseases Act in 1910 (Fleming, 1989). However, much of the discursive legacy about promiscuous women as vectors of sexually transmitted disease remained, along with legislation that prohibited soliciting and brothel-keeping. Sex workers are now challenging this legislation for two reasons: it discriminates against women, and it conflicts with official AIDS policy, which advocates inclusivity, empowerment, and the "enablement" of marginalized groups.

Methodology

The formal methods of data collection for this case study were semi-structured interviews of key informants and analysis of epidemiological and documentary data. The two principal organizers of the NZPC were interviewed separately on several occasions during 1994, either by telephone or in person, as were four members of the Christchurch branch of the NZPC, and relevant health sector and community workers. Surveillance data on HIV/AIDS in New Zealand were obtained from the Epidemiology Group at the University of Otago, New Zealand. Documentary sources included the Collective's HIV prevention magazine, *Siren*, resource material from the NZPC's national and regional offices, selected news items from *The Press* and *The Christchurch Mail*, a parliamentary submission on the decriminalization of prostitution laws in New Zealand, academic papers on sex work in professional journals such as the *New Zealand Medical Journal*, and *Working Girls*, written by a board member of the Wellington branch of the NZPC.

My contact with members of the Christchurch NZPC was initiated in 1993, after which I attended formal gatherings and social occasions and kept apace with national NZPC events.[2] Such high-contact research activity is possible in New Zealand where AIDS work is characterized by informality and inter-sectoral collaboration, a phenomenon that has facilitated New Zealand's response to HIV/AIDS (Davis & Lichtenstein, 1996). Although this networking calls for care to avoid problems of researcher bias, a major outcome has been both the support and surveillance of agency operations. For this reason, mandated evaluations of agency programs are rare, and can be refused if considered by AIDS organizers to be intrusive, unnecessary, or stigmatizing. Evaluations can be negotiated by the agencies themselves. The NZPC is a case in point: a recent attempt by epidemiologists to test HIV seropositivity among sex workers was successfully resisted on the grounds that it would "add to the stigma and tell us nothing we didn't know." (Healy, 1998). For sex workers, the epidemiologists' moves to test for HIV infection were disempowering and strongly hinted at nineteenth-century stigmatization of "promiscuous" women. In the spirit of compromise, however, epidemiologists were granted restricted access to HIV data collected through NZPC health clinic sites.[3] It should be noted that there have been no reported cases of autochtonous HIV infection among New Zealand-born prostitutes since AIDS surveillance began in 1983 (Dickson, 1998).[4]

The Prostitute as AIDS Icon

The word "prostitute" has often been ascribed to women whose sexual activities brought them to the notice of health authorities (Brandt, 1988; Plant, 1990; Lichtenstein, 1996). In the AIDS epidemic, sex workers were depicted as vectors once HIV infection was known to be heterosexually transmitted. In his paper "AIDS and syphilis: The iconography of disease," Gilman (1988, p. 107) explained the response as:

> [The] shift—from male victim to female source of pollution—clearly repeats the history of the iconography of syphilis. A new group has now been labeled as the source of disease: women, but not all women, only those considered to be outside the limits of social respectability. Even while acknowledging heterosexual transmission, the attempt is made to maintain clear and definite boundaries so as to limit the public's anxiety about their own potential risk.

In New Zealand, the reaction to sex workers and their trade in the HIV/AIDS epidemic followed the overseas example. In a letter to a New Zealand newspaper, for example, it was asserted by one correspondent that "brothels are like fireworks. They only need one cracker to set off a blaze of HIV infection" (Fechney, 1994). The irony of this letter is that brothels, as such, do not exist in New Zealand. In another example, 67 percent of the respondents in a 1989 national survey replied that prostitutes were to blame for "catching" diseases, up from 60 percent in 1987 (Chetwynd, 1992).

This discursive legacy resulted in epidemiological scrutiny in the HIV/AIDS epidemic, and in prostitutes being "seen as so contaminated that their bodies are virtual laboratory cultures for viral replication" (Treichler, 1988, p. 45). The legacy and its stigmatizing outcomes in the HIV/AIDS epidemic have given rise to a feminist critique of the meaning of the words "prostitute" and "prostitution" and a search for less pejorative terms to describe commercialized sex. Patton (1994, p. 53) has argued that the word "prostitute" represents risk as well as derogation for many women, because the "misapplication of early epidemiology [of HIV/AIDS] resulted in increased policing and harassment of women identified as 'prostitutes' in many locales around the world." While the distinction has been made between "prostitution" as non-voluntary sexual labor in poorer countries, and sex work as voluntary employment in some Western countries, this article reflects the practice of some researchers and feminists who use the term "sex work" in the broader sense "because it is both general and non-pejorative" (Plant, 1994, p. xiv). The use of "sex work" instead of "prostitution" also reflects the preference of the New Zealand Prostitutes' Collective, whose organizers argue that "prostitute implies 'dirty' and can lead to lower self-esteem—it gives a criminal label. 'Sex worker' implies that a person sells his or her services" (NZPC service sheet, 1995).

New Zealand's Sex Industry and Laws

An estimated 8,000 women work as prostitutes in New Zealand, most of whom are aged between 18 and 30 years old.[5] By far the largest number of sex workers is female, although there are some transvestites and transsexuals involved in street prostitution, and some escort agencies that cater to gay men (NZPC submission to parliament, 1990). While women do operate as "ship girls,"[6] street workers, or escorts, most sex work is carried out in massage parlors owned or operated by men (Jordan, 1991). It is estimated that men comprise about 75 percent of the total sex industry in New Zealand as owners, workers, managers, and receptionists.

Sex work is legal in New Zealand. However, soliciting is a crime under Section 26 of the Summary Offenses Act 1981. A number of other crimes relating to sex work co-exist; they include brothel-keeping, pimping, procuring, and living off the earnings of prostitution. Pimping in New Zealand is rare. NZPC organizers maintain that the New Zealand sex industry is different from that of many other countries in that local sex workers have an unusual degree of personal independence from the proprietors of sex businesses. Sex workers do not have the status of employees and are not, in general, associated with pimps.

The prostitution laws prohibit brothel-keeping, sex palaces, and household operations (women working from their homes). Sex workers who work as escorts, street walkers, or in massage parlors "own" their services because the law prohibits their earnings from being procured by pimps or managers of parlors. However, parlor operators often extract payment from sex workers in the form of shift fees, laundry money, late fees, and room rent. Sex workers in parlors are paid directly by clients; massages are provided free. While New Zealand sex workers experience some exploitation, it is generally considered to be less than that encountered elsewhere (Jordan, 1991). In part, this lack of exploitation is attributed to actively enforced anti-pimping laws. However, one sex-industry commentator has stated that "it is virtually impossible to work as a prostitute [in New Zealand] and stay within the law" (Jordan, 1991, p. 10). Invisibility among sex workers exists for historic reasons and because legal sanctions are occasionally enforced.

As noted, laws to prohibit soliciting in New Zealand were a nineteenth-century response to the syphilis epidemic. The laws targeted women on the basis that they, rather than men, were the initiators of paid sex, and that society should be protected from female sexual predators. The gender bias implicit in the early prosecutions meant that most women coming to official notice had been labeled as prostitutes prior to their arrest (Jordan, 1991). The continued existence of these laws has prompted one parliamentarian to remark: "[These laws] fail to take into account the clients and the employers. That seems like a law drafted by men, to protect men, and it's most definitely unfair to women" (from a 1992 parliamentary speech by the Hon. M. Williamson). The NZPC's goal to reform the soliciting laws is an effort to reverse the misogyny that frames women's sexuality and to assert one's "right" to practice sex work.

Community organizing by New Zealand sex workers was unknown before the HIV/AIDS epidemic. Sex work was largely invisible, prostitutes were marginalized, and street workers were harassed rather than protected by the police. Condom use was practiced by individual sex workers rather than advocated by employers, community activists, or the health sector. Sex workers were responsible for their own sexual health and did not have access to dedicated clinics or physicians. Despite this lack of organizational support, the incidence of sexually transmitted disease among New Zealand sex workers was low because "most [sex workers] were careful in the precautions they took" (Jordan, 1991, pp. 265–266). The lack of disease can also be attributed to the virtual absence of the sex-for-drugs exchange, a known risk factor in the transmission of sexually transmitted disease in the United States (Bloor, 1995; Patton, 1994; Plant, 1990).

Reframing Eve: Sex Workers as Activists/Organizers

The New Zealand Prostitutes' Collective was formed in 1987. This collaborative effort between the New Zealand government and local sex workers was prompted by the government's fear of the spread of HIV/AIDS to the heterosexual population, and by sex workers' anxieties about the effects of this new disease on their health and livelihood. The collaboration gave sex workers a long-awaited opportunity for organizational empowerment, and the means by which to function as a collective "voice."

For sex workers, "empowerment" was a critical concept that provided a rationale for their organizational and political activities. It was directly linked to the philosophy of enablement as articulated by The Ottawa Charter (see Note 2). This concept was formally adopted by the National Council on AIDS (NCA), a twenty-three-member national committee appointed by the New Zealand government to make recommendations on AIDS policy. The NCA defined enablement as:

> The process of enabling people to increase control over, and to improve, their health. To reach a state of complete physical, mental and social well-being, an individual or group must be able to identify and to realize aspirations to satisfy needs, and to change or cope with the environment. [The Ottawa Charter] identifies five interdependent areas for action to promote health: (1) building healthy public policy; (2) creating supportive social environments; (3) strengthening community action; (4) developing personal skills; and (5) re-orienting health services. (The New Zealand Strategy on HIV/AIDS, 1990, p. 35)

The process that emerged from this health promotion paradigm led to an AIDS partnership in New Zealand between the community, government, and health sectors (Lichtenstein, 1997). For the NZPC, "enablement" became "empowerment" through the collaborative mechanisms involved in creating supportive social environments, strengthening community action, and developing personal skills.

The events surrounding the establishment of the Prostitutes' Collective are recounted by an organizer in this excerpt from *Working Girls*:

> The end of 1987 saw the beginning of what was to become the NZPC. A core group of sex workers, although we had not begun to call ourselves that, began to meet in pubs, private homes, massage parlors, on the street, and typically New Zealand, on beaches, to discuss in a semi-serious way the forming of an organization specific to the needs of sex-industry workers. At this time a few sex workers were invited to meet with the AIDS Task Force of the Department of Health. AIDS, of course, was something we had all heard about. Our wallets were beginning to register its effects, and certainly it was becoming another reason for the wider community to stigmatize us further.... The Department of Health began to woo us in earnest. They were quite clearly committed to enlisting sex workers as educators for the prevention of HIV/AIDS.... We agreed with the department on objectives, signed contracts and eventually the funding starting to trickle through. We set about establishing community bases, first in Wellington in 1988, then in Auckland in March 1989. (Jordan, 1991, pp. 271–272)

The NZPC was offered funds, infrastructure, and support by government in return for pro-active HIV prevention work. Once established, the Collective provided a number of services to sex workers, clients, and to the public. Sex workers were offered safer-sex information and supplies such as condoms, dental dams, and lubricants, often from the premises of drop-in centers, by outreach to street and parlor workers, or in the form of community magazines. HIV testing, advice, and counseling services were also provided. The Collective's role included safer-sex education for health providers and the public. Typically, NZPC branches have a drop-in center where safer-sex information and health and support services are provided. In Christchurch, for example, the drop-in center operates on week-days, from early afternoon to night.

Coffee and company are available, together with an on-site STD clinic and access to a needle exchange service, inexpensive condoms and lubricant, legal services, and an HIV/AIDS counselor at specified times. The services are used by both female and male sex workers and their clients.[7]

In the words of one organizer, 1988 was a time of "coming out." Sex workers sought legitimacy and status through their own activities and through their contacts with political leaders, health and government officials, medical professionals, and academics. Organizers gained confidence by collaborating with community and public health workers in the provision of health services and by participating in inter-organizational and research activities. They also acted as advocates in the public arena, most notably in favor of the repeal of soliciting and brothel-keeping laws. The move toward decriminalization followed the realization that soliciting laws inhibited the ability of NZPC organizers to gain access to workers, and to distribute condoms when such items were seen as evidence of prostitution by police and the courts.

Central to the Collective's HIV prevention and self-empowerment goals is the production of a health-promotion discourse that focuses on safer-sex and other harm-reduction practices. For sex workers, this discourse is manifested in the Collective's magazine *Siren* (Sex Industry Rights and Education Network), in self-protection measures such as the "Ugly mugs" list,[8] and in outreach and activities such as advocacy, networks, and drop-in centers. The discourse focuses on safety and risk and advises sex workers to "Be Careful Out There. Practise Safe Sex. Look After One Another." (*Siren*, 1994, p. 30).

The NZPC's "Take Care" discourse is framed by the fear of acquiring HIV infection from clients and of other occupational hazards. Concern about client behavior and the effects of stigma appears in this excerpt from *New Internationalist* by NZPC organizers Catherine Healy and Anna Reed:

> [I]t's still the sex workers who are perceived by many to be a major reservoir of infection, the vectors of the transmission of HIV/AIDS into the general population. In the early days of AIDS it was inevitable that the sex industry would be scrutinized. The media in our own country—Aotearoa/

New Zealand—ran stories that whipped up hysteria against prostitutes, with images of the "vengeful AIDS victim...a crazed hooker on revenge trip against all punters." We have yet to hear about the crazed punter hell-bent on infecting prostitutes. (Healy and Reed, 1994, p. 17)[9]

This lament is representative of the NZPC's occupational discourse, in which information is presented in ways that challenge or "reverse" common beliefs about prostitution. This "reverse discourse" not only presents information or perspectives from an alternative point of view, but it is often used for political purposes. In the case of the NZPC, reverse discourse is a strategy that is used for protection as well as empowerment. The strategy fulfills Sullivan's requirement for "accounts of prostitution which assert the will and agency of prostitutes...which refuse the notion that women sell themselves in prostitution, and which reconfigure prostitution transactions" (Sullivan, 1995, p. 197). An apt example of the NZPC's reverse discourse is a health promotion poster claiming that "The Best Sex is Paid Sex."

In the NZPC's "reverse discourse" presentation, risk is posited as external to the sex worker in the form of clients, the police, sex industry personnel, and the public. It is embedded in statements about "crazed punters" who "put holes in condoms for their own cheap thrills" (*The Christchurch Mail*, 1994, p. 1). To offset such risks, members of the NZPC offer detailed advice on a range of health, safety and civil rights issues. The advice includes warnings about police demands for incriminating photographs of sex workers and information about alarm systems for women working as "escorts"; methods for dealing with predatory or abusive taxi drivers, clients and massage parlor operators; the safe use of tampons and other devices; and STD prevention. An ever-present sense of personal threat is apparent in the headings of articles which read "Danger in the workplace," "Escorts Alarmed!," "Surviving the Street," and "What Gets on My Goat!" (all in *Siren*, April 1994).

NZPC organizers draw on the expertise of health workers, police, government officials and other experts in the field to support their health and safety efforts. An excerpt from *Siren* reads: "A representative of Land Transport [The New Zealand Department of Transportation] met with the NZPC and gave us some hints on how to choose a taxi and what to do if something goes wrong" (*Siren*, April 1994, p. 20). A sense of risk, in this instance, led NZPC organizers (as informed citizens) to draw on governmental expertise. The NZPC's designated role as providers of tax-funded public services to sex workers evokes a sense of legitimacy (and entitlement) by such incremental means. A reading of items entitled "This list is published by Land Transport" and "Land Transport met with NZPC" suggests that meetings between NZPC and Land Transport officials were conducted on a peer basis, and that members of the NZPC operated as equals rather than as stigmatized mendicants of government favors.

A sense of legitimacy is also enhanced by the provision of multi-agency health services at the drop-in centers. In the words of NZPC organizers Healy and Reed: "At one of our centers we've set up a medical clinic where we carry out anonymous HIV-testing for sex-workers. Can you imagine how empowering it is for prostitutes to interview doctors and nurses to ascertain their suitability for staffing our clinic?" (Healy & Reed, 1994, p. 17). The language of empowerment suffuses literature produced by the Collective, and notions of threat and risk are countered with strategies designed to promote self-esteem. One strategy involves teaching sex workers self-defense techniques. As reported in a local newspaper, "the NZPC has produced a video instructing sex workers on self defence and health issues hoping to empower people in a potentially dangerous situation" (Espiner, 1994, p. 5). Spokeswoman Anna Reed invoked the "legitimacy theme" in the article by saying:

> I'm looking forward to the day that a woman can put on her CV that she has worked in the sex industry and has good communication skills, she's a good listener, a good reader of body language and that these things be recognized as the skills they are. (Healy & Reed, 1994, p. 17)

This statement epitomizes Foucault's "reverse discourse" axiom and the NZPC's empowerment strategy: in referring to the non-sexual aspects of prostitution, the organizers align sex work with other service sector jobs such as banking, hotel, and sales work that depend upon interpersonal skills.

The sex workers' generalized sense of risk is mirrored by society's fears about the moral and medical risks associated with prostitution. For members of the public who believe the "disease-bearing prostitute" axiom, sex workers who call themselves safer-sex experts are engaging in risible double-speak. For sex workers, the image of the "Healthy Hooker" is far from oxymoronic. Rather, it is a proud assertion and a repudiation of the disease-bearer image in the HIV/AIDS epidemic. True to the empowerment methods of the NZPC, this repudiation takes the form of self-advocacy, and a determination to reverse negative images associated with prostitution. In this vein, Healy and Reed assert:

> [T]here is now near-universal use of condoms by sex workers in industrialized countries. This is having a far greater impact on sexual culture than all the chats in doctors' clinics. We can't prove it, of course, but it is probable that prostitutes have been more successful in safer-sex education than all the television advertisements put together. After all, the best way for someone to learn something is to do it. So it follows, the best way for a man to start to feel OK about condoms is to have someone put one on him, and then proceed to give him a pleasurable experience. (Healy & Reed, 1994, p. 16)

This rhetoric may be considered more than self-aggrandizement by members of the NZPC. It serves to present a corrective perspective by those on whom an unpalatable stigma has been foisted. In the case of New Zealand's politicians, the rhetoric has succeeded to the extent that several parliamentarians have presented the NZPC's perspective to officials and colleagues in an effort to repeal the soliciting laws. In the case of one parliamentarian, his support of the NZPC was such that he announced: "In fact, the Prostitutes' Collective believes that it has done at least as much as all the advertising campaigns [in New Zealand] to popularise condoms amongst heterosexuals" (Parliamentary speech, The Hon. Maurice Williamson, 1992).

One of the NZPC's HIV prevention mottos is "No Joe, no go," or no condom = no sex (Healy & Reed, 1994, p. 16). This motto is an example of assertive action-taking in the interests of self-protection, and was formulated after sex workers became frustrated with condom-shy clients. The New Zealand government plays an active role in this campaign by funding the NZPC for condom distribution. The NZPC seeks out sex workers in the streets, massage parlors, escort agencies, and other venues to guarantee this portion of their funding (Healy, telephone communication, February 15, 1998).

To all accounts, the "No Joe, no go" motto is not merely rhetoric, but accurately reflects the practice of New Zealand sex workers in their professional lives. Dr. Helen Moriarty, Medical Officer for Sexual Health Services and for the NZPC in Wellington since 1995, has noted that "Sex industry workers in New Zealand are very safety conscious, and are far more conscientious about condom use and safe sex practices than the average person. I can count on the fingers of one hand the number of STD infections that have been transmitted through sex work in that time" (Moriarty, 1998). Although it is difficult to assess the efficacy of the "No Joe, no go" campaign in absolute terms, the low incidence of sexually transmitted disease and HIV infection among female sex workers suggests that there is a shared behavioral commitment to safer-sex. This finding is replicated in Britain, where Gorna notes:

> [O]ne of the remarkable features of prostitution in the UK, confounding most public perceptions, is the extremely low level of HIV infection and the extremely high level of safer-sex practice. A London study recruited 280 women who worked in a range of indoor and street settings: just two women tested HIV-positive, and both had a history of injecting drugs. (Gorna, 1996, p. 267)

The New Zealand sex workers' low STD and HIV incidence rates are claimed as proof of their ability to control the paid sexual encounter. However, this claim is mirrored by the well-documented inability by other women to do the same. For example, Holland et al. (1994, p. 62) have stated that young women they studied lacked the ability to control sexual encounters, and others have maintained that women are often powerless to determine condom use in the heterosexual encounter (Lupton, 1994). There is also the perception that sex workers, rather than respectable women, use condoms (Holland et al., 1994, p. 77).

The purported success of the NZPC's safer-sex policy is, to some extent, dependent on the business nature of sex work, where the prostitute is the "provider" of a desired "product" (sex). This business paradigm, of course, is deemed unsuitable for women in their private lives. The transactional nature of sex work serves to provide leverage to women engaged in prostitution: the leverage also promotes survival techniques such as safer-sex. Thus, safer-sex serves two purposes: self-protection and "product enhancement" (i.e., "clean" women for male clients). By insisting on safer-sex, New Zealand prostitutes have assumed the role of "women who draw the line," a role traditionally ascribed only to "respectable" women. In so doing, they contravene the image of irresponsibility traditionally allotted to the whore. The self-control paradigm adopted by sex workers for physical and economic survival in the HIV/AIDS epidemic is not only proving useful for political advocacy, but is also providing a challenge to the notion that self-control for women requires an asexual respectability during a sexual epidemic.

Reverse Discourse: The Survey as Strategy

The activities of sex workers in New Zealand have been little studied, except in relation to anti-prostitution legislation such as the 1869 Contagious Diseases Act, or to the nineteenth-century history of immigration. Surveys about or relating to sex work have been a feature of the HIV/AIDS epidemic in New Zealand mainly since 1991. While studies have been initiated by academics, several have been initiated by the sex workers themselves or by sex workers and academics as collaborators. The dialogue that has emerged between sex workers and socio-behavioral researchers in the HIV/AIDS field has been facilitated by the intersectoral collaboration as featured in New Zealand's response to HIV/AIDS since 1985 (Lichtenstein, 1997). The visibility afforded the NZPC through this process has given organizers access to such tools of research as surveys, reports, and evaluations, while providing academics with new areas of study.

Research prior to 1993 tended to focus on evaluation of the NZPC or its magazine, rather than on the dynamics or health risks of sex work (see Glaisyer et al., 1994). In 1993, however, social scientists from the Christchurch School of Medicine collaborated with NZPC organizers to undertake a pilot study of 30 male clients of female sex workers. The research was unusual because it focused on the clients of sex workers rather than on the sex workers themselves. It also investigated safer-sex dynamics between the worker and client. The spotlight fell on male clients because their "pivotal existence in the world of sex work" had been ignored (Gilling, 1994), and because it had been reported that they were often reluctant to take the initiative in condom use during paid sexual encounters (Plumridge et al., 1997).

The results of the survey were unequivocal: they pointed to the clients' overwhelming lack of interest in HIV prevention and their refusal to consider the health risks even though "many used commercial sex services on their travels in countries where HIV infection rates were higher and condom use much lower than in New Zealand" (Gilling, 1994). The clients were described as being passive, as lacking accurate knowledge about transmission of HIV, and as careless in their primary relationships with wives or partners. Although almost half were white-collar workers, most clients were reported to lack the desire or ability to communicate with sexual partners. It was also reported that "the initiative in [condom] use appeared to be with the sex workers: the sex worker both supplied the condom and put it on in most cases" (Chetwynd & Plumridge, 1994, p. 352). The researchers concluded that the findings of the pilot survey were disturbing because "clients of sex workers were a key element linking the world of commercial sex with the broader community. This pivotal position meant they had considerable potential to spread HIV" (Chetwynd & Plumridge, 1994, p. 352).

In New Zealand, as elsewhere, the sexual behavior of heterosexual men in the HIV/AIDS epidemic has often been ignored. This bias continues despite an upsurge in socio-behavioral AIDS research in New Zealand and overseas.[10] The pilot study represents a shift from viewing prostitution as an atomized female activity in which disease is transmitted from female worker to male client, to one in which the sex worker is more accurately located within a client-sex worker-sex industry dynamic, and in a way that highlights the behavior of clients. For New Zealand sex workers the results of this research are invaluable, if only because the data have been promulgated through scientific channels rather than by activist polemic, thus gaining scientific weight in the eyes of policymakers, legislators and health officials. Lupton (1994, p. 3), in citing van Dijk (*Racism and the Press*), refers to this "mainstreaming" thus: "The opinions of minority groups are rarely reported, and if they do receive attention they are often presented as partisan, whereas elite news actors or groups are presented as 'neutral.'"

Writers Sander Gilman (1988), Paula Treichler (1988), Simon Watney (1988), and Douglas Crimp (1988) have independently argued that HIV/AIDS is an epidemic of blame. Research into AIDS commonly focuses on "risk behavior" as a means of identifying "modes of HIV transmission," thus promoting the idea that "risk groups" are the vectors of disease. The New Zealand pilot study is no different in this respect: the clients' safer-sex behavior was investigated and found wanting, and they have been blamed for risking their own, sex workers', and other women's health. With the locus of blame transferred from sex worker to client, the prostitute has been interpolated as safer-sex expert, earning credit for her pro-active stance in reducing the risk of HIV transmission. In the "epidemic of blame" paradigm, it is the client (rather than the sex worker) who becomes the "dangerous element in the sexual exchange" (see Chetwynd & Plumridge, 1994, p. 352). Like the bisexual man engaging in anonymous, man-to-man sex, it can be inferred that the male client places all women at risk through his refusal to wear condoms except when confronted by the responsible sex worker. Sex workers can be seen to provide a public service by protecting themselves and clients from disease, and by offering safer-sex education to men who lack knowledge about HIV/AIDS. In addition, "bad" women can be seen to protect "good" women from the ravages of disease, since heterosexual men have been exposed as potential HIV vectors.

The researchers concluded the New Zealand pilot study by stating that further research should be done into "what stopped these men using condoms" (Chetwynd & Plumridge, 1994, p. 353). This recommendation contributed to a de-emphasis of the prostitute's role as HIV vector. It also helped reframe notions about sex work by drawing attention to heterosexual men's sexual attitudes and praxis. The move exemplifies how a discourse of resistance can be produced through challenges to popular ideology. In the case of the pilot survey, the sex industry became the conduit through which subversive knowledge could be extrapolated, shaped according to scientific norms, then broadly articulated through the medical and popular media. Since "bad" and "good" women in New Zealand are differentiated less by class than by sexual praxis in the HIV/AIDS epidemic, the gap between both is being strategically narrowed by the sex workers' campaign to be seen as protectors of the public health.

Conclusion

This article has presented some of the ways in which "Eve" imagery has been reframed by New Zealand sex workers for political and HIV prevention purposes. Traditional imagery draws on longstanding beliefs about disease-bearing prostitutes; it emerged in nineteenth-century measures to control syphilis, and has underscored the New Zealand government's decision to fund sex workers for HIV prevention work in the 1980s and 1990s. Paradoxically, it also provided leverage to New Zealand's sex workers for their activist agenda. In reframing the discourse about prostitution, New Zealand sex workers offer a positive way of viewing sex work as life-enhancing rather than as a dangerous activity. The NZPC's putative success in promoting safer-sex activities among themselves, their clients and the wider public is evident in the absence of HIV infection that has been recorded among New Zealand born sex workers and their clients (Lichtenstein, 1996; Dickson, 1998). The sex-workers' activist and HIV prevention agendas have resulted in improved relations with police, judges, politicians, health officials, and the New Zealand public.

The emergence of the sex workers' "voice" in the HIV/AIDS epidemic through survey research, activism, health promotion and inter-sectoral collaboration is embryonic but unique in New Zealand's history. To place this phenomenon in perspective, sex workers have yet to obtain the legal reforms obtained by gay men. Homosexual activity between consenting males over the age of sixteen has been legal in New Zealand since 1986, and discrimination against gay men and women and HIV-positive individuals in housing, employment, and services has been illegal since 1993. Community activists, such as the gay men who sought changes to legislation during the "crisis" years of the HIV/AIDS epidemic in New Zealand (1985–1990) have been more successful in their efforts to secure reform than have sex workers. In part, this delay is due to the absence of political activism by sex workers during the early years of New Zealand's HIV/AIDS epidemic and, in part, to political events in 1990 that resulted in defeat of the pro-reformist Labour Party. For sex workers, stigma also retards law reform. The Director of the New Zealand AIDS Foundation, Warren Lindberg, has claimed that sex workers and illicit drug users in New Zealand are more stigmatized than gay men (Lindberg, 1988). The NZPC's political future is therefore uncertain and must be measured against growing local conservatism over social issues such as immigration and crime. The political and economic climate is also less conducive to AIDS organizing because of two unrelated factors: a waning concern about HIV/AIDS and reduced government spending on health delivery and programs. On a positive note, the NZPC's funding has been increased for 1998, and the reform of soliciting laws is about to be debated in parliament. However, the optimistic portrayal of the legitimization of sex work in New Zealand in this article is provisional. A longer term evaluation is needed to judge the progress of reform and to gauge the public's perception of sex work after ten years of the existence and political advocacy of the NZPC.

Notes

Funding for the research that formed the basis of this article was provided by the Health Research Council of New Zealand.

1. The Ottawa Charter on Health Promotion was written at the International Conference on Health Promotion at Ottawa, Ontario, Canada, in November 1986. The conference was sponsored by the World Health Organization (WHO), Welfare Canada, and the Canadian Public Health Association.

2. The writer of this article is a New Zealander who wrote her Ph.D. dissertation on organizational and discursive responses to HIV/AIDS in New Zealand, and who has since emmigrated to the United States.
3. This study of HIV seroprevalence among sex workers was nested within a larger, unlinked, anonymous seroprevalence study of STD clinic attendees that is currently being analyzed. The study was performed in four major cities in New Zealand in 1996 and 1997 by epidemiologists at the AIDS Epidemiology Group, Department of Preventive and Social Medicine, University of Otago Medical School, Otago, New Zealand. Enrollment in the NZPC sub-study was voluntary and did not include all clinic attendees at time of testing.
4. Nigel Dickson of the AIDS Epidemiology Group, Department of Preventive and Social Medicine, University of Otago Medical School, New Zealand, has noted that "Surveillance of people with HIV infection suggests no discernible HIV infection among New Zealand born female sex workers" (E-mail communication: February 17, 1998).
5. Based on NZPC estimates (from a speech by The Hon. Maurice Williamson, Assoc. Minister of Health, August 27, 1992). The number of male sex-workers is much smaller. According to this figure, about one in every 150 women in New Zealand between the ages of 18 and 40 is employed in some form of sex work.
6. Most ship girls are Maori or Polynesian. Ship girls provide services onboard (National Council on AIDS [NCA] minutes, No. 9, p. 4).
7. This information was supplied by organizers at the Christchurch Branch of the New Zealand Prostitutes' Collective.
8. A list of abusive clients is kept by the NZPC and is supplied to sex-workers on request. Information includes descriptions of abusive clients (age, height, appearance, distinguishing features, ethnicity, occupation), their vehicles, and other relevant details about weapons, and so on.
9. Catherine Healy is National Coordinator of the NZPC and a World Health Organization consultant on sex work to Pacific rim countries such as Vietnam and Thailand. Anna Reed is an NZPC organizer who engages in collaborative research about HIV-related topics and who presents the results of the research and her NZPC expertise to the media and to various conferences. The two organizers are committed activists, and arguably the most high profile members of the NZPC.
10. In the 1994 bibliography "Social Research on HIV/AIDS in New Zealand," for example (see references), there were no listed studies that specifically referred to adult heterosexual men's sexual behavior, although separate sections were devoted to adolescents, the sex industry, injecting drug users, and gay men.

References

AIDS—New Zealand (May 1991–November 1997). Newsletter, Issues 9–35, AIDS Epidemiology Group, Department of Preventive and Social Medicine, University of Otago Medical School, New Zealand.

Bloor, M. (1995). *The sociology of HIV transmission*. London: Sage.

Brandt, A. (1988). From social history to social policy. In Fee, E., & Fox, D. (Eds.), *AIDS: The burdens of history* (pp. 147–171). Berkeley: University of California Press.

Chetwynd, J., & Plumridge, E. (1994). Knowledge, attitudes and activities of male clients of female sex workers: Risk factors for HIV. *New Zealand Medical Journal*, 107, 351–353.

Chetwynd, J. (1992). Changes in sexual practices and some HIV related attitudes in New Zealand: 1987–9. *New Zealand Medical Journal*, 105, 237–239.

Crimp, D. (1988). AIDS: Cultural analysis/cultural activism. In Crimp, D. (Ed.), *AIDS: Cultural analysis/cultural activism* (pp 3–16). Cambridge: MIT Press.

Davis, P., & Lichtenstein, B. (1996). Introduction: AIDS, sexuality and the social order in New Zealand. In Davis, P. (Ed.), *Intimate details and vital statistics: AIDS, sexuality and the social order in New Zealand*. Auckland, New Zealand: Auckland University Press.

Dickson, N. (1988). AIDS Epidemiology Group, Department of Preventive and Social Medicine, University of Otago Medical School, New Zealand. (Telephone Communication: February 15, 1998.)

Espiner, G. (1995). Sex workers "just ordinary people." *The Christchurch Mail*, January 7, p. 5.

Fechney, L. (1994). Safe sex. (Letter to the editor.) *The Christchurch Mail*, November 21, p. 11.

Fleming, P. (1988). Fighting the "red plague": Observations on the response to venereal disease in New Zealand 1910–1945. *New Zealand Journal of History*, 22, 56–64.

Fleming, P. (1989). "Shadow over New Zealand": The response to venereal disease in New Zealand 1910–1945. Unpublished Ph.D. dissertation, Massey University, Palmerston North, New Zealand.

Foucault, M. (1978). *The history of sexuality: An introduction*, vol. 1. New York: Random House.

Gilling, N. (1994). Sex workers' clients "pivotal" to HIV. *The Press*, September 21, p. 3.

Gilman, S. L. (1988). AIDS and syphilis: The iconography of disease. In Crimp, D. (Ed.), *AIDS: Cultural analysis, cultural activism* (pp. 87–107). Cambridge: MIT Press.

Glaisyer, N., Chetwynd, J., & Plumridge, E. (1994). Social research on HIV/AIDS in New Zealand: A bibliography 1984–1993. Report to the Health Research Council of New Zealand.

Gorna, R. (1996). *Vamps, virgins and victims: How can women fight AIDS?* London: Cassell.

Healy, C. (1988). National Coordinator, New Zealand Prostitutes' Collective, Wellington, New Zealand. (Telephone Communication, February 15, 1998.)

Healy C., & Reed, A. (1994). The Healthy Hooker. *The New Internationalist*, 252, 16–17.

Holland, J., Ramazanoglu, C., Scott, S., & Thomson, R. (1994). Desire, risk and control: The body as site of contestation. In Doyal, L., Naidoo, J., & Wilton, T. (Eds), *AIDS: Setting a feminist agenda* (pp 61–79). London: Taylor and Francis.

Jordan, J. (1991). *Working Girls*. Auckland: Penguin Books.

Kehoe, J. (1992). Medicine, sexuality, and imperialism. British medical discourses surrounding venereal disease in New Zealand and Japan: A sociohistorical and comparative study. Unpublished Ph.D. dissertation, Wellington, Victoria University, New Zealand.

Lichtenstein, B. (1996). The iconography of Eve: Epidemiologic discourse in New Zealand's response to HIV/AIDS. Unpublished Ph.D. dissertation, Christchurch, University of Canterbury, New Zealand.

Lichtenstein, B. (1997). Tradition and experiment in New Zealand AIDS policy. *AIDS and Public Policy*, 12, 79–88.

Lindberg, W. (1998). New Zealand National Strategy. Paper presented at the Australian AIDS Conference, Tasmania, Australia.

Lupton, D. (1994). *Moral threats and dangerous desires: AIDS in the news media*. London: Taylor and Francis.

Moriarty, H. (1998). Medical Officer for the Sexual Health Services, Wellington, New Zealand, and the New Zealand Prostitutes' Collective, Wellington, New Zealand. (E-mail communication February 17, 1998.)

National Council on AIDS (1990). *The New Zealand strategy on HIV/AIDS, 1990*. Wellington, New Zealand: Department of Health.

National Council on AIDS (1990). Minutes 9, August 30.

————. (1988). Minutes 1, April 28.

New Zealand Prostitutes' Collective (1990). New Zealand Prostitutes' Collective working group on occupational regulation regarding The Massage Parlors Act. Submission to the New Zealand Parliament, July.

New Zealand Prostitutes' Collective service sheet (1995). August 7.

Patton, C. (1994). *Last served? Gendering the HIV pandemic*. London: Taylor and Francis.

Plant, M. (1990). *AIDS, drugs and prostitution*. London: Routledge.

Plumridge, E.W., Chetwynd, S.J., & Reed, A. (1997). Control and condoms in commercial sex: Client perspectives. *Sociology of Health and Illness*, 19, 228–43.

Sex Industry Rights and Education Network (1995). *Siren*. Magazine of the New Zealand Prostitutes' Collective, Wellington, New Zealand, September.

————. (1994). *Siren*. April.

Sullivan, B. (1995). Rethinking prostitution. In Caine, B., & Pringle, R. (Eds.), *Transitions: New Australian feminisms*. Sydney: Allen & Unwin.

The 1994 New Zealand Yearbook (1994). Government Printer, Wellington, New Zealand.

Treichler, P. A. (1988). AIDS, homophobia, and biomedical discourse: An epidemic of signification. In Crimp, D. (Ed.), *AIDS: Cultural analysis, cultural activism*. Cambridge: MIT Press.

Watney, S. (1988). The spectacle of AIDS. In Crimp, D. (Ed.), *AIDS: Cultural analysis, cultural activism*. Cambridge: MIT Press.

LONG-TERM CONSUMPTION OF "X-RATED" MATERIALS AND ATTITUDES TOWARD WOMEN AMONG AUSTRALIAN CONSUMERS OF X-RATED VIDEOS

Roberto Hugh Potter
Department of Sociology, Social Work, and Criminology
Morehead State University, Morehead, KY 40351

This article examines the results of a survey of 380 purchasers of X-rated videos throughout Australia. Of specific interest is the impact of pornography consumption on general attitudes toward women, as measured by items taken from the 1984 Australian National Social Science Survey. Analysis of the data indicate that variables measuring pornography consumption have no statistically significant impact on agreement or disagreement with "traditional" or "nontraditional" statements about women's roles and affirmative action. Age and educational attainment of the respondent prove to be the best predictors of response. The results are discussed in relation to previous results of studies of exposure to pornography and attitudes toward women, as well as the abandonment of this line of research by feminist and religious advocates of pornography censorship or prohibition.

Introduction

The history of social science pornography-related research has typically shadowed the moral/philosophical/legal discourses on sex. Perhaps the most damning indictment of pornography is its reputed link to violence against women (and children) and the fostering of negative attitudes toward women. For nearly two decades, a driving force in the study of the effects of consuming "pornographic" materials has been the impact of such materials on attitudes and behaviors toward women. This interest is often derived from the philosophical and political assertions of feminist writers, as well as prior research. Radical feminist authors, especially, have posited a direct causal link between "pornography" consumption and a wide range of both general and specific harms to women.

In the early 1990s, faced with equivocal evidence for the pornography-violence link, philosophical/legal arguments (especially feminist) have shifted focus from physical violence against women to the more systemic violence of discrimination against women engendered through pornography. The work of Edwin Schur (1965, 1983, 1988) is one of the best exemplars of the inter-relationship between social science work and feminist philosophy on pornography. In his earlier work, Schur (1965) included pornography among his category of "crimes without victims." By 1983, and especially in 1988, he had squarely identified pornography as a key contributor to the devaluation of and violence against women in American society. Many of the arguments developed by Schur and others are yet to be subjected to empirical test, however. The aim of this article is to test the effect of long-term consumption of pornographic materials (especially X-rated videos) on attitudes toward women. Data collected from an Australian sample will be used to test the assumptions put forward by theorists and prior researchers. The social science research and philosophical debate will be examined briefly prior to the empirical portion of the article.

Attitudes Toward Women: Social Science Evidence
of the Harm Caused by Pornography

Research studies on the consumption of pornographic materials and attitudes toward women have been of two basic types: laboratory experiments or ecological-level statistical studies. Laboratory studies generally utilize "volunteers" from introductory psychology courses or advertise for "subjects" in local newspapers. Their indicators of attitudes include such items as the prison sentences given to hypothetical rapists by subjects who have been exposed to various amounts of "pornographic" material (Zillmann & Bryant, 1984); the degree of electrical shock experimental subjects are willing to administer to a research confederate following exposure to "pornographic" materials and perhaps being angered; and the reported "likelihood of rape" (LR) among subjects in research settings (Malmuth & Ceniti, 1986; Boeringer, 1994). The ecological-level studies utilize various indicators of the status of women and other indicators of theoretically relevant variables, such as "adult" magazine sales, to explore the relationship between "pornography" sales and women's statuses or rape rates.

Laboratory Studies

The laboratory studies often put forward as exemplars of support for the link between pornography and negative attitudes toward women include those conducted by Zillmann and Bryant (1984, 1988). It is asserted that these experiments involving six hours or less of exposure to pornographic materials demonstrated decaying support for women. In fact, much of the research (Zillman & Bryant, 1984, 1988) focused on support for "family values." By this, Zillman and Bryant (1988) often meant that those in the experimental conditions where exposure to "sexually explicit" videos were shown demonstrated higher acceptance of non- and extra-marital sex, lowered the evaluation of marriage, and believed that sexual repression might lead to health problems. Experiments with college students conducted by Garcia (1986) found that exposure to "different types of sexual material" actually led to more "liberal" views toward women, which is exactly what Zillman and Bryant seem to decry in their research.

In the 1984 study, 80 male and 80 female university students were randomly assigned to either "no exposure," "nil," "intermediate," or "massive" exposure groups. Those students in the "intermediate" exposure group viewed two hours, twenty-four minutes (144 minutes total) of "erotic" films over a six-week period. Students in the "massive" exposure group watched twice that amount, or four hours, forty-eight minutes (288 minutes total), of erotic films over a six-week period. Subjects in the "no exposure" group were subjected to the full 228 minutes of "non-erotic" videos. Those in the "nil" group viewed no films and were only brought into the experiment during the assessment of attitudes or mock trial portion.

Part of the research dealt with prison sentences handed out to hypothetical rapists by participants in the various exposure categories. Zillman and Bryant note that the greater the exposure to pornographic materials the lower the prison sentences assigned to hypothetical rapists. This effect held for both men and women in the exposure groups. A similar relationship to attitudes toward accessibility of "explicit erotic films" and exposure category is also reported. That is, those who saw more erotic film did not express the same level of evaluation of such material's offensiveness, "pornographic" content, or need to restrict its availability to minors or from broadcast as those who saw none. Finally, Zillmann and Bryant (1984) did find that support for the women's liberation movement decreased with "massive" exposure to non-violent pornographic material. Zillmann and Bryant relate these differences to the degree of exposure to sexually explicit materials in the experiment.

Other studies (e.g., Fisher & Barak, 1991) have failed to replicate such findings using scales specifically designed to measure attitudes toward women following exposure to a wide range of pornographic materials. As noted above, Garcia (1986) found that his results were generally in the direction of increased "liberalism" toward women in society. Donnerstein, Linz, and Penrod (1987) summarize the research to that point as showing very little evidence that exposure to "pornographic" materials substantively changed participants' minds about women. Boeringer (1994; see also Felson, 1996) found that, consistent with earlier research, exposure to "soft-core pornography" was negatively related to the reporting of actual rape behavior and likelihood of rape (LR). He did find, however, that exposure to "hard-core violent and rape pornography" were most strongly related to respondents' reported actual sexual coercion and aggression, as well as to reported LR.

Ecological-Level Studies

Baron (1990) examined the relationship between circulation rates of "soft-core pornographic" magazines and gender equality in the fifty United States. Using indices of gender equality (including politics, economics, and legal rights), Baron sought to determine whether women would achieve less in states with higher "adult" magazine sales than in those with lower sales. This followed earlier work (Baron & Strauss, 1984) in which it was shown that states with higher "adult" magazine sales also had higher rape rates. Later analyses, including a measure of the sales of other magazines aimed at the male market (e.g., hunting and fishing, adventure magazines), revealed a much weaker relationship between sales of "adult" magazines and rape rates. Baron and Strauss then concluded that it was a "hypermasculine" climate that was responsible for the variation in rape rates rather than simply the sales of "pornography."

In the 1990 study, Baron found that sales of "adult" magazines were related to attitudes toward women in the opposite manner predicted by anti-pornography feminists. In those states with higher sales figures for "adult" magazines, women's accomplishments in the economic, political, and legal rights areas was actually higher than in states with lower sales figures (comparable results to Garcia's laboratory work). The best explanatory variable in Baron's (1990) model was the proportion of the state's population who were Southern Baptists, a measure of religious fundamentalism supporting sexual inequality (according to Baron). Gentry (1991) tested Baron and Strauss's results at the Standard Metropolitan Statistical Area-level (SMSA) and found that the association between "adult magazine" sales and rape rates fell below statistical significance. She concluded that the unit of measurement might play a greater role in the association than previously believed.

State of the Field

Evidence in support of a causal link between "pornographic" materials and aggression or attitudes toward women is at best scant. Even those to whom the strongest evidence is attributed admit this weakness (Donnerstein, Linz and Penrod, 1987). Several critics have outlined the methodological and technical shortcomings of such research (e.g., Baron, 1990; Fisher & Barak, 1991; Felson, 1996). Curiously, it can be seen that, with regard to attitudes toward women at least, the empirical research evidence to date tends to find consistently that increased exposure to "pornography" leads to more "liberal" attitudes toward women. As Zillmann and Bryant (1988, p. 542) note:

> Clearly, the findings we have presented cannot be discussed in a value vacuum. Dependent upon the reader's values regarding sexuality and marriage, they will be welcome news, decadent aberrations, or anything in between.... Our objective is not to support and fortify the one or the other value position. Rather, it is to understand what effects the prolonged consumption of pornography has, and exactly how these effects come about. We hope that a better understanding of the effects under consideration, as well as of their mediation, will aid those who ponder the question of pornography's social and societal impact and lead to more informed, less irrational debates concerning this volatile issue.

And, to that end, Zillmann and Bryant (1984, p. 136) write: "We cannot hope to gain much understanding by conducting one-exposure, one-session studies. We shall have to conduct longitudinal investigations. There is no alternative."

To date most studies of the "harm" of exposure to pornography have employed experimental or statistical designs believed to control for the impact of exposure to pornographic materials and other related variables. Little research into the "harm" done to attitudes toward women by consumption of "pornography" has involved regular consumers of materials identified as pornographic. The great majority of the research utilized university students. Although their ages are rarely presented, it could be assumed that they are at most in their early twenties, on average. The community volunteers utilized do tend to be older, but no measures of prior exposure to pornographic materials are used as a control variable in the analyses. Thus, one of the key shortcomings of prior research is the use of respondents who have had relatively little time to be exposed to pornography.

The study described here addresses the issue of long-term consumption of "pornographic" material through the use of long-term consumers in their "natural" environment. The current study is not longitudinal in its design, however. Rather, it measures the impact of length of reported consumption of "pornographic" materials on certain attitudes among regular consumers of these materials. This is an attempt to address some of the shortcomings of prior laboratory research and to gather further information about the impact of pornography consumption on attitudes toward women. Four items measuring attitudes toward women were included on a detailed questionnaire utilized in a national study of Australian consumers of X-rated videos completed by a nationwide availability sample of persons purchasing X-rated videos. These questions had been used previously on the General Social Sciences Survey (Kelley, Cushing & Headley, 1987), providing some nationally comparable data.

Methods

Setting

Australia presents an excellent setting in which to study the effects of non-violent sexually explicit materials ("pornography"). The content of all films, videos, video games, books, and magazines is "classified" by the Office of Film and Literature Classification (OFLC). Before such products can be made available (legally, at least) for public consumption, they must be rated. The X-rating is applied to sexually explicit videos, but forbids violence of any kind (OFLC, 1991). X-rated materials are available by mail-order only in the Australian states, but may be purchased in "adult shops" in the two territories. The distributors of X-rated videos are politically organized, offering a central body with whom the author coordinated the study from which these data are taken. See Potter (1996a) for a fuller discussion of these factors.

Participants

"Theoretical sampling" (Glaser & Strauss, 1967; Strauss &

Corbin, 1990) suggests that in order to study the effects of pornography consumption one should sample persons who consume these products. Determining how many people consume such materials and how best to obtain information about them presented the first problem in conducting this research. The exact number of persons who consume pornographic materials in Australia is unknown and the subject of speculation. One major distributor claimed to have 120,000 names on his mailing list, although he pointed out that only about 20,000 (16.66 percent) of those were "regular" customers. The largest retailing group offered similar figures for its mailing list. Other retailers' claims ranged downward to at least 10,000. However, such lists may not capture those who visit "adult" shops in Sydney, Melbourne, Canberra, or other cities where such shops are legal but where the sale of X-rated videos is not. Nor would mailing lists capture people who might be members of "swap clubs" that operate in some communities. Overall estimates by industry representatives are in the area of 800,000 consumers of X-rated videos and a total of 2 million consumers of "pornography" (Wilson, 1995). Australia's total population is around 18 million people.

A fuller description of the methodology for the study is detailed elsewhere (Potter, 1996a), as is a full demographic description of the respondents (Potter, 1996b). Briefly, the respondents were overwhelmingly male (90 percent; n = 338), and the average age was 39 years (range from 18 to 78), with women being on average five years younger. Respondents tended to be in intact marriages (41 percent; n = 156) or never married (33 percent; n = 123). About 10 percent of the respondents indicated that they were gay or lesbian. Nearly one-third (31 percent; n = 113) reported having children under the age of 18 living in their homes. Just over half (51 percent; n = 114) of the respondents reported having a high school or lower educational attainment. The largest proportion of the respondents (44 percent; n = 154) were in professional or managerial occupations, with higher overall income than the average Australian resident. It should be noted here that, on average, the respondents had been viewing X-rated videos for fourteen years (women for eleven years).

The questions used in this study were taken from items included in the 1984 General Social Science Survey conducted by the Australian National University (Kelley et al., 1987). While they are not as comprehensive and specific as some scales used in the research outlined above, the responses of the X-rated video consumers can be compared to responses of a representative sample of the Australian population on the same questions. There are problems with this approach (e.g., the different time frames and sampling techniques, response category differences), so that the comparisons must be considered with caution.

Procedure

The survey was conducted with the cooperation of one of the largest mail-order distributors of X-rated videos in Australia. Two "adult" shops in Canberra (associated with the large mail-order house) agreed to place survey forms into customer purchases during the same time period covered by the mail-order survey. A total of 1,887 survey forms were shipped to the distributors as follows: 1,750 forms to be mailed to customers from the Darwin-based merchant, and 137 forms to be distributed at the two shops in Canberra. The mailings began from Darwin in late September and ended in late October 1992. The questionnaires in Canberra were handed out over a two-week period in mid-October 1992.

The method of distribution was the insertion of survey forms and post-paid return envelopes into packages of videos being shipped to customers. By agreement with the distributor no access to the names or addresses of those to whom the questionnaires were delivered was made available to the researcher. No follow-up reminders or second questionnaires were to be mailed. This fact was mentioned in the cover letter of the questionnaire, drafted by the distributor and the researcher. All possible steps were taken to guarantee anonymity of the respondents, also spelled out in the cover letter. The merchants estimated a return rate ranging from 1 percent to 5 percent.

Three hundred eighty (20 percent) useable survey forms were returned. Several other forms were returned, one from as far away as the Netherlands, but were not completed (two further forms arrived in early 1994). By usual survey standards, this is not an overwhelming response rate. However, given the nature of the subject matter, the survey design employed, and the exploratory nature of the study, it provides a first glimpse at those who consume X-rated videos in Australia.

Despite its methodological limitations, this study is important because, for the first time in the published literature, people who actually and actively consume "pornographic" materials were surveyed. There is a degree of self-selection here, to be sure. However, these are not individuals whose exposure is limited to walking by a newsstand and glimpsing covers of magazines, or covers ("slicks") of video cassettes on the rack of a video store. These are consumers who took the time to place an order for material (or browse the Canberra store shelves), paid for that material, and had it delivered to their homes. Previous studies primarily have taken university students and exposed them to brief clips or readings of "pornographic" material, whether or not these "subjects" were interested in the material outside of the experimental setting. Perhaps one of the best ways to summarize this is that the current sample is comprised of motivated, paying customers, whereas most previous experimental studies involved passive "subjects."

The Statements

Items A (WPREF, hiring preference for women) and B (WEARN, women should earn as much as their husbands) are viewed as opinion statements that support "non-traditional" attitudes toward women (see Table 1). That is, agreement with these two statements represents support for women occupying non-traditional roles in society and affirmative action for women. Items C (DEVOTE, married women should devote most of their energies to their families) and D (WCAREER, women should not attach too much importance to their own careers) are viewed as opinion statements which support more "traditional" attitudes toward women. Agreement with these two statements is taken to

indicate that respondents hold traditional views of women's social roles. Finally, item E (DEGWOM, all women are degraded
by pornography) is an attempt to assess consumers' attitudes toward a basic tenet of anti-pornography feminism (and fundamentalist) belief about pornography and attitudes toward women.

Results

Frequency and Bivariate Analysis

The responses of the X-rated video consumers to the statements
are presented in Table 1. The far right-hand column presents the
overall responses of the 1984 respondents for comparison purposes. Item A, regarding preferential treatment of women in hiring decisions, is the only statement to which the X-rated video
consumers expressed attitudes that might be considered less supportive of women than those of the GSSS respondents. The GSSS
format employed a Likert scale response format that resulted in
up to 22 percent of respondents registering no definite response.
Most of these were "neither," rather than missing responses or
refusals. The current survey only included a "Don't Know" response category.

When the "Don't Know" and "Neither" categories are removed
in the statement regarding preferential hiring of women, the real
difference in responses appears to be in the strength of disagreement between the two samples. There is a 20 percentage point
difference in the "strongly disagree" category between the
samples. However, 90 percent of the consumers and 92 percent
of the GSSS respondents disagree with the statement to some
degree. There is still a significant statistical association between
the groups and response categories ($X^2 = 48.22$, df = 3, p<.001).
In written comments, the video consumers noted that while such
remedies may be needed in some circumstances, they would still
rather see people compete on merit rather than rely on an affirmative action approach.

On items B, C, and D, the attitudes expressed by the X-rated
video consumers are consistently in a direction more supportive

TABLE 1
Attitudes toward Women among X-rated Video Consumers

A) Women should be given preferential treatment when applying for jobs.

	Total		Males		Females		GSSS	
	%	n	%	n	%	n	%	n
Strongly Disagree	36	(121)	37	(110)	30	(11)	16	(483)
Disagree	54	(182)	54	(161)	54	(20)	58	(1721)
Agree	5	(18)	5	(15)	5	(2)	5	(153)
Strongly Agree	4	(12)	3	(9)	8	(3)	1	(40)
Don't Know	2	(7)	2	(6)	3	(1)	20*	(592)
		(340)		(301)		(37)		(2926)

B) I approve of a married woman earning money in business or industry even if she has a husband capable of supporting her.

	Total		Males		Females		GSSS	
	%	n	%	n	%	n	%	n
Strongly Disagree	2	(7)	2	(7)	0	(0)	4	(128)
Disagree	5	(18)	6	(17)	3	(1)	20	(594)
Agree	66	(225)	66	(200)	64	(23)	53	(1564)
Strongly Agree	25	(87)	25	(75)	33	(12)	9	(278)
Don't Know	2	(5)	2	(5)	0	(0)	14*	(413)
		(342)		(304)		(36)		(2777)

C) A woman should devote almost all her time to her family.

	Total		Males		Females		GSSS	
	%	n	%	n	%	n	%	n
Strongly Disagree	22	(75)	20	(60)	42	(15)	5	(162)
Disagree	59	(202)	62	(187)	36	(13)	43	(1270)
Agree	12	(39)	12	(36)	8	(3)	27	(802)
Strongly Agree	4	(14)	4	(11)	8	(3)	5	(162)
Don't Know	3	(10)	3	(8)	6	(2)	20*	(583)
		(340)		(302)		(36)		(2979)

D) A married woman should not attach much importance to a career.

	Total		Males		Females		GSSS	
	%	n	%	n	%	n	%	n
Strongly Disagree	32	(111)	31	(94)	46	(17)	8	(250)
Disagree	48	(166)	50	(153)	32	(12)	43	(1266)
Agree	9	(31)	9	(27)	11	(4)	23	(688)
Strongly Agree	6	(21)	5	(16)	11	(4)	4	(118)
Don't Know	4	(14)	5	(14)	0	(0)	22*	(648)
		(343)		(304)		(37)		(2853)

E) X-rated (NVE) videos degrade all women.

	Total		Males		Females	
	%	n	%	n	%	n
Strongly Disagree	55	(187)	57	(174)	35	(13)
Disagree	37	(125)	34	(103)	59	(22)
Agree	2	(6)	1	(4)	3	(1)
Strongly Agree	6	(20)	6	(19)	3	(1)
Don't Know	1	(4)	1	(4)	0	(0)
		(342)		(304)		(37)

Notes: Comparison with General Social Science Survey data.

*GSSS utilized a Likert scale approach, a Likert-type was utilized in the present study.

Some rounding errors result in totals exceeding or falling below 100 percent.

of women than those expressed by the representative sample of Australians (GSSS) asked the same questions a few years earlier. Cursory inspection of the data indicates that the X-rated video consumers provided more support for the less traditional attitudes than did the GSSS sample. The statistical analyses of the responses (again, excluding the "Neither" and "Don't Know" categories) confirm the association between the two groups and their expressed attitudes toward women, with significant X^2 values (p<.001). While one would hope that general attitudes toward women have improved over this time period, it is unlikely that they would have increased to the extent found here.

Finally, item E, regarding the degradation of women by X-rated videos, sought to solicit responses to one of the primary contentions of anti-pornography feminists and religious fundamentalists. Those who responded to this question overwhelmingly rejected the assertion that X-rated videos degrade all women. While men and women overall disagreed with this statement, the reversal in strength of disagreement is quite interesting and begs further study, as do other differences in the strength of opinions held by male and female X-rated video consumers.

The results presented in Table 1 do not provide initial support for the hypothesis that long-term consumption of "pornography" leads to or is associated with negative attitudes toward women. To test the ideas further, variables thought to be important in predicting such attitudes were subjected to a correlational analysis. The results are presented in Tables 2 and 3.

The interrelationships among the dependent variables, or attitudes toward women, are presented in Table 2. From a strictly technical point, the strength of the correlations (r values) shows that, while statistically related to each other, most variables appear to be measuring different aspects of attitudes toward women. The highest correlation in Table 2 is between women devoting time to their families and women not placing too much emphasis on their own careers (r = .67), the two "traditional" opinion statements.

The correlation coefficients among the dependent variables and theoretically important independent variables are presented in Table 3. Of particular interest for this study are the relationships

TABLE 2
Correlations among the Attitude towards Women Variables

	DEGWOM	WPREF	WEARN	DEVOTE	WCAREER
DEGWOM	1.000				
WPREF	.293***	1.000			
WEARN	−.165**	−.110*	1.000		
DEVOTE	.184***	.240***	−.224***	1.000	
WCAREER	.299***	.322***	−.240***	.672***	1.000

Notes: *p < .05; **p < .01; ***p < .001.

TABLE 3
Correlations among the Attitudes toward Women Variables
and Selected Independent Variables

	DEGWOM	WPREF	WEARN	DEVOTE	WCAREER
AGE	.090	.143**	−.143**	.190***	.209***
RELGTH	.060	.044*	−.039	.062	.026
EDUC	−.032	−.032	.180***	−.119*	−.182***
INC	−.031	−.067	.171***	−.065	−.141**
OCODE	.044	.011	.134**	−.086	−.073
LGTVMAG	.027	.110*	−.124*	.199***	.149**
LGTVX	.087	.014	−.092	.177***	.191***
OFTENVX	−.025	.010	−.062	.099	.066
HOUSE	−.000	−.033	−.022	.047	.048

Notes: *p < .05 ; **p < .01;***p < .001.

among the indicators of "pornography" consumption (length of viewing X-rated videos, length of reading "adult" magazines, and the frequency of watching X-rated videos) and the various attitudes toward women. LGTVX measures the number of years respondents have been watching X-rated type movies (mean = 14.7 years). LGTVMAG measures the number of years respondents have been reading "adult" magazines (mean = 21.8 years). OFTENVX measures the frequency with which the respondents watch X-rated movies (mean = less than once per week). Standard sociodemographic variables (age, education, income, and occupational category) are also included in the correlations, as they may help to predict the attitudes. Finally, for those who are in relationships, the length of the relationship (RELGTH) is included (mean = 10.22 years).

For Item A (giving women preference in hiring), there are two statistically significant relationships, although neither is very strong. The number of years that respondents have been reading "adult" magazines is the only consumption variable significantly related to preferential hiring support ($r = .11$, $p < .05$). Thus, the longer people have been reading "adult" magazines the more they agree that women should be given preferential treatment in hiring decisions. This appears to run counter to the hypothesis that consumption of "pornographic" materials is associated with anti-female attitudes. The more strongly related variable to preferential hiring support is the age of the respondent ($r = .148$, $p < .01$). That is, the older the respondent the more likely he or she is to agree with preferential hiring for women.

Item B, approval of women earning money even if their husbands are capable of supporting them, has several variables significantly related to it, although the correlations are weak. The number of years reading adult magazines is again the only consumption item significantly related to this attitude ($r = -.124$, $p < .05$). Here we find that the longer respondents have been reading "adult" magazines the less likely they are to approve of a woman earning money if she has a husband capable of supporting her. This would appear to be consistent with the hypotheses of anti-pornography feminism about pornography and attitudes toward women. Sociodemographic variables are more strongly (though still weakly) related to support for this statement. The educational attainment of the respondent ($r = .180$, $p < .001$), reported income of the respondent ($r = .171$, $p < .001$), and occupation of the respondent ($r = .134$, $p < .01$) all show positive relationships with support for married women earning money. That is, as one's educational/occupational attainment and income increase, so does support for a woman to earn money even if her husband is capable of supporting her. The age of the respondent, on the other hand, shows a significant negative relationship ($r = -.143$, $p < .01$) with this statement. As age increases, respondents are less supportive of women earning money when they have husbands capable of supporting them.

The first of the more traditional statements (Item C or DE-VOTE) concerns women devoting most of their time to their family. Here we find that both the number of years respondents have been reading adult magazines ($r = .199$, $p < .001$) and the number of years they have been viewing X-rated videos ($r = .177$, $p < .001$) are significantly and positively related with supporting the statement. This means that the longer respondents have been consuming these types of materials the more they agree that a woman should devote most of her time to her family. These are again supportive of arguments of anti-pornography feminists. The same (though slightly stronger) relationship is observed with the age of the respondent ($r = .199$, $p < .001$). The older the respondent, the stronger the agreement with this statement. Only the level of educational attainment ($r = -.119$, $p < .05$) shows a significant relationship in the opposite direction. The higher the educational attainment, the more respondents disagreed with the statement.

Item D, the idea that women should not attach much importance to their own careers, is the second traditional statement. Here we again find the number of years reading adult magazines ($r = .149$, $p < .01$) and the number of years of watching X-rated videos ($r = .191$, $p < .001$) to be significantly and positively related to the statement. Respondents who have been consuming "pornographic" materials for longer periods more strongly agree that women should not attach much importance to a career. This again is supportive of assertions by anti-pornography feminists. The age of the respondent ($r = .209$, $p < .01$) is again the most strongly positively related variable to support for the statement, such that as age increases so does agreement with the statement. And, we again find significant negative associations between educational attainment ($r = -.182$, $p < .001$), reported income ($r = -.141$, $p < .01$), and support for the statement. As these two increase, support for the statement decreases.

The final indicator of attitudes toward women is Item E, "X-rated (NVE) videos degrade all women." None of the variables show either a significant or a strong relationship to this statement.

Indicators of consumption of "pornographic" materials appear to indicate no association in the direction predicted by anti-pornography feminism with two of the five attitude statements, pref- erential hiring of women and the belief that X-rated videos de- grade all women. The most consistently associated of the consumption variables is the indicator of how long respondents had been reading "adult" magazines. Its association is in the pre- dicted direction on three of the five measures of attitudes toward women. The measure of how long respondents had been watch- ing X-rated movies shows the expected association in only two of the attitudinal statements. It should be noted that the frequency with which respondents report viewing X-rated videos shows no significant association with any of the opinion statements. At the bivariate level we appear to have some support for predictions made by anti-pornography feminist writers.

Educational attainment, income, and occupational category also show significant relationships to the idea that married women should be allowed to earn money through employed work. Education and income show similar relationships with allowing women to attach importance to their own careers. Edu- cation is significantly related to agreement with notions of women's devotion to their families. All of these relationships are such that, as attainment on each increases, support for non- traditional views of women's roles is increased. This is consis- tent with "liberal" notions about the impact of education and its associated benefits.

The most problematic of the variables for anti-pornography feminism is age of the respondent. It is the only variable that shows a significant relationship with four of the five variables. With the exception of preferential hiring for women, age is always associ- ated with support for the more traditional views of women's so- cial roles. Complicating this is the high level of correlation between age and both the number of years consuming adult magazines ($r = .86$, $p < .001$) and X-rated videos ($r = .62$, $p < .001$). The same relationship does not hold for the relationship between age and frequency of viewing X-rated videos ($r = .04$, $p < .43$). It will remain for a multivariate analysis to determine whether the ef- fects of length of consumption are important, or whether they are artifacts of the respondents' ages.

Multivariate Analysis

In an attempt to unravel the associations among the various in-dependent variables and the dependent variables (attitudes toward women), separate ordinary least squares regression models were created. The independent variables used as predictors were age of the respondent, educational attainment, occupational category, fre-quency of viewing X-rated videos, income, length of their current relationship, political party supported in the previous national elec-tion, and number of years the respondent had been watching X-rated videos. Where cases had missing values, the mean value for the particular variable was substituted. A cross-tabulation demon-strated that those who had zero (0) value on the length of relation-ship variable (RELGTH) were indeed those who reported not currently being in a relationship, rather than being missing data.

The number of years of reading adult magazines was omitted from these models because of its high intercorrelation with age ($r = .85$). This high degree of relationship suggests that this vari-able might be measuring essentially the same phenomenon as the age variable and, as age precedes the likelihood of reading such material, the broader measure of age was left in the model. Al-though the number of years of watching X-rated videos and age correlate at a level which might indicate some dangers of multicolinearity ($r = .66$), it is borderline. The decision to leave the number of years of viewing X-rated videos in also offers two measures of "pornography" consumption. In the end, this is a judgment call on the part of the researcher. However, as the pri-mary interest in this research was X-rated videos, the decision to err on this side was made.

The first regression model regressed support for preferential hiring of women on the independent variables. This model failed to attain statistical significance, and predicted almost none of the variance ($R^2 = .03$). That is, this model tells us almost nothing about predicting the respondents' attitudes toward women being given preferential treatment in hiring decisions.

The results of regressing support for married women earning their own money even when their husband could support them on the independent variables produced unclear results. It may be noted that the overall model attains statistical significance ($F = 3.730$, $p < .001$), although the explained variance is only 8 percent ($R^2 = .075$). Examining the individual predictors, the age of the respondent and educational attainment prove to be statistically significant. Increasing age is associated with opposition to the statement that a woman should be able to earn money in business regardless of her husband's capacity to support her. As educational attainment increases, however, so does agreement with the statement. Age and educational attainment appear to play opposing roles in attitudes expressed on this statement.

Next, support for the statement that a woman should devote most of her attention to her family was regressed on the independent variables. Again we find that the model is statistically significant ($F = 3.397$, $p < .001$) but still explains little of the variance ($R^2 = .069$). Only the age of the respondent has a significant impact. As age increases, so does agreement with the statement that a woman should devote most of her time to her family.

Support for the idea that a woman should not attach much significance to her own career was regressed on the independent variables. This model is also highly statistically significant ($F = 5.447$, $p < .0001$) and explains more of the variance than any other model, but still not much ($R^2 = .106$). The age and educational attainment of the respondent are again the strongest predictors of this attitude, again in different directions. Educational attainment appears to be the strongest independent predictor ($B = -.155$) such that, as educational attainment increases, so does disagreement with the statement that a woman should not attach much importance to a career. The impact of age ($B = .146$) is that when age increases, so does agreement with the statement.

Discussion

The preceding results do not demonstrate support for the hypothesis that long-term consumption of "pornographic" materials negatively influences general attitudes toward women. Variables measuring pornography consumption drop out of predictive significance when age and educational attainment of the respondents are controlled for simultaneously. The effects of these two variables are in the same direction of "liberal" or non-traditional attitudes toward women demonstrated by researchers cited earlier. These results provide no support for the contention that consumption of sexually explicit materials leads to a more generalized and insidious hatred of women.

It can be seen from the regression analyses that, while we are able to generate statistically significant models for three of four attitudinal variables, we are not able to explain much about why people hold these attitudes. What is of particular interest for this article is that *none* of the measures of "pornography" consumption shows any statistically significant relationship to any of the attitudinal responses from those surveyed. Age most consistently predicts agreement with the more "traditional" statements about women's roles in society. That is, the older respondents are more likely to favor "traditional" roles, except in the case of preferential hiring of women. Educational attainment consistently predicts agreement with the "less traditional" role statements, and disagreement with the "traditional" ones.

The present study is another example of a failure to find a demonstrable link between consumption of pornography and negative attitudes toward women. There are two aspects of this research that make it unique in addressing this issue. First is the use of "regular" consumers of X-rated videos who have a truly longitudinal consumption history in a society with definable notions of an "X-rating." Second is the use of statements that tap more subtle aspects of institutional sexism rather than potential physical harm. And, as noted above, the consumption variables show no statistically significant impact on the attitudes toward women measured in the study.

Given the consistent failure of social science research to demonstrate this link between consumption of, or exposure to, pornography and attitudes toward women, one is left to wonder how it has become a staple of "conventional wisdom." Altimore (1991) addresses several aspects of this question in his analysis of how the social science research has been used by the Meese Commission in the United States and the media coverage of pornography-related issues. Downs (1989) provides a more detailed study of the specific political processes by which the Dworkin and MacKinnon ordinance was shepherded through two U.S. jurisdictions. An analysis based in a social constructionist technique should help in further understanding why and how such information is used to establish "harm" in the minds of those in the general public (if it is) and comes to be enacted into legislative programs. An analysis of these processes focusing on a "moral crusade" and "social constructionist" approach is presented in greater detail in Potter (1996a).

The theme to be developed here regards the abandoning of research such as this to study the impact of pornography consumption on empirical social behavior, as opposed to expressions of possible intent or constrained laboratory responses. Critiques of the social science research examining the impact of pornography exposure on attitudes toward women have shown that this research tradition has provided little evidence of harmful effects. The use of the purported evidence of the harmful effect of pornography exposure on attitudes toward women has been examined to show how (particularly) anti-pornography feminists have tried to construct pornography as a harmful social problem (see also Gray, 1982; Altimore, 1991; Potter, 1996a).

As a body of evidence to support the need for censorship of sexually explicit material, the social science research itself is of little value (Itzin, 1992). The use of this material by anti-pornography groups, both feminist and religious, has managed to somehow avoid the consistent lack of a demonstrated link between exposure to or consumption of pornographic material and negative attitudes toward women. The use of such material in the construction of a social "reality" in which such a link is alleged to exist deserves further and fine-grained analysis.

The aim of such an analysis is not to denigrate the efforts of feminists and others to point out the social desirability of equal treatment of women. Rather, such an analysis should enable us to better understand how the knowledge produced in the academic sphere is used outside that arena as a resource in shaping public opinion and possibly social action. Weaver (1992) has advocated switching from the rigorous requirements of social science standards of "proof" (roughly equivalent to the "beyond a reasonable doubt" standard of criminal trials) to a "balance of probabilities" standard (roughly equivalent to the standard of a civil trial) to make policy-relevant decisions on pornography. Goldsmith (1993) has admitted that social science will not provide the "smoking gun" needed to convince the public to censor pornographic material. She, too, advocates abandoning the rigors of social science in favor of a more politically expeditious remedy. Concomitant with this line of reasoning has been the approach of either ignoring or dismissing evidence contradictory to the position held by the "advocacy" writers. Such techniques abandon the norms of social science in favor of the adversarial approach of legal arguments. That is, "make your case, ignore any inconvenient information, and denigrate anyone who would contradict you." On three continents, then, we see a move to ignore or downplay social science evidence that is not supportive of the anti-pornography position by moving to a more directly political line of action.

Many anti-pornography feminists reject the assertion that their claims of "harm" from "pornography" are "moral" claims. However, several works in the social constructionist tradition (e.g., Gusfield, 1963, 1981; Becker, 1973) have pointed out the role of "moral entrepreneurs" in seeking to establish "normative dominance" of a particular group's definition of morality on the rest of a given society. In Gusfield's (1963) work on temperance movements, it was shown that women played a major role in temperance movements in the United States that culminated in Prohibition. More recently, Leong (1991) has outlined the similarities between the leadership provided by women in the anti-pornography campaigns and previous "moral crusades" in the United States and Great Britain.

Schneider (1984), responding to concerns that "morality" does not imply behavior, notes that morality, for sociologists, is a matter of behavioral accomplishment. That is, morality is more than an abstract code of conduct, it is an implied "correct" way of behaving; one that is constantly open to negotiation among groups with varying degrees of power and other social resources. Thus, conceptions of "morality" are central to any group seeking to change the way in which behavior is structured.

Perhaps the reason pornography remains such a powerful field for rhetoric and action by both feminists and fundamentalists is the symbolic role it plays for both. For fundamentalists, it is one of the tangible embodiments of evil to which they can point as needing change. When anti-pornography feminists attack pornography and seek to present it as a social issue or problem, they are metaphorically attacking patriarchy, a constructed explanation of social differences attributed to social interpretations of biological sex. Pornography is observable, some would say pervasive and immediate, and allegedly profitable for those who produce and distribute it. These are themes developed by Brown (1992) and Potter (1996a). Perhaps it is also time to consider the role pornography has played in the development of feminist jurisprudence (e.g., MacKinnon, 1985; Smart, 1989) and the attack on social science research from all sides (Altimore, 1991).

References

Altimore, M. (1991). The social construction of a scientific myth: Pornography and violence. *Journal of Communication Inquiry,* 15 (1), 117–133.

Baron, L. (1990). Pornography and gender equality: An empirical analysis. *Journal of Sex Research,* 27 (3), 363–380.

Baron, L., & Strauss, M. A. (1984). Sexual stratification, pornography, and rape in the United States. In Malamuth, N., & Donnerstein, E. (Eds.), *Pornography and sexual aggression.* Orlando: Academic Press.

Becker, H. S. (1973). *Outsiders: Studies in the sociology of deviance.* New York: Free Press.

Boeringer, S. (1994). Pornography and sexual agression: Associations of violent and nonviolent depictions with rape and rape prolicivity. *Deviant Behavior,* 15, 289–304.

Brown, B. (1992). Symbolic politics and pornography. *Economy and Society,* 21(1), 45–57.

Childress, S. A. (1991). Reel "rape speech": Violent pornography and the politics of harm. *Law & Society Review,* 25(1), 177–214.

Donnerstein, E., Linz, D., & Penrod, S. (1987). *The question of pornography.* New York: The Free Press.

Downs, D. (1989). *The new politics of pornography.* Chicago: University of Chicago Press.

Felson, R. B. (1996). Mass media effects on violent behavior. *Annual Review of Sociology*, 22, 103–28.

Fisher, W. A., & Barak, A. (1991). Pornography, erotica, and behavior: More questions than answers. *International Journal of Law and Psychiatry*, 14, 65–83.

Garcia, L. T. (1986). Exposure to pornography and attitudes about women and rape: A correlational study. *Journal of Sex Research*, 22, 378–385.

Gentry, C. S. (1991). Pornography and rape: An empirical analysis. *Deviant Behavior*, 12, 277–288.

Glaser, B., & Strauss, A. (1967). *The discovery of grounded theory: Strategies for qualitative research*. Chicago: Aldine.

Goldsmith, M. (1993). Pornography and sexual violence. *Quadrant*, November, pp. 26–31.

Gray, S. H. (1982). Exposure to pornography and aggression toward women: The case of the angry male. *Social Problems*, 29, 4, 387–398.

Gusfield, J. R. (1963). *Symbolic crusade: Status politics and the American temperance movement*. Urbana: University of Illinois Press.

Gusfield, J. R. (1981). *The culture of social problems*. Chicago: University of Chicago Press.

Itzin, C. (Ed.) (1992). *Pornography: Women, violence and civil liberties—A radical new view*. Oxford: Oxford University Press.

Kelley, J., Cushing, R. G., & Headley, B. (1987). *Australian National Social Science Survey 1984*. Canberra: Social Science Data Archives, The Australian National University.

Leong, W. T. (1991). The pornography "problem": Disciplining women and young girls. *Media Culture and Society*, 13, 91–117.

MacKinnon, C. (1985). Pornography, civil rights, and speech: Commentary. *Harvard Civil Rights-Civil Liberties Law Review*, 20, 1–70.

Potter, R. H. (1996a). *Pornography: Group pressures and individual rights*. Sydney: The Federation Press.

Potter, R. H. (1996b). Potential criminals?: Australian consumers of X-rated videos. *Behavioral Sciences and the Law*, 14, 231–243.

Schneider, J. W.(1984). Morality, social problems, and everyday life. In Kitsuse, J. I., & Schneider, J. W. (Eds.), *Studies in the sociology of social problems*. Norwood, N.J.: Ablex Publishing Co.

Schur, E. (1965). *Crimes without victims*. Engelwood Cliffs, NJ: Prentice-Hall.

Schur, E. (1983). *Labeling women deviant: Gender, stigma, and social control*. Philadelphia: Temple University Press.

Schur, E. (1988). *The americanization of sex*. Philadelphia: Temple University Press.

Smart, C. (1989). *Feminism and the power of law*. London: Routledge.

Spector, M., & Kitsuse, J. I. (1977). *Constructing social problems*. Menlo Park, CA: Cummings Publishing Co.

Strauss, A., & Corbin, J. (1990). *Basics of qualitative research: Grounded theory procedures and techniques*. Newbury Park, CA: Sage.

Weaver, J. (1992). The social science and psychological research evidence: Perceptual and behavioural consequences of exposure to pornography. In

Itzin, C. (Ed.), *Pornography: Women, violence and civil liberties*. Oxford: Oxford University Press.

Wilson, P. (1995). *In defence of pornography*. Sydney: University of New South Wales Press.

Zillmann, D., & Bryant, J. (1984). Effects of massive exposure to pornography. In Malamuth, & Donnerstein (Eds.), *Pornography and sexual aggression* (pp. 115–138). Orlando: Academic Press.

Zillmann, D., & Bryant, J. (1988). Pornography, sexual callousness, and the trivialization of rape. In Kimmel, M. (Ed.), *Men confront pornography* (pp. 207–218). New York: Crown Publishers.

Sex Work and Sex
Workers (Sexuality and
Culture, Vol 2) 1999

SEX, BEACH BOYS, AND FEMALE TOURISTS IN THE CARIBBEAN

Klaus de Albuquerque
*Department of Sociology, College of Charleston
Charleston, SC 29424*

This article explores the relationships between beach boys, rent-a-dreads, and female tourists in the Caribbean. I argue that these relationships should be correctly termed "sex tourism"; however, unlike South East Asia, where degradation and exploitation of sex workers by tourists is common, sex tourism in the Caribbean is generally mutually beneficial. I maintain that one of the prime motivations propelling Euro-American women to the Caribbean is the racialized sexual fantasy of black male hypersexuality—a fantasy that Caribbean societies encourage and sustain through song and dance.

Prologue

One of the most enduring calypsos (satirical songs usually of a political or sexual nature often employing double entendres) played at tourist resorts throughout the Caribbean is entitled *The Big Bamboo*. The calypso is about a woman who cannot be appeased by anything, sugarcane or coconuts; instead, all she wants is the big bamboo. Of course, the Calypsonian clutches himself appropriately at the verses invoking the big bamboo and directs his attention to the women in the audience, who nervously titter while their male counterparts look uncomfortable. Hsu (personal communication) argues that the song "sets up a sexual rivalry between tourist men (read 'white, ex-colonial') and Caribbean men." It also subtly reinforces the popular myth of the sexual endowment, and presumable sexual prowess of the black Caribbean male and the performance demands made upon him by his female counterpart.

The sexual power of the Caribbean male is a major theme in West Indian music, but it is in contemporary Jamaican dance halls that lyrics involving penis size and sexual performance have reached new heights of explicitness. So successfully has the sexual power of the Caribbean male been communicated through song and music videos, that some female tourists literally get off the plane single-mindedly embarked on the holy grail (the search for the big bamboo).

Introduction

As tourism has evolved into the largest global industry (WTO, 1997), supplanting the trade in oil and arms, there has been mounting concern over its environmental and socio-cultural costs (Harrison, 1992; de Albuquerque & McElroy, 1992, 1995). One of the social costs that has received increasing attention is the degradation and exploitation of women and children that often accompanies one form of tourism, namely, sex tourism. Part of the larger social phenomenon of prostitution, sex tourism is simply one facet of the global sex trade, where destinations are marketed, usually unofficially (although Thailand and the Philippines at one stage even sponsored sex tourism as national policy), for their sexual attractions, and travel is undertaken mainly to engage in some kind of sexual activity. Gay (1985, p. 34) estimates that between 70 percent and 80 percent of male tourists who travel from Japan, Australia, Western Europe, and North America to Asia do it solely for sexual entertainment. Today, there are few places in the world immune from sex tourism, and hot new sexual Meccas (for example, Havana and Budapest) emerge yearly.

Two Separate Realities

The extensive literature on sex tourism, both popular and academic, portrays some very different realities. The popular writing invariably presents highly emotive accounts of the sexual exploitation and degradation of Third World women and children followed by attempts to mobilize action through a number of Third World ecumenical organizations and their local affiliates. These organizations have lobbied governments in South and Southeast Asia to end the worst abuses of sex tourism. However, they have met with little success, as sex tourism is big business—US$20 billion alone in Thailand if one takes into account what Thai men also spend on prostitutes (Kruhaug, 1997).

The popular literature (print and electronic) on sex tourism also has its seamier side—from articles in porn "zines" to racy sexual guide books touting new-found sexual Meccas, providing tips on where to stay and what to experience, reporting on prevailing prices for services, and sounding updates on sexually transmitted diseases.

The academic literature is also fraught with some of the same moralism and sensationalism (Ericsson, 1980), largely because it tends to be rather strongly ideological, written from either a Third World (Truong, 1990), Neo Marxist (Britton, 1982; Ong, 1985; Cincone, 1988; Leheny, 1995) or Feminist perspective, in which prostitution is simply treated as another example of masculine power and privilege (Hawkesworth, 1984; Enloe, 1989; Hill, 1993). In fact, so dominant is the portrayal of sex tourism as deviant and exploitative that the academic discourse has generally ignored the liminal, mutually beneficial, and in some cases, companionship and romance aspects of sex tourism (Cohen, 1986; Ryan & Kindler, 1996b; Pruitt & LaFont, 1995). While sexual fantasy is often viewed as an important element in sex tourism (Ryan & Kindler, 1996b), with the exception of O'Connell Davidson (1995), researchers have not addressed the issue of racialized sexual fantasy as the primary fantasy element motivating sex tourists. Karch and Dann (1981) allude to this when they reenact the encounters between Barbadian beach boys and female tourists.

The academic discourse has also focused its attention almost entirely on male tourists, neglecting the fact that women are traveling in greater numbers, and independently of men, and are seeking sexual encounters free from the strictures traditionally imposed by their own cultures (Pruitt & LaFont, 1995).

Female Sex Tourists: A Growing Constituency

Male sex tourists vastly outnumber their female counterparts and are far more visible. Nevertheless, with women traveling in greater numbers, some of them are looking for, and paying for, sex—a growing phenomenon that has received very little attention in the academic literature on tourism (Pruitt & LaFont, 1995) and even less in the popular literature.

Shipboard and shore romances, the stuff of romance novels, predate the advent of mass travel by economically and socially emancipated European and North American women. Wealthy white women have always been able to escape to the tropics (Bermuda, the Bahamas, the Virgin Islands, etc.) over the last 100 years or so for the duration of the winter season. There they found willing local companions. However, they did so discreetly, drawing minimum attention to themselves and their companions.

The entry of women as consumers into the sex tourism market dates to the early 1960s when Scandinavian, British, and German women began to travel on their own or in groups to Italy, Spain, and Greece. In Greece, a special term, "kamaki," evolved to describe Greek men, many of them fishermen, who regularly had sexual relations with tourist women (Vassilikos, 1978). Zinovieff (1991) contends that through "kamaki" Greek men can find sexually willing tourist women in an otherwise sexually restrictive society and can therefore enhance their social and material status among their peers. Sometimes "kamaki" can escape their subsistence way of life by marrying a wealthy tourist and occasionally choosing to follow her abroad. Selanniemi (1997) estimates that there are approximately 4,000 foreign women married to Greek men in Rhodes.

With the emergence of long haul package tours in the 1970s, European women have been able to travel further afield—to the Gambia (Harrell-Bond, 1978; Wagner & Yamba, 1986), Kenya, Ghana, Jamaica, Barbados, Brazil, Thailand, Philippines, Indonesia (Bali) and India (Goa)—to find willing young men to provide them with sexual services in exchange for money, gifts, food, drink, and entertainment.

That female sex tourism is tied to greater female economic power, and concomitant gender emancipation with its new gender and sexual identities, is best demonstrated by Japanese female tourists who currently make up 43 percent of all Japanese traveling abroad (Leheny, 1995). Often dubbed "office ladies," they go on group tours and, free of the constraints of their patriarchal home society, are proving to be as sexually adventurous as their male counterparts and Euro-American women—engaging in liaisons with young Thai, Indonesian, Australian, Hawaiian, Guamanian, Brazilian, British, and Jamaican men (Hashimoto, 1997; Gray, 1997; Patterson, 1997). Gray (1997) describes Japanese secretaries lining up in the sand to choose Hawaiian life guards, while Hashimoto (1997) maintains that female Japanese tourists approach young British males in London more discreetly and pay for their food, drink, and accommodation, but not for sexual services. In Jamaica, I have witnessed, for many years now, young Japanese women, who are reggae-dance-hall aficionadas, attending the various music festivals in the company of "rent-a-dreads" (male prostitutes sporting long knotted hair known as "dread-locks"). Here the attraction is cultural, Jamaican music and the Rastafarian lifestyle, and not based on any quest for the mythical big bamboo—that racist mythology being tied to European colonization of Africa and slavery in the New World ("Mandingo," the "buck" negro).

Scope of Analysis

What follows is an observational study of female sex tourism in two popular Caribbean destinations—Barbados and Jamaica. (For the sake of comparison, it also briefly examines male sex tourism in the Dominican Republic, Jamaica, and Cuba. The focus is largely on female sex tourism in Barbados as the Jamaican case has been reasonably well covered by Pruitt and LaFont [1995].) I argue that female sex tourism is essentially no different from its male version, and attempts by feminists (Pruitt & LaFont, 1995) to distinguish it by labeling it "romance tourism" are disingenuous and smack of the kind of essentialism popular in some academic circles. I also enumerate those areas where sex tourism in Barbados and Jamaica differs from conventional sex tourism (epitomized in South East Asia) and note that this is not because of the gender of the clients (females) but rather because there is no organized system of prostitution in Caribbean countries, the Dominican Republic excepted. I maintain that there are few differences between male and female sex workers in the Caribbean and also examine whether indeed beach boys in Barbados or rent-a-dreads in Jamaica can be considered prostitutes, as both groups and their female clients refuse to recognize their activities as prostitution.

I contend that the prime motivation for sex tourism is sexual fantasy, particularly sexual fantasy as it is derived from racist mythology—the hypersexualized black male, the hot mulatta, or the demure and subservient Asian girl. This racialized sexual fantasy, although originally a production of the white world, has been skillfully manipulated in the Caribbean through songs like *The Big Bamboo* and the promotion of the mulatta or black woman as "mucho caliente" (very hot).

Researching Sex Tourism

Like other sex research, research into sex tourism has been largely qualitative, often involving extensive face to face interviews with sex workers, third parties, or brokers (pimps, taxi drivers, concierges, bartenders, etc.) (see Cohen, 1986, 1993). What is conspicuously absent from the research on sex tourism, as it is from the more general research on prostitution, is the client's perspective. Ryan and Kinder's (1996b) work represents one of the few attempts to interview clients who visited massage parlors in Wellington, New Zealand.

In the Caribbean context, formal interviews of any kind (face-to-face, telephone, etc.) will not elicit much information on sexual matters because of the general reluctance to discuss things sexual with non-acquaintances. Researching sex tourism in the region requires a number of stratagems—all of which were employed in this study—including lurking, overhearing conversations, careful observation, the development of long-term relationships with key respondents such as beach boys, rent-a-dreads, hotel managers, beach wardens, hotel security guards, beach vendors, and so on. It is even more difficult to obtain the clients' perspective in research on sex tourism than on conventional prostitution because of the transience and greater anonymity of the clients. Most of them visit for seven days or less and are certainly uninclined to talk to a researcher and give a formal interview while on vacation. At best, one can carefully observe and overhear clients in their interactions with each other and with sex workers, and attempt to engage them in brief informal conversations by posing as a friendly local or another tourist.

The research whose results I describe here was carried out over an extensive period of time—10 months in Barbados and periodic visits to Jamaica, beginning in 1970. Maintaining my invisibility as a researcher was difficult and, of course, prevented me from sometimes accessing crucial information. Nevertheless, I was able to make careful observations of the interactions between beach boys or rent-a-dreads and female tourists. I was also able to develop a number of key respondents among beach boys, as well as hotel security guards, beach vendors, guest house operators and small hoteliers, taxi drivers, and assorted individuals who were knowledgeable about the beach boy-female tourist phenomenon.

The information on sex tourism in the Dominican Republic and elsewhere in the region contained in this article was gleaned from numerous visits over my twenty-seven-year experience in the Caribbean.

My research is deficient in hard facts on clients. Regarding interviews with clients, in Barbados, I spoke to one German woman who travels every winter to pick up beach boys, and I spoke to two young British women (I gave them a lift back to their hotel from the Reggae Lounge after one of them had had an altercation with her beach boy).

Sex Tourism in the Caribbean

In the Caribbean context, it is much more productive to view sex tourism as part of the well-known liminal complex of sun, sea, sand, and sex. This is not to imply that sex is everywhere available and is always part of the vacation fantasy. In fact, the region, with the exception of the Dominican Republic, has no organized sex industry, no sex tours, and no involvement of third parties; sex workers are autonomous and solicit on their own. The region also has a long history of mass tourism and a fairly ambivalent attitude towards tourists. Not surprisingly, tourists are treated rather matter-of-factly, sometimes even churlishly, and not with the servility common among the liveried classes in Asia. Additionally, Caribbean female and male sex workers are socially much more aggressive than are their Asian counterparts and therefore more capable of dictating the nature of their sexual encounters with visitors. They also are quick to exploit the racialized sexual fantasies of Euro-Americans by feeding such myths as that of black hypersexuality. So tourists are regaled by songs about *The Big Bamboo* or *Stamina Daddy* (*Buju Banton*) who can perform sexually all night.

There are some interesting gender variations on who becomes a sex worker in the Caribbean based on prevailing sexual mores. In the sexually more restrictive Catholic countries, such as the Dominican Republic, Cuba and, to a lesser degree, Haiti, sex tourists are primarily male while the sex workers are overwhelmingly female. However, in the more sexually permissive, English-speaking, predominantly Protestant countries, where males and females come of sexual age in their early teens and sexual mores are more relaxed, sex workers are more likely to be male and sex tourists female.

The Dominican Republic has the oldest history in the region as a sex tourism destination. Prostitution here is an outgrowth not only of poverty, but also of a sexually restrictive culture afflicted by the well-known Latin American sexual double standard—the machismo/marianismo complex—where young women, particularly from the middle and upper classes, are expected to be virgins before marriage, yet their prospective male partners are required to be sexually experienced.

The advent of mass tourism has brought a whole new clientele to the bars, clubs, and bordellos that dot the Dominican landscape. So large is the Dominican sex industry that young women have become one of the principal exports of the country, to be found most everywhere in the region and further afield—Panama, Venezuela, Argentina, Florida, New Jersey, New York, and, increasingly, Western Europe.

In Cuba, sex tourism is a more recent outgrowth of the rapid expansion of tourism and the dire circumstances in which most Cuban families find themselves (O'Connell Davidson, 1996). Jamaica has a number of clubs in Kingston, Ocho Rios, and Montego Bay catering to foreign male tourists and local businessmen (the latter use these clubs primarily for entertaining associates). However, as a sex tourism destination, Jamaica is primarily known for its male sex workers. Pruitt and LaFont (1995, p. 425) recount an expression that has developed in Germany: "The men go to Thailand and the women go to Jamaica."

In most other English-speaking Caribbean islands where tourism is the major industry or fairly well developed, there are invariably a small number of young men who are eager to sell their services, sexual and otherwise, to female tourists. For them this is simply another subsistence/survival strategy in a region with perennially high rates of unemployment and underemployment.

Contemporary female sex tourists who visit the Caribbean have a wide range of social characteristics: from young women in their late teens to elderly dowagers, the less affluent to the very wealthy, and from lowly office workers to university professors. Many are married or have regular boyfriends at home. They are also drawn from many different countries—the United States, Canada, Britain, Holland, Germany, Denmark, Sweden, France, Switzerland, Italy, Belgium, Venezuela, and Japan—and are frequent travelers to warm weather destinations.

For the purposes of this article, I am categorizing female sex tourists into four types: the "first timers" or "neophytes"; the "situational sex tourists," who, according to O'Connell Davidson (1996), do not travel with the specific intention of buying sex but avail themselves of the opportunity when it arises; the "veterans," who travel explicitly for anonymous sex and usually find multiple partners; and the "returnee," who visits specifically to be with one man met on an earlier trip and with whom she has established some sort of ongoing relationship. "Neophytes" and "situational sex tourists" often graduate to become "veterans" or "returnees."

To my knowledge, there have been only three published accounts of female sex tourists and male sex workers in the Caribbean. They are the articles by Karch and Dann (1981) and Pruitt and LaFont (1995) previously referred to, and a short piece by Gibbings (1997). The latter notes (p. 13) that "sex tourism in Tobago mainly involves European and North American women and local men," and focuses primarily on its relatively high price tag— 218 persons, mostly male, tested positive for HIV between 1990 and 1996, a period corresponding with Tobago's tourism boom. Gibbings (1997, p. 13) mentions the case of a Swiss visitor who was deported as an "undesirable" after she announced on local television that "she was HIV positive and had engaged in unprotected sex with numerous local men."

Beach Boys and Female Tourists in Barbados

Since the early 1970s, Barbados has become a well-known destination for female tourists in search of what Karch and Dann (1981) amusingly dub "close encounters of the Third World." Males, mostly young, who cruise the various beaches in search of unattached tourist women are known as "beach boys." They are easily recognizable by their ubiquitous T shirts, swimming shorts (boxer style), beach sandals (Tevas are the fashion), gold chains and bracelets, sunglasses (Oakleys or Ray-Bans, preferably), and athletic builds. Some have bleached hair, and there are a few "nubbies" (baby dreadlocks), but seldom any heavy dreadlocks of the kind that are *de rigeur* among male sex workers in Jamaica. Some rent out beach chairs and umbrellas. Others are vendors of coconuts, aloe vera, coral, and assorted handcrafted jewelry. A few deal drugs. The largest number by far work for water sports related businesses—water skiing, sail boat rentals, jet ski rentals, glass bottom boats, and the numerous daily charter boats. Some own jet skis, which they rent out, but most others operate jet ski rentals for absentee owners. The jet ski operators cruise the various West Coast and South Coast beaches soliciting tourists for jet ski rides. They work either part-time, seasonally, or full-time, but at wages that cannot afford them their fairly ostentatious lifestyle—the latest clothes and shoe fashions, jewelry, meals and drinks at beach bars/restaurants catering to tourists, and almost nightly entertainment.

Hustling female tourists for drinks, meals, cigarettes, entertainment, gifts, and money becomes a way for these young men to maintain their enviable (in the local youth context) lifestyle. However, no beach boys whom I knew relied solely on hustling female tourists to make a living. When queried about this, they pointed out that it was an irregular living even at the height of the tourist season. They also invariably rejected the notion that they were somehow prostitutes dependent on female tourists to augment their meager incomes. Instead, they emphasized that they gave the women a "good time" and showed them around Barbados, acting very much like personal tour guides.

As in any group, there is a great deal of variation among beach boys in terms of their sources of income, their presentation of self, commitment to hustling female tourists, long-term goals, choice of clients, honesty and dependability (important for referrals), and so on.

Setting the Stage

The beach is usually the stage where first contact is made. Since most beach boys are involved with beach/water-related activities that are not too demanding, they have ample time to observe and interact with tourists. To draw the attention of prospective female clients, they use a number of different strategies: performing stunts on jet skis, beach calisthenics to show off a particularly well muscled body, mock wrestling matches, sprints on the beach with one another, and spirited games of beach paddle ball. One particular beach boy with dreadlocks, who frequented Carlyle Bay, would strip down to a skimpy bathing suit (he was well endowed), and would advertise himself by engaging in the kind of acrobatic paddle ball that would have even the most jaded tourist watching. Despite being fairly unattractive, he was seldom seen without a white female tourist in tow and, like many West Indian males, he liked his women on the large side.

Sizing up Potential Clients

As Karch and Dann (1981) note, there are many important cues beach boys use to size up a prospective client. Is she alone or accompanied by another female or other females? An unaccompanied woman laying on a beach towel not particularly interested in her reading material is a choice target for striking up a conversation. More than one woman raises the "numbers" problem, eventually requiring cooperation from other beach boys. Even before the initial verbal encounter, a beach boy is able to glean critical information about a potential client—her nationality (by her physical appearance, beach/swim attire, reading material, beach paraphernalia, etc.), and her relative affluence (jewelry, beach attire, bearing, etc.).

This sizing up is important; beach boys have a hierarchy of preferred clients based on nationality, affluence, age, and attractiveness (Worrell, 1995). A relatively wealthy, attractive thirty-something French Canadian tops most lists (see also Karch & Dann, 1981, p. 252). My informants report that French Canadian women have few racial inhibitions, are sexually enthusiastic, and are usually very generous. Germans and other Europeans rank below French Canadians. Young Brits are fine in a pinch; they like to have a good time but are usually on a tight budget. Mature and older Brits are preferable. Young white American women are at the bottom of the hierarchy since they often come with too much racial baggage and are generally first timers unaware of the rules of the game. Their black counterparts are preferable if they appear relatively affluent, but sporting a black female tourist around does not enhance a beach boy's status as much as having a white woman on his arm. As one beach boy informed me: "I can get a black girl anytime." In addition, although Barbados is a predominantly black society, the color complex looms large. As a result, light skin, straight hair, and Caucasian features are valued highly in partners.

The Approach

Having sized up his prospective client from a distance, the beach boy wanders over nonchalantly and smiles (a return smile is a good sign). My informants told me that there were several standard ice breakers in their repertoire. "Is this your first visit to Barbados?" "How are you enjoying your stay?" "How do you like the beach?" "Would you like to use some aloe on your skin?" "Sorry to bother you, but can I have a cigarette?" (Karch & Dann, 1981, also report this last one). If the response is friendly, the exchange continues in predictable fashion.

For the beach boy this is a well-rehearsed script, but for the neophyte female tourist there is always some hesitancy, as the game and her role in it are unfamiliar. As soon as the second series of questions is dispensed with (e.g., "Do you have a boyfriend or husband who is here with you?") and the female tourist shows continuing interest, the beach boy quickly steers the conversation towards finding ways to spend time together away from the public space of the beach. Going for a jet ski ride is a good feeling-out process since the beach boy can easily gauge the woman's physical interest in him by how tightly she holds him around the waist as he puts the jet ski through its paces. If the woman shows some reluctance in continuing the conversation, the beach boy might beat a quick retreat or play the race card—"Don't you like talking to a black man?" The latter often puts the woman on the defensive and, to prove she is not a racist, she continues the conversation.

Sometimes beach boys use a more direct approach and work into the conversation the question, "Have you ever had sex with a black man?" Depending on facial cues and any verbal response, the beach boy still has a way to back out if the cues are negative or the response un-encouraging. If the response is "yes," the beach boy's studied rejoinder is, "Then you know what it is like." If the response is a simple "no," the beach boy's scripted reply goes like this: "You should try it. You know what they say about us black men, and it is true." The latter reply is, of course, designed to appeal to any racialized sexual fantasy the female tourist might be harboring.

The feeling out process for a situational female sex tourist is simpler, for she is already aware of the rules of the game. For the veteran female sex tourist, adept at being picked up by or picking up beach boys, these preliminary conversations are predictable and amusing. Such women are not averse to cutting the conversation short and getting down to business or, if the first beach boy is not to their liking, inquiring about another who may have caught their fancy. These female tourists are the equivalent of O'Connell Davidson's (1996) "macho men sex tourists," since their transactions are explicit and focused. To quote O'Connell Davidson (1996, p. 45), they "find them, feed them, fuck them, and forget them."

Priming the Female Client

A neophyte may not initially realize that this encounter is going to cost her money, but she soon catches on when the beach boy asks her to pay for his drinks and food, and informs her that he does not have a car and that she will have to rent one or pay for taxis. Once this understanding is reached, the task of priming the client can begin. A number of drinks, some smokes (marijuana), and dancing at a club, particularly "bumping and wining" (gyrating hips and bottom) to a soca tune or "grinding" (slow, close dancing) to a dance hall number, are enough to prime any neophyte.

For the situational sex tourist and the veteran sex tourist, all this priming with drinks and dancing is unnecessary. Situational sex tourists usually stay with one beach boy for the duration of their vacation and are more inclined to see the relationship as genuine and reciprocal (see O'Connell Davidson, 1996). To them, companionship and even the possibility of a holiday romance become just as important as sex. These women are unlikely to see themselves as engaging in prostitution. Veteran sex tourists, on the other hand, prefer to keep their contacts with beach boys to a minimum—a few drinks, sex, and perhaps something to eat, with a handsome tip, really payment for services, but generally couched as a gift or payment for the taxi and meal. No sleeping over. The next day they may choose another beach boy. Indeed, multiple relationships characterize veteran sex tourists. Returnees, in contrast, are committed to one beach boy and come back laden with gifts. They may be met at the airport by their beach boy, usually stay in guest houses or small hotels, and while they may have romantic sentiments towards their beach boy lovers, these are seldom reciprocal. Like most young West Indian males, beach boys are notorious for their lack of commitment to women and, although a beach boy might have an "official" local girlfriend, she has to grudgingly share him with many other women. A few of my informants indicated that some beach boys had several foreign "girlfriends" and often had to juggle around their visits so they were not on the island at the same time.

But many female sex tourists are just as promiscuous as beach boys. I have witnessed female tourists at night clubs abandon the beach boy they were with to pick up another who had just caught their fancy. Sometimes this provokes a verbal altercation, especially if the beach boys are from different beaches, but the jilted beach boy soon calms down, and he is off immediately, prospecting on the dance floor, trying to find an unattached tourist.

Initiating Sex

As West Indian males are used to making the first sexual overture and dictating the nature of the sexual encounter, Barbadian beach boys like to be in control of deciding when sex will occur, how, and where. Too much public display of a sexual nature by female tourists (except on the dance floor) is seen as unbecoming and in bad taste. Sex is a very private affair to be conducted indoors and, since their place of abode is often off limits, because they live at home or with a girlfriend, the preferred location is the woman's hotel room or vacation apartment. Thus, the hotel where a woman is staying is critical, as many upscale hotels strictly forbid beach boys from visiting guests in their rooms and discourage them from the grounds of the hotel. Beach boys therefore find it useful to have friendly relations with hotel security guards so that they can be surreptitiously smuggled in late at night.

Like most West Indian males, beach boys prefer straight sex; few deviations from the missionary position, and no cunnilingus (the West Indian male aversion to this is well known). Thus, unlike female prostitutes who may take pains to accommodate their client's every sexual fantasy, beach boys approach sex with female tourists as if they are doing them a favor. Fellatio performed on them by the female tourist is acceptable. Foreplay is limited. The sexual service provided is clearly permeated with emotional indifference.

Everold Hosein, in a study of young Caribbean women's feelings about their sexual lives, conducted in-depth interviews with 112 women in twelve Caribbean countries, including Barbados and Jamaica. Hosein reported that most women indicated that they often faked orgasms, that there was little foreplay (except on the dance floor), and that the men were usually in a rush to have sex and were ignorant about female sexuality (*The Barbados Advocate*, 21 February 1995, p. 15). In fact, women in the study described the men's approach to sex as the RSBS approach—"ram, slam, bang, scram." Hosein concluded that most women in the study did not have a satisfying sex life. The reaction to the Hosein study throughout the region was predictable: men complained that the study was not scientific, the sample size was too small, and the women interviewed were all up-tight, cold women.

In Barbados, a phone-in on the survey conducted by the *Daily Nation* (March 1, 1995, p. 17A) newspaper found many men complaining that the thirteen Bajan (Barbadian) women interviewed were all lesbians. One man opined that Bajan women were frigid and cold. Another noted, if "Caribbean men are so bad in bed, why is it that beach bumming is an occupation that brings droves of foreigners to our shores every year?" (ibid.). The latter statement raises the interesting issue of the intersection of race with sexual mythology and reality. Many white women come to the Caribbean in pursuit of the racialized fantasy of black male hypersexuality, yet Caribbean women in the Hosein survey who experience the daily reality of black male "hypersexuality" spoke out about insensitive and ignorant lovers. The paper reported that an increasing number of women were turning to masturbation and the use of sexual aids like vibrators (ibid.). Either Caribbean women are sexually more demanding and less easily satisfied than Euro-American women, or the latter, in pursuit of a racialized fantasy embodied in the myth of the big bamboo, are prepared to reify the sexual experience as another pleasurable holiday activity. This is probably the case of the male stud as an insensitive lover, but how does it explain why some female tourists maintain contact with their beach boys, send them money, and return to visit periodically? Obviously, these women must be experiencing sexual fulfillment or other kinds of fulfillment in their relationships. Pruitt and LaFont (1995) suggest that there might be two other factors at work—the relationship as an instrument for the woman to have a "brown baby," and a misguided kind of liberalism that seeks to save these men from a life of poverty.

Maintaining Contact

A small number of female tourist-beach boy liaisons are maintained after the vacation is over through telephone calls, letters, remittances of money, and periodic visits back to Barbados ("returnees"). These long-term relationships are more likely to develop between mature, financially secure women and older beach boys, who are themselves looking for some security. Several of my informants would routinely place collect calls to their "girlfriends" overseas, their prime motive being to ask for money. Those who had telephones would also periodically receive calls from their love-struck female friends. The romance, if it existed, was primarily in the mind of the female tourist turned "girlfriend." The beach boys' motivations for continuing the relationship were entirely economic—the receipt of regular or irregular monetary remittances to help with the bills, and a convenient contact person from whom to request outboard motor or jet ski parts, clothes, shoes, and other items that are much cheaper abroad. In a few cases that have become the stuff of beach boy legend, foreign girlfriends have bought jet skis and, in one case, a speedboat for their beach boyfriends, and have helped set them up in their own water sports businesses. (I was never able to determine the veracity of this, but Worrell [1995] also reported hearing the same.) This is not to say that all beach boys view their foreign girlfriends in an instrumental light. My informants did tell me about several true romances between beach boys and tourists; however, they were far fewer than Pruitt and LaFont (1995) indicate is the case for Jamaica.

My informants also told me of a number of beach boys who did marry foreign tourist women, essentially to get out of Barbados, and who obtained landed immigrant status in Canada, Britain, or one of the European countries, or a green card (an immigrant card) for the United States. The majority of these marriages did not last—the Barbadian men found it difficult to adjust, because of cultural differences and racism, and they had trouble finding jobs with their limited skills. Also, the relationships, also, out of the context of the holiday environment where they had first developed, soon soured. The majority of these men eventually returned to Barbados. (Worrell [1995] reported hearing the same thing from her informants.)

Occasionally, the women themselves move down to Barbados to continue the relationship. Again, most of these relationships do not last—their beach boys, like many young Bajan men, are uninclined to stay home nor will they give up their local girlfriends or abandon hustling tourist women. So these women move on to a succession of local men and sooner or later return home, sometimes pregnant or with an infant in tow.

Rent-a-Dreads and Female Tourists in Jamaica

Pruitt and LaFont (1995) have provided a fairly detailed account of female tourists and rent-a-dreads in Jamaica in an article entitled "For Love and Money: Romance Tourism in Jamaica." Without wishing to duplicate their observations, I would like to point out where our observations and interpretations differ.

Rent-a-dreads are the Jamaican equivalent of Barbadian beach boys. However, they differ from Bajan beach boys in a number of ways. They are invariably unemployed, significantly poorer (no Teva sandals or Ray Ban sunglasses), have less formal education, and most are migrants from rural areas living in shacks on "capture land" (land squatted on) ringing the tourist resort towns of Ocho Rios, Montego Bay, and Negril. They are also easily identifiable by their long dreadlocks.

Rent-a-dreads are familiar fixtures at most tourist beaches (for example, Doctors Cave in Montego Bay or the long stretch of beach at Negril) and haunts, where, like Bajan beach boys, they attempt to pick up tourist women. They use roughly similar techniques in setting the stage, sizing up potential clients, approaching these clients, and priming them. Like beach boys, they are extremely adept at "sweet talking" women ("chatting up" to use the Jamaican equivalent). In addition, a significant number have learned a smattering of German, and this serves them well with German tourists. Unlike beach boys, rent-a-dreads generally single out mature female tourists who are likely to have more money and be interested in one relationship for the duration of their vacation. But they are not averse to relationships with younger tourist women if the opportunity presents itself.

Rent-a-dreads have an advantage over Bajan beach boys, because Jamaica is more likely to attract tourists who are reggae dance hall aficionados and who, through Jamaican music, have some insight, albeit superficial, into Jamaican culture and an appreciation of Rastafarianism (belief in the divinity of Haile Selassie, the former emperor of Ethiopia, and in "natural" living free from all the evils of modernity). Therefore, many female tourists who come to Jamaica are already favorably disposed to men with dreadlocks.

The various music festivals in Jamaica (Reggae Sunsplash, Reggae Sumfest, and so on) attract tourists from around the world, but particularly from North America, Britain, and Japan. Female tourists who are traveling alone or with other females find it advantageous to link up with a rent-a-dread, who not only serves as a "culture broker" (Pruitt & LaFont, 1995) but who can also negotiate taxis and tickets to the various shows, ward off persistent vendors and assorted hustlers, and generally provide protection in an environment where tourists are often victimized by crime. For these services, female tourists usually provide drinks, meals, cigarettes, tickets to the nightly shows (which are very expensive), transportation, gifts, and a monetary tip. If they are looking for sex as well, there are greater expectations regarding gifts and money.

Japanese females who come to the reggae festivals are known to be big spenders but are considered to be shy sexually and sometimes uninclined to enter into a sexual relationship with their respective rent-a-dreads. Young, white American females are also considered to be poor prospects—at best a rent-a-dread can cadge a cigarette or a drink from them. During the North American spring break, when hundreds of college students come down to the North Coast of Jamaica, rent-a-dreads complain about the very slow business. German and other European female tourists traveling alone or with other females are considered prime prospects, as are mature Americans and Canadians. Black American women are viewed as being interested in long-term relationships and as good vehicles to obtain a much coveted U.S. green card (through marriage), and they have been coming down in greater numbers ever since Terry McMillan extolled the virtues of Jamaican men. Terry McMillan is the author of *Waiting to Exhale*, a book that takes black American men to task for their lack of commitment to their women and now a successful movie that has appealed largely to black female audiences. While she herself was on a vacation in Jamaica, she met a young Jamaican man and a blossoming romance ensued. She subsequently married the man and has suggested on television that professional black American women, whose prospects of finding a suitable marital partner at home are slim, should follow suit.

Conclusion

McMillan's experience would tend to support Pruitt and LaFont (1995, p. 423), who argue that the liaisons between female tourists and rent-a-dreads are constructed "through a discourse of romance and long-term relationships" and that there is an "emotional involvement usually not present in sex tourism." Yet, my long-term observations of the rent-a-dread phenomenon suggest that the "discourse of romance" tends to be part of the performance pattern and becomes increasingly more transparent as time progresses. (McMillan's relationship was relatively new at the time of her public pronouncements.) Jamaican males who enter into relationships with female tourists have a different agenda, money not love, and a ticket out of Jamaica. Likewise, female tourists, the vast majority of whom are white, have their own agenda, which I have observed as being largely sexual and based on the racialized fantasy of black hypersexuality—the big bamboo. Theirs is a quest, and how better achieved than through multiple encounters?

Pruitt and LaFont (1995, p. 435) acknowledge that "tourist women often seem fickle, turning from one man to another," and that many men "describe feeling used by foreign women." They also recognize that relationships that extend "beyond the casual vacation romance" often lose their bloom and lead to "disappointment and conflict" (p. 434). Yet, they insist on framing the relationships between female tourists and rent-a-dreads as romance, thereby implying that there are gender differences: female tourists engage in "romance tourism" while male tourists engage in "sex tourism." In other words, women are incapable of approaching sex casually and unemotionally, while men prefer to have anonymous sex and avoid romantic entanglements. On the contrary, my research in the Caribbean indicates that there are few gender differences and that the majority of both female and male tourists are looking for casual sex with no entanglements based on some racialized sexual fantasy—hot mulattas/black women for men in the case of the Dominican Republic and Cuba (O'Connell Davidson, 1996), and the big bamboo for women. Yes, female tourists and male tourists do get emotionally involved with local sex workers on occasion, but this is the exception rather than the rule (see Cohen, 1986; O'Connell Davidson, 1996).

There are very few differences between male and female sex workers in the Caribbean. Both tend to initiate encounters with tourists, use similar sizing up and approach strategies, although their venues might be different, prime their clients on the dance floor, and generally initiate sex.

If sex tourism in the Caribbean differs from conventional sex tourism as we have come to know it from research in South East Asia, it is because there is no organized sex industry in the region (the Dominican Republic excepted), no specific sex tours, sex hotels, pimps, or other third parties. Instead, sex workers are autonomous (O'Connell Davidson, 1996) and free to construct whatever type of relationship with clients that provides them with the benefits they seek. O'Connell Davidson (1996, p. 44) describes situations in which Cuban sex workers often put up male tourists in their own rooms and, as well as granting them sexual license, act as "guide, companion and interpreter" (in some cases even cook and do laundry) all for a little food, drink, entertainment, soap, clothing, plus a little cash. Sometimes young Cuban females will have sex with a male tourist for as little as a meal or a bar of soap (O'Connell Davidson, 1996). The price paid for sex in Cuba, Barbados, or Jamaica is thus highly variable and often does not involve cash, but this does not make this relationship different from conventional prostitution. What is occurring meets Gagnon's (1968) definition of prostitution: granting sexual access relatively indiscriminately in return for money or goods.

Given the ad hoc nature of the sex industry in the Caribbean, it is not surprising that sex workers seldom consider themselves to be prostitutes. Beach boys in Barbados define what they do as "showing female tourists a good time," and bristle at the suggestion that because they receive goods and/or money in exchange for sexual services, they are essentially male prostitutes. Likewise, their clients, from neophytes to situational sex tourists to returnees, define their contacts with beach boys as involving companionship, emotion, and reciprocity, certainly not prostitution. In the wider Barbadian society, while most people would recognize what beach boys do as prostitution, they use euphemisms to describe it ("beach bumming," "hustling"). (Prostitution is illegal in Barbados.) The same is true of rent-a-dreads and female tourists in Jamaica, where the term "hustling" is used to describe the activity of male sex workers. In Cuba, a similar situation exists. Rather than being called "putas" (whores), a term that has strong pejorative connotations, female sex workers who solicit tourists are called "jiniteras" (literally "jockeys," because they are viewed as "riding" tourists) (O'Connell Davidson, 1996).

Sex tourism in the Caribbean is also different in that it seldom involves the kinds of exploitation and degradation commonly associated with sex tourism in Asia. Although sex workers and their clients might have different motivations, the relationships are generally mutually beneficial. If exploitation does occur, it tends to be symmetrical. I know of numerous cases in which beach boys and rent-a-dreads used the language of romance to get female tourists to marry them just so they could get a green card/landed immigrant status, only to abandon these women once their immigration status was secure. I have also heard of Dominican sex workers doing the same thing to European and North American men. But Dominican women are just as likely to arrive in Europe anticipating a new life, only to find themselves abandoned by their husbands/future husbands, and having to resort back to prostitution to pay for their fares home.

As the number of women traveling alone or in groups increases (witness the Japanese case) and as these women seek to redefine gender roles and power relationships, they realize that sex is a commodity that they too can purchase. In doing so, particularly in societies in the Caribbean where men are afflicted by the machismo complex, they subvert traditional male power by controlling those things beach boys and rent-a-dreads want most—money and access to North America and Europe. Beach boys and rent-a-dreads usually try to reassert their power by attempting to control the sexual encounter, taking charge of the tourist's vacation, engaging in flattery and insincere declarations of love, and by skillfully manipulating the racialized sexual fantasies of their clients. (Female sex workers in the Caribbean are also able to subvert the economic power of their male clients in similar ways.) The older and less attractive the client, the more likely the flattery, declarations of love, and manipulation of racialized sexual fantasies are able to afford sex workers greater power over their clients. Thus, the relationships between sex workers and clients in the Caribbean are much more complex than the literature on sex tourism in Asia would indicate, and sometimes it is difficult to determine who is being "found, fucked, and forgotten." For the most part, however, sex tourism in the Caribbean involves the intersection of mutual interests—the fulfillment of a racialized sexual fantasy in exchange for money and/or goods.

References

Britton, S. (1982). The political economy of tourism in the Third World. *Annals of Tourism Research*, 9, 331–58.

Cincone, L. (1988). *The role of development in the exploitation of Southeast Asian women: Sex tourism in Thailand.* New York: Women's International Resource Exchange.

Cohen, E. (1986). Lovelorn "farangs": The correspondence between foreign men and Thai girls. *Anthropological Quarterly*, 59, 115–127.

Cohen, E. (1993). Open-ended prostitution as a skillful game of luck, opportunity, risk and security among tourist oriented prostitutes in a Bangkok "soi." In Hitchcock, M., King, V., & Parnwell, M. (Eds.), *Tourism in Southeast Asia*. London: Routledge.

de Albuquerque, K., & McElroy, J. (1992). Caribbean small-island tourism styles and sustainable strategies. *Environmental Management*, 16(5), 619–632.

de Albuquerque, K., & McElroy, J. (1995). Alternative tourism and sustainability. In Conlin, M., & Baum, T. (Eds.), *Island tourism: Management principles and practices* (pp. 23–32). Chichester, England: Wiley.

Enloe, C. (1989). *Bananas, beaches and bases: Making feminist sense of international politics*. Berkeley: University of California Press.

Ericsson, L. (1980). Charges against prostitution: An attempt at a philosophical assessment. *Ethics*, 90, 335–366.

Gay, J. (1985). The patriotic prostitute. *The Progressive*, 49(3), 34–36.

Gagnon, J. (1968). Prostitution. *International Encyclopedia of Social Sciences*, vol. 12. New York: MacMillan and Free Press.

Gibbings, W. (1997). The high cost of sex tourism. *Contours*, 7(10), 13–14.

Harrel-Bond, B. (1978). A window on the outside world: Tourism as development in the Gambia. *American Universities Field Staff Reports*, Africa Series, No. 19.

Hall, M. (1992). Sex tourism in South-east Asia. In Harrison, D. (Ed.), *Tourism and the Less Developed Countries* (pp. 64–74). London: Belhaven Press.

Harrison, D. (1992). Tourism to less developed countries: the social consequences. In Harrison, D. (Ed.), *Tourism and the less developed countries* (pp. 19–34). London: Belhaven Press.

Hawkesworth, M. (1984). Brothels and betrayal: On the functions of prostitution. *International Journal of Women's Studies*, 7(1), 81–91.

Hill, C. (1993). Planning for prostitution: An analysis of Thailand's sex industry. In: Turshen, M., & Holcomb, B. (Eds.), *Women's lives and public policy: The international experience*. Westport, CT: Greenwood Press, pp. 133–144.

Karch, C., & Dann, G. (1981). Close encounters of the Third World. *Human Relations*, 34(4), 349–268.

Kruhaug, N. (1997). AIDS epidemic. *Dagbadet,* October 6, 1997. Reprinted in *World Press Review*, January 1998.

Leheny, D. (1995). A political economy of Asian sex tourism. *Annals of Tourism Research*, 22(2), 367–384.

McClintock, J. (1992). Sex and tourism in Cuba. *Hemisphere*, 5(1), 27–28.

O'Connell Davidson, J. (1996). Sex tourism in Cuba. *Race and Class*, 38(1), 39–48.

Ong, A. (1985). Industrialization and prostitution in Southeast Asia. *Southeast Asia Chronicle*, 96, 2–6.

Pruitt, D., & LaFont, S. (1995). For love or money: Romance tourism in Jamaica. *Annals of Tourism Research*, 22(2), 422–440.

Ryan, C., & Kinder, R. (1996a). The deviant tourist and the crimogenic place: The case of the tourist and New Zealand prostitute. In Pizam, A., & Mansfeld, Y. (Eds.), *Crime and international security issues* (pp. 23–35). Chichester: Wiley.

Ryan, C., & Kinder, R. (1996b). Sex, tourism and sex tourism: Fulfilling similar needs? *Tourism Management*, 17(7), 507–518.

Troung, T. (1990). *Sex, money and morality: Prostitution and tourism in Southeast Asia*. London: Zed Books, Ltd.

Vassilikos, V. (1978). *Ta Kamakia*. Athens: Kaktas.

Wagner, U., & Yamba. B. (1986). Going North and getting attached: The case of the Gambians. *Ethnos*, 51, 199–222.

World Tourism Organization (1997). *Tourism market trends 1997*. Madrid: World Tourism Organization.

Zinovieff, S. (1991). Hunters and hunted: Kamaki and the ambiguities of sexual predation in a Greek town. In Loizos, P., & Papataxiarchis, E. (Eds.), *Contested identities: Gender and kinship in modern Greece* (pp. 203–220). Princeton, NJ: Princeton University Press.

INVISIBLE MAN: A QUEER CRITIQUE OF FEMINIST ANTI-PORNOGRAPHY THEORY

Jody Norton
Department of English Language and Literature
Eastern Michigan University, Ypsilanti, MI 48197

Catharine MacKinnon, Andrea Dworkin, and other anti-pornography "feminists" (the term in this case is a misnomer) claim that sexuality in Western societies is constituted as the eroticization of dominance and subordination— relations that define masculine and feminine gender roles. I argue that MacKinnon's colleagues' model of male dominance and female subordination reduces the indefinite complexity of power dynamics within heterosexual and homosexual relations to a mechanical binary system that explains little more than the most abusive situations. In order to maintain their position that sexuality amounts to male abuse of women and that pornography represents the essence of sexuality, MacKinnon et al. must make men in pornography invisible (and incomprehensible) except as the occupants of a monolithic position as perpetrators of sexual violence. I conclude that the anti-pornography arguments of MacKinnon, Dworkin and others are unconvincing because of the gross over-simplification of categories on which the logic of their arguments depends.

Introduction

In her essay, "Desire and Power," Catharine MacKinnon argues that "[s]exuality is the social process that creates, organizes, expresses, and directs desire" (MacKinnon, 1987, p. 49). It turns out that desire is itself "created by...social relations." The "erotic," whose character is unspecified, "defines sex [sexualizes sex?] as an inequality, hence as a meaningful difference" (p. 50). From these somewhat incoherent beginnings, MacKinnon produces the idea that sexuality, in our culture, amounts to the eroticization of dominance and subordination. Inequalities of power are certainly one common dynamic in sexual activity, but only one. MacKinnon insists, furthermore—in my view illegitimately—that this dynamic is unequivocally gendered as male dominant/female subordinate. In "Pornography: On Morality and Politics," she claims that the male homosexual can be fully explained by a butch/femme model. She fails to address autoeroticism in either this essay or in "Desire and Power."

MacKinnon's male dominant/female subordinate model collapses any ambiguity in the power relations between heterosexual partners (let alone same sex partners), and in doing so denies the complexity of subordination itself. Reviewing MacKinnon's book, *Only Words*, in *The Women's Review of Books*, Leora Tanenbaum points out that subordination comprises "a vast category open to greater subjective interpretation than abuse or degradation, which imply the presence or threat of violence" (Tanenbaum, 1993, p. 30).

As is well known, MacKinnon, Andrea Dworkin, John Stoltenberg and others understand pornography as performing a continuing causal role in the maintenance of sexuality as domination/subordination, and of the social inequality of women in general. As David Downs writes, "The feminist theory of pornography is derived from the feminist theory of sexuality: pornography reflects and reinforces the subordinating structure of male sexuality and power" (1989, p.36). In *Only Words*, MacKinnon argues that pornography should be declared unconstitutional, and therefore illegal, because it violates the equality provisions of the Fourteenth Amendment.

The Model Ordinance that MacKinnon and Dworkin coauthored, and that was passed by the Minneapolis City Council in 1983 before being vetoed by the mayor, defines pornography as

the graphic sexually explicit subordination of women through pictures and/or words that also includes one or more of the following: (a) women are presented dehumanized as sexual objects, things, or commodities...(e) women are presented in postures or positions of sexual submission, servility, or display. (MacKinnon, 1993, pp. 121–122)

The language of the Ordinance adds that "the use of 'men, children, or transsexuals in the place of women' is also pornography" (p. 122).

However, MacKinnon needs, for the sake of her fundamental argument about the nature of sexuality in American society, to maintain that: "Gender is sexual" (MacKinnon, 1989, p. 197) and, crucially, simply binary: "Male dominance is sexual" (p. 127); and "Pornography constitutes the meaning of...sexuality" (p. 197). She must make men in any kind of pornography invisible except insofar as they can be said to occupy a monolithic role as perpetrators of sexual violence. In attempting to present pornography as not simply expressive but constitutive of the oppression of women, MacKinnon constructs an accordion-style argument, in which pornography, sex, and women finally come to mean virtually the same thing: abuse. "Pornography is masturbation material," MacKinnon writes. "It is used as sex. It therefore is sex" (MacKinnon, 1993, p. 17). She adds that "to express eroticism is to engage in eroticism, meaning to perform a sex act. To say it is to do it, and to do it is to say it. It is also to do the harm of it" (p. 33).

Thus, because pornography is sex, the harm of the representation is equivalent to the harm of the act. And if the act itself must be heterosexual and dominant/subordinate (and therefore unequal and oppressive) in order to qualify as sexual, by MacKinnon's definition, then sex as an act becomes inherently and universally harmful, as is indicated in the progressive slippage in MacKinnon's reference to "the positioning of sex words in sexual abuse, in abuse as sex, in sex as abuse, in sex" (MacKinnon, 1993, p. 58).

A "logical" effect of this "slippery slope" argument, in which sex and its representations occupy an identical ontological status, is that the human participants are included in the conceptual meltdown: "Once you are used for sex, you are sexualized. You lose your human status. You are sex..." (p. 67). However, again due to the needs of MacKinnon's political argument, only some of those who are sexualized in fact lose their "human status." Men retain their humanity (though invisibility) and women become the inhuman, the abused who are sex. This becomes fully clear when MacKinnon refers, in "Pornography: On Morality and Politics," to "sex—that is, women" (MacKinnon, 1989, p. 209).

In *Only Words*, MacKinnon does not propose an alternative form of sex for an envisionable—or even a utopian—future, except in the form of yet another negative, and absolute, pronouncement: "In a society in which equality is a fact...[s]ex between people and things, human beings and pieces of paper, real men and unreal women, will be a turn-off" (MacKinnon, 1993, pp. 109–110). In other words, "these abuses," as she indiscriminately labels pornographic texts, will not be erotic.

In her essay, "Erotica vs. Pornography," Gloria Steinem writes: "pornography is...about an imbalance of power that allows and even requires sex to be used as a form of aggression" (Steinem, 1993, p. 36). Elsewhere, she states, "all pornography is an imitation of the male-female conqueror-victim paradigm" (p. 35). And in fact, according to Gayle Rubin,

> A great deal of anti-porn propaganda implies that sado-masochism is the underlying and essential "truth" towards which all pornography tends. Porn is thought to lead to S/M porn which in turn is alleged to lead to rape. (1993, p. 26)

Are Steinem, MacKinnon, et al. correct in their claim that all pornography represents aggression, or are they not? I want to pursue the issue of power relations in pornographic representations through a series of related questions, the most general of which is whether statements of the kind that begin "All pornography is...," or "All pornography does..." are coherent. In other words, does pornography always represent and/or commit the same act? The consequence of a negative answer to this question will be to mandate an analysis of pornography that is considerably more complex and flexible than those of the leading feminist anti-pornography theorists in terms of its conception of variations in gender construction; the relevance of historical, cultural, personal, and socially contextual factors in the meaning of sexual acts; and the significance of race, of ethnicity, of class, of age, of ideology, and so on.[1]

I have chosen to focus the following discussion on the possibility of differentials in gender and power relations. Perhaps the most obvious opening question then, is whether all pornography is about male domination of women.

Pornography and Male Domination

Take, for example, a photograph depicting a woman performing oral sex on a man. A quick-and-dirty anti-porn analysis of this image might argue that what we were looking at (the assumption being that "we" are male) was an instance of the subordination of a woman to the subjectivity of, and for the pleasure of, a man—an act often accompanied by economic exploitation and sometimes by the actuality or threat of violence.

Let us acknowledge that the material circumstances under which the act was performed presumably did involve payments to both actors, and certainly may have involved force, real or implied, and let us focus on the meaning of the text, as a representative event. Although MacKinnon is quite right in insisting that the acts depicted in pornographic photographs, films, and videotapes actually have to be performed (simulations aside) in order for the product to be made, we all need to acknowledge that a series of photographs, or even a single picture, is never simply reality, or even a record of reality (assuming—unreasonably, in the light of modern physics and poststructural theory—that there is a reality as such). It is a representation, and therefore open to interpretation, which is never stable, even if no overt narrative has been constructed by the producer. The viewer is free (within the limits of her own construction, life experience, and so on) to position herself as observer, as participant (through her imagination), or as some combination of both.

One of the intriguing aspects of oral sex, I would argue, is precisely the fact that it is never unambiguously clear who is doing what to whom. Is the woman being subjugated by the phallus? Or is she devouring it? A woman who has a man's penis in her mouth and his testicles in her hand is arguably in a position of considerable power.

If the argument is that domination here takes the shape primarily of objectification, is it clear that the man is less objectified than the woman? If so, why do we see her face—the mirror of the soul—but his penis (nothing more than a part-object, a fetish, a piece of meat)? Is it clear, furthermore, that it is only conceivable that the male is getting sexual pleasure from this interaction?

What would change, though, if we found that, in fact, the "woman" is a man? If we understand this biological male to be transgendered, we can ask all the same questions: Is this, in effect, a "woman" being subjugated by the phallus, etc.? However, if we know that the "woman" is cross-dressed but not transsexual, we might choose to argue: 1) s/he may self-identify as a gay male, and 2) in the world of the text, s/he may be the one actively seeking this particular sexual interaction, and gaining pleasure from it. We might hypothesize the male figure as simply allowing, rather than actively desiring, someone he knows is not a "real" woman to have oral sex with him (though straight tricks, at least, do not always know the "true" sex of the persons with whom they are having sex).[2] We might even understand this as a picture of a "normal" young man—perhaps a college student—being sexually abused by a perverse but potent Svengali who is not what s/he appears to be. Thus, the range of possible meanings for the "same" situation seems quite different.

Now consider a photograph of two men engaged in a homosexual sex act in which, as in the previous situation, one of the "men" is cross-dressed—in this case, the one who is being fellated, rather than the fellator. Is this a representation of a man subordinating a "woman" to his presence and power? Clearly, the center of attention would be the "woman's" phallus, on which the man is performing a "feminine" action. Is this a picture of a man seeking unconscious mastery of his own (phallic) mother? But his dominance must be attained by an act of submission—to a man! The relations of power here seem even more complex and ambiguous than those of the previous male/"female" oral sex act. And we may feel moved, at this point, to question whether we are justified in maintaining MacKinnon's assumption that sexuality is, and means, solely male domination and female subordination—

an assumption that comes to seem intuitively less and less satisfactory as we read images such as these.

If, in fact, there *is* any gendered inequality in the above relations—and it doesn't seem in the least obvious to me that there is—is the subordination (say, of the receptor's role) inherently abusive? This is even less clear. And the question itself raises the more general question of whether real or role-played difference in power—even where such difference reflects gender or gendered desire—is by definition oppressive, exploitative, violent, and so on. Leora Tanenbaum writes of MacKinnon:

> She is unable to envision a healthy sexuality that includes voluntary subordination. To her, female sexual subordination is necessarily degrading. But why can we not distinguish between voluntary and involuntary subordination, between consent and coercion? (1993, p. 30)

Why indeed? Not as a cover-up for male violence, but as a recognition of the erotics of power.

Next let us consider a photograph of a run-of-the-mill, not very committed job of cunnilingus. Is this too a picture that can only mean "a man is abusing a woman for another man's pleasure"? Who can say for sure that the consumer/viewer is male? Or that the woman in the world of the text feels abused, or that she is being abused? By no means do all of the straight women I know feel abused when a man of whom they are fond performs cunnilingus on them. Perhaps the man feels abused in having to perform a sex act from which he derives no pleasure.

We should continue to ask the question: Does all pornography mean the same thing? And, in particular: Is all pornography about male domination of women? Although the answer to the second of these questions, at least, would obviously appear to be *no,* it is still possible to argue for a butch/femme explanatory model of gay porn. So, let us add the further question: Can gay male porn be accounted for as the domination by one man of a feminized and subordinate other male, even when transsexuals and transvestites are not involved?

Take the case of a photograph that shows a boy ("all models are 18 years or older," as the magazines say) performing oral sex on a man. As with the woman performing oral sex on a man, it would not be immediately clear that the boy is being dominated or subjugated by the man. If he is the object of the camera's gaze, he is the subject of the dramatic event. The man, on the other hand, is secondary (his head not appearing in the photograph) and, as an individual, is nowhere to be seen. Who is doing what to whom? Who is the dominant partner? Is it perhaps the man who is in the passive, subordinate, faceless, feminine role? The meaning of the picture, and the power relations it depicts, are ambiguous.

Now reverse the relation: a man performs oral sex on a boy. The man is bigger and older than the boy, yet he is kneeling and the boy is standing above him; he is the receptor, the boy is the penetrator. In this photograph the boy is the spatially dominant image. Does such a picture depict the domination of a feminized and subordinate other male by a man? If so, is the boy the "man"? Is the meaning of it, then, the same as the meaning of the previous photograph in which the boy was the receptor of the phallus?

Let us ask a broader version of the butch/femme question. Are power relations between actors/participants in gay porn in all cases unequal? Think of a photograph that depicts one young, blond man having oral sex with another young, blond man. There is no apparent age difference between the two men—indeed, they appear as though they might be twins. In fact, there is no basis, except for the parceling out of easily reversible roles, on which to argue that one man is the dominant subject of the pornographic image, the other the subordinate object. In "Pornography Without Power?," Chris Clark suggests that "sex without power is often portrayed in gay porn where the relation between two partners has the possibility of gender equality" (Clark, 1991, p. 283).

Finally, who would hold the power in a photograph showing three males—boys, young men—each performing oral sex on the other. All appear to be roughly the same age. No one appears to be in control; all are simultaneously receptors and penetrators. Does this picture have the same, and only the same, meaning as woman/man? Or "woman"/man? Or man/woman? Are the gender relations identical to those in all the other situations that have been discussed? Are the material and symbolic power differentials identical? Is the same "man" always, essentially, dominating, subordinating, exploiting, violating the same "woman"? Essentially—and I would argue that it *is* essential—the answer is *no*.

Conclusion

There are two central conceptual problems that beset the anti-pornography theory of MacKinnon and Dworkin. The first is that typically, in their work, men are treated as Man—with a degree of essentialism no significant feminist thinker would dream of applying to the subject of women. Man is demonized as a kind of Moloch—huge, cruel, all-powerful—whose pleasure is the violation of women. Paradoxically, all individual men tend to disappear in the shadow of this monstrous Man. Men, as such, become invisible, both as subjects of discourse and as historical individuals. It seems to me that this replacement of the materiality and particularity of men with a relentless condemnatory reification is an extremely aggressive move, and one that reveals the urge to a very masculinist domination in the work of MacKinnon and Dworkin. A putatively liberating discourse that in fact effaces men is no more feminist, in spirit, than a patriarchal discourse that effaces women. On the contrary, it is reactionary, androphobic, and oppressive.

Adrienne Rich states, in "Compulsory Heterosexuality and Lesbian Existence," that the essay was written "in part to challenge the erasure of lesbian existence from so much of scholarly feminist literature, an erasure which I felt (and feel) to be not just anti-lesbian, but anti-feminist in its consequences" (Rich, 1993, p. 227). Though I know Rich would not want to conflate gay male and lesbian issues, it seems to me that her sense of the anti-feminist applies as well to the erasure of gay, and for that matter, straight, bi, or trans males and trans women, from discussions of sexuality and oppression (except, of course, as victimizers). A discourse that purports to speak generally about oppression and gender, and which unsparingly castigates men while virtually ignoring the ambiguous economic and political, as well as sexual, locations of males in heterosexual pornography, and the entire field of gay pornography, and which, finally, depends on a thoroughly reductive and essentialist model of masculine gender, can only very oddly be described as feminist, if that term is to continue to connote broad ethical and liberationist commitments.

At the same time that they reduce men—gay, straight, or in between, to paraphrase John Money—to a single meaning (violent misogyny), MacKinnon, Dworkin, et al. reduce the genre of pornography to a similarly monolithic phenomenon. MacKinnon writes:

> In pornography, the violence is the sex. The inequality is sex. The humiliation is sex. The debasement is sex. The intrusion is sex. Pornography does not work sexually without gender hierarchy. If there is no inequality, no violation, no dominance, no force, there is no sexual arousal. (MacKinnon, 1989, p. 211)

On the other hand, Linda Williams cites David Pendleton as arguing that the structure of gay porn, at least, is not hierarchical but

> rhapsodic and combinatory—a series of sexual acts which, in contrast to the relatively purposeful, problem-solving nature of heterosexual pornography, are paratactic, lacking hierarchy and ultimate goals—except, that is, for the goals of visible orgasm. (Williams, 1993a, p. 245)

Not only is pornography uniformly violent and hierarchical, according to MacKinnon, it is also, as I have pointed out, strictly gendered:

> [E]xactly what is defined as degrading to a human being, however that is socially defined, is exactly what is sexually arousing to the male point of view in pornography, just as the one to whom it is done is the girl regardless of sex. (MacKinnon, 1989, p. 211)

The images I have analyzed, however, seem ambiguously gendered in some cases, and undifferentiated as to gender in others. Social and symbolic hierarchies, when present at all, are indeterminate. And one must strain one's interpretive imagination a good deal to conceive these images as violent.

My purpose in this essay has not been to advocate for pornography so much as to critique what I consider to be a socially and intellectually irresponsible body of discourse on the subject. It will perhaps be useful, however, in closing, to offer three ideas.

The first addresses the harm that pornography, as such, supposedly causes. In his balanced analysis of the Minneapolis Ordinance, titled *The New Politics of Pornography*, David Downs observes that "no strong correlations have yet been demonstrated between harmful effects and non-degrading and non-violent sexually explicit materials" (Downs, 1989, p. 23).

The second idea proposes the socio-aesthetic merits of pornography as a genre. Richard Dyer writes, in "Coming to Terms: Gay Pornography":

> A defence of porn as a genre (which...is not at all the same thing as defending most of what porn currently consists of) would be based on the idea that an art rooted in bodily effect can give us a knowledge of the body that other art cannot. (Dyer, 1992, p. 123)

The third idea addresses specifically gay pornography. Linda Williams notes that there is, in these years of kiddie porn panic and AIDS phobia, a widespread "agreement to hate homosexuals" (1993b, p. 59). She concludes:

> If we do not want to be in the business of condemning the sexuality of villainous others, we need a better sexual politics. This sexual politics must be aware of the diversity of sexual fantasies which cannot be simplified into an easily scapegoatable aggression, perversion or evil. One way to explore this diversity would be to become aware that pornography is no monolith, that it has a history, and that in that history it has appealed to many more "bodies and pleasures" than are dreamt of in any feminist anti-pornography philosophy. (Williams, 1993b, p. 59)

As Eve Kosofsky Sedgwick simply and profoundly points out, "People are different from each other" (1990, p. 22). Pornographies are different from each other, too. To lose sight of this fact is to create theoretical confusion. Conceptual inadequacy and political tunnel vision produce rancor and misunderstanding rather than insight, in readers and audiences, and are therefore counterproductive with respect to the goal of freeing women, men, and transpeople from all forms of sexual and political aggression—forms that notably include aggressively sectarian discourse.

References

Clark, C. (1991). Pornography without power? In Kimmel, M. S. (Ed.), *Men confront pornography* (pp. 281–284). New York: Meridian.

D'Emilio, J. (1992). *Making trouble: Essays on gay history, politics, and the university.* New York: Routledge.

Downs, D. (1989). *The new politics of pornography.* Chicago: University of Chicago Press.

Dworkin, A. (1989). *Pornography: Men possessing women.* New York: Plume.

Dyer, R. (1992). *Only entertainment.* New York: Routledge.

MacKinnon, C. (1987). *Feminism unmodified: Discourses on life and law.* Cambridge: Harvard University Press.

MacKinnon, C. (1989). *Toward a feminist theory of the state.* Cambridge: Harvard University Press.

MacKinnon, C. (1993). *Only words.* Cambridge: Harvard University Press.

Rich, A. (1993). Compulsory heterosexuality and lesbian existence. In Abelove, H., Barale, M. A., & Halperin, D. M. (Eds.), *The lesbian and gay studies reader* (pp. 227–254). New York: Routledge.

Rubin, G. S. (1993). Thinking sex: Notes for a radical theory of the politics of sexuality. In Abelove, H., Barale, M. A., & Halperin, D. M. (Eds.), *The lesbian and gay studies reader* (pp 3–44). New York: Routledge.

Sedgwick, E. K. (1990). *Epistemology of the closet.* Berkeley: University of California Press.

Steinem, G. (1993). Erotica vs. pornography. In Buchwald, E., & Fletcher, P. R. (Eds.), *Transforming a rape culture* (pp. 31–45). Minneapolis: Milkweed.

Tanenbaum, L. (1993). Contested connections. *The Women's Review of Books*, December, 29–31.

Williams, L. (1993a). Pornographies on/scene: or diff'rent strokes for diff'rent folks. In Segal, L., & McIntosh, M. (Eds.), *Sex exposed: Sexuality and the pornography debate* (pp. 233–265). New Brunswick, NJ: Rutgers University Press.

Williams, L. (1993b). Second thoughts on "Hard core: American obscenity law and the scapegoating of deviance." In Church, P., & Gibson, R. (Eds.), *Dirty looks: Women, pornography, power* (pp. 46–61). London: British Film Institute.

Notes

1. Linda Williams notes: "Donna Haraway once said in passing that one should not 'do' cultural studies of objects to which one is not vulnerable" (Williams, 1993b, p. 57). As a male-to-"female" transperson, I believe I'm to some extent "vulnerable" to the attractions of most forms of pornography, on the levels both of identification and desire.

2. In other instances, tricks may knowingly opt for cross-dressed males, or transwomen, in preference to GGs (genuine girls).

THEORIZING PROSTITUTION:
THE QUESTION OF AGENCY

Melanie Simmons
*Department of Sociology, Florida State University
Tallahassee, FL 32306*

There is a debate within feminism regarding the *agency* of prostitutes. This debate is between what I refer to as the Prostitutes Rights (PR) and Feminists Against Systems of Prostitution (FASP) movements. Both groups are feminist and are concerned with the welfare of prostitutes, although their analyses differ fundamentally. The cause of this conflict is incommensurate theoretical views of the agency of prostitutes. The PR perspective sees "sex workers" as active decision makers who "choose" to engage in prostitution. From this perspective, "sex work" is an occupational choice among other gendered and discriminated forms of work available to women. The FASP perspective views "prostituted women" as compelled by their social circumstances into prostitution, so that the involvement of women in prostitution is essentially nonconsensual. I identify five similarities and seven differences in the perspectives of FASP and PR. Proponents of PR are concerned with *choice* and the *individual* women. FASP members stress *coercion* and the *institution of prostitution.* These different levels of analysis help explain the incommensurability of language while blurring the distinctions between choice and coercion. In fact, their mutual concern for the welfare of prostitutes and their vision of a changed state provide common goals and arenas for concerted action.

Introduction

There is a debate within feminism concerning the *agency* of prostitutes. The words "consent" and "choice" are commonly used to describe agency, which is the ability of a person to make choices and take action under the social and economic constraints that impede these choices. This article reviews the agency-structure logics that separate two feminist camps. I refer to the two groups as the Feminists Against Systems of Prostitution movement (FASP) and the Prostitutes Rights movement (PR). Members of the FASP camp argue that the agency of prostitutes is constrained by patriarchal oppression, whereas members of the PR group argue that prostitutes are less constrained and freely choose prostitution. This difference in conceptions of agency leads to a difference in how prostitution should be viewed and what should be done to improve the lives of prostitutes.

Although some authors have explored the intricacies of this debate (Baldwin, 1997; Bell, 1994; Perry & Sanchez, 1998; Sanchez, 1998a, 1998b, 1998c; Scambler & Scambler, 1997; Shrage, 1989, 1994; Zatz, 1997), variation between the two movements in terms of the agency of prostitutes has not been fully addressed. For purposes of explanation, I compare the views of two complex categories of activists as ideal types in order to explore variation between FASP and PR. Differences among these two groups stem from incommensurable theoretical frameworks.

In the service of each camp's political stand, I use their own words and phrases in describing their perspectives. I define a prostitute as a person who engages in sexual acts for hire; FASP members often refer to these women as "prostituted" or in prostitution. The FASP camp takes the position that prostitutes have limited agency but have the right to sexual integrity and autonomy. This agency-constrained perspective is not new and has its roots in early twentieth century feminism (Barry, 1979,1995). Ideally for FASP, prostitution should be eliminated. They argue that no woman in a sexist society, which all Western societies are, can make "free" and fully informed decisions about engaging in prostitution. The notion that a woman might freely "choose" such work is problematic because only those women who are compelled by circumstances will make such a choice. This camp argues that true choice by women to prostitute themselves is impossible. Short of their goal of eliminating prostitution, FASP members seek to criminalize and punish "procurers, pimps, tricks, and johns."

Echoing the abortion debate, the PR activists declare that women should have the right to decide what they do with their bodies. They take the position that adult, able-bodied, rational women and men who want to engage in "sex work," as they often characterize it, have a right to do so without being criminalized, pitied, or confined to red light districts. They argue that sex workers are people who choose prostitution over a range of other kinds of possible work activities. The term *sex worker* is also used to ally the PR camp with other workers such as pornography actors and erotic dancers. The goal of the PR activists is to decriminalize all aspects of prostitution. They want prostitution taxed and regulated as any other service business. Finally, they seek more legal and socio-cultural rights and, ideally, respect for sex workers (Nagle, 1997).

Both movements are concerned with the welfare of prostitutes, although they have different perspectives. Within the logic of each perspective, arguments of what should be done about prostitution make sense. From the perspective of the FASP group, however, the hopes of the PR group are illogical and wrong headed, and vice versa. Theoretical differences explain the inability of these two groups to coordinate their efforts to improve the lives of prostitutes.

The Agency and Structure Debate

Central to my analysis is the question, "Where do the two feminist groups fall on a continuum running from unrestricted agency to unmitigated structure?" To set the stage for this analysis, I briefly define agency and structure and summarize some of the issues that sociologists and others debate concerning the association of human agency to structures.

Agency

If a member of society had total and completely free agency, this person could make choices without any constraints being placed on his or her behavior. For example, a girl as an unrestrained agent can decide whether she wants to be a brain surgeon, the CEO of a major corporation, or a prostitute. If she is totally free to choose, she knows all her options, and she can choose one as readily as the other (March & Olsen, 1989). Most scholars would have problems with this scenario; they would say that a girl's choices are shaped by her race, age, social class, intelligence, nationality, physical appearance, health and so on. Agency is therefore a relative term. People make choices, but they make them within particular circumstances, many of which entail constraints. Totally free agency is thus an ideal. Philosophers, social scientists, and the two feminist groups—PR and FASP—differ in their views of the degree to which people have agency. As I describe below, PR activists view prostitutes as having more agency than the FASP proponents accord. My analysis frames agency as a continuum with less restrained agency on one end and more restrained agency on the other (Alexander & Geisen, 1987, p. 4; Hays, 1994, p. 62).

Structure

Competing with agency, or free choice, as an explanation for human behavior, many philosophers, academics, and others view people as mostly responding to a priori situations, more than influencing those situations. People who emphasize social structures as shaping human activity generally focus first on the constraints that an individual faces when making choices or taking action. As an extreme, a person who is totally shaped by structure would make no choices; she or he would merely do as circumstances dictated, slavishly propelled along by external forces (Mayhew, 1980, 1981). As Mayhew describes it, people are like rabbits who run across a field; they run into whatever holes present themselves as possibilities, but they do not consciously "select" which holes to enter. From a structural determinist perspective, people are shaped by circumstances more than they are shapers of them. As with agency, most philosophers and activists reject an extreme structuralist position. Some favor a strong structural perspective, however, and emphasize the impact of structural circumstances on individuals' perceptions, beliefs, and practices. Viewing structure also as a continuum, my analysis explores how the PR perspective accords less importance to social structures in the experiences of prostitutes while the FASP perspective accords more importance to it.

FASP and PR Perspectives and the Agency-Structure Debate

The FASP perspective's stronger structuralist view sees women as controlled or at least compelled by their social environments. Prostituted women can be understood as socially constrained individuals whose involvement in the sex industry is more a consequence of their gender, age, social class, education, and so on, than by the choices they have made. In this view, these women were economically compelled, lured by false claims, or duped into prostitution and, once involved, found it difficult to leave. FASP activists see prostitution as little more than rape and celebrate prostitutes for simply surviving the situation (Barry, 1979, p. 46; 1995, p. 293; Baldwin, 1997, p. 123; 1992, p.70).

The activists of the PR perspective agree that women are constrained by poverty, job discrimination, and segregation and, as a result of these constraints, some women choose to engage in sex work. The PR group stresses that sex workers consent to prostitution and have power within the sexual encounter as they negotiate the service and fee. The PR perspective leans towards a stronger view of agency than FASP. The PR movement does not see unmitigated structure nor completely free agency. I believe that their perspective fits in the theoretical center of the structure/agency continuum. The PR perspective finds sex workers as agents because they have alternate courses of action (to engage in sex work or not) and make conscious (or unconscious) choices among an available set of structural alternatives (Hays, 1994, pp. 61–62).

Similarities

Welfare of Prostitutes

Both the PR and FASP perspectives are concerned with the well-being of prostitutes (Table 1). Activists in both groups have organized conferences, lobbied governments, and written books about their views of the ways to improve the lives of prostitutes. The FASP group seeks to protect women from the sex industry and from what they see as inherently violent, intrusive sex in prostitution. It seeks to protect women and punish pimps and johns. The PR group wants to empower sex workers through decriminalization. It expects to organize sex work so that prostitutes are safe, healthy, and prosperous.

Feminist Perspectives

TABLE 1
Similarities between the Feminists Against Systems of Prostitution and the Prostitutes Rights Movements

	Feminists Against Systems of Prostitution (FASP)	Prostitutes Rights (PR)
Welfare of Prostitutes	Concerned with general well-being of prostitutes. Organize conferences, write books, and attempt legal reforms.	Concerned with general well-being of prostitutes. Organize conferences, write books, and attempt legal reforms.
Feminist Perspectives	MacKinnon influenced feminism	Sex positive feminism
Prostitution as Exploitation	Prostitution is the symbol of female sexuality and exploitation. The woman is bought and sold for men and male desire. Sexuality is the primary social sphere of male power.	Sexual and economic exploitation is associated prostitution. Discriminatory law enforcement and the illegality of prostitution are the major source of exploitation.
Depenalization or Decriminalization	Some support depenalizing (undefined) prostituted women.	Decriminalize the sellers, buyers, and managers of prostitution.
Opposition to Legalization	Oppose legalization of prostitution as in Northern Europe and Nevada. When prostitution is legalized, there is an increase in trafficking in women and children from the developing world.	Oppose legalization (regulation) as in Northern Europe and Nevada. Regulated prostitution often allows no choice in clientele, no right to refusal or to fair earnings, no freedom of movement.

The FASP group is generally viewed as more assertively feminist, but the PR group also argues from a feminist perspective (Table 1). The two groups share four feminist principles:

1. They agree that women have certain common characteristics and are treated in a particular and often negative way in society.
2. They believe women should be able to define for themselves what characteristics and behaviors are appropriate for women.
3. They recognize that it is a "man's world" where men define a "good" woman as one who meets their expectations, serves and pleases them, and abides by the rules they have created. In this third principle, the PR proponents argue that no one, neither men nor women, have the right to define what a good woman is. The FASP proponents focus more on the power of men to define and manipulate women into that which they would not have defined for themselves.
4. Both groups desire to make change in society in order to end the unjust power that allows others to define what women can do, say, or be. Feminists, in general, believe that change requires struggle and a social movement to effect change so that women can fulfill their own destiny (Feree & Hess, 1994, pp. 32–33). Thus, PR and FASP proponents support the wider feminist movement that works for structural change (Bell, 1994, p. 73; Jenness, 1993, p. 65).

PR and FASP also differ on several feminist issues. Members of the PR camp call themselves "sex positive feminists." They do not find female sexual experiences and pleasure problematic. The FASP perspective, inspired originally by MacKinnon (among others), conceives of women's sexual desires and expression as constructed by a patriarchal society and thus not of their own making (MacKinnon, 1989, pp. 127–128).

Prostitution as Exploitation

Claims about sexual and economic exploitation are central to the causes of prostitution (see Table 1). PR activists agree with this claim, but their concerns deal mostly with inequity caused by laws and law enforcement practices (Bell, 1994; Sanchez, 1998c). Alexander states that "Prostitution exists, at least in part, because of the subordination of women…[which] is reflected in the double standard of sexual behavior for men and women, and is carried out in the discrepancy between women's and men's earning power" (Alexander, 1987, p. 188). According to PR members, prostitution may or may not be exploitative for women who practice it depending on the situation (Bell, 1994, p. 124). The PR camp stresses that imprisonment, court imposed debt, and law enforcement officers are the primary vehicle for the exploitation of prostitutes. The failure of police to arrest men involved in solicitation illustrates exploitation and gender discrimination in the legal system (Jenness, 1993, p. 52).

Members of the PR movement do not want clients or managers to be arrested, however. If prostitution is decriminalized, they believe police harassment would decrease and sex workers would be able to rely on the police for protection rather than be oppressed by them. More protection would mean less violence against sex workers (Jenness, 1993, p. 74; Scott, 1987, p. 100). Thus, the PR stance is that discriminatory law enforcement and the illegality of prostitution are major causes the explotation of women sex workers. PR activists focus on laws because they trust the ability (agency) of prostitutes to shape their environment (structure).

Additionally, the relatively narrow emphasis on sexual and economic exploitation by PR activists is congruent with a rights discourse (Bell, 1994). The PR movement concludes that prostitution is symptomatic of women's oppression in society but does not offer a critique or analysis of the structural conditions that produce gender, class, and race inequality. Nor can it, Bell argues. "A discourse premised on the extension of basic human and civil rights...as far as it may go in changing the identity and status of the claimant group and even in undoing the traditional concept of rights, can only act as an intervention. It is an act of micropolitics concerned with its specific struggle,...and not with a change in any totality" (Bell, 1994, p. 111). PR does not attempt to change gender relations in society. Rather, its goals are to reform inequities of law enforcement and bad laws.

The FASP group is concerned with much more than inequity of law enforcement and laws. FASP does not associate prostitution with work, as does the PR camp. For FASP members, prostitution is what women are forced into when they are desperate. Prostitution is a model for female sexuality in a patriarchal society (Wynter, 1987; Baldwin, 1992, p. 46). Arguing from a FASP perspective, Wynter states that "Prostitution isn't like anything else. Rather everything else is like prostitution, because it is the model for women's condition, for gender stratification, and its logical extension, sex discrimination. Prostitution is founded on enforced sexual abuse under a system of male supremacy that is itself built along a continuum of coercion, fear, force, racism, and poverty" (Wynter, 1987, p. 268).

Prostitution is more than a job or a type of sexuality. For MacKinnon and Barry, women's sexuality is a mirror of male desire. Prostituted women, like all women, do not have sexuality for themselves but for the men who purchase them (MacKinnon, 1987, p. 59; Barry, 1995, p. 22; Bell, 1994, p. 80). Bought and sold for a price, women do not possess their own sexuality. Rather, they experience sexual violence (Barry, 1979; Baldwin, 1992; Dworkin, 1981; MacKinnon, 1987) or are essentially enslaved (Barry, 1995).

"Depenalization" or Decriminalization of Prostitution

For FASP, the issue of depenalization versus decriminalization is unclear (see Table 1). Originally, FASP members argued that prostitution should be decriminalized, meaning that women who practice prostitution should not be arrested or punished by the state for their poverty and sexual exploitation (Raymond, 1997, p. 5). To others, it is not clear that decriminalization would serve women's interests (Baldwin, 1992, p. 79, 1997, pp. 124–125). Recently, the Coalition Against Trafficking in Women began to support the undefined term, "depenalization," of prostitutes (see http://www.uri.edu/artsci/wms/hughes/catw/empower.htm). An example of depenalization is that sponsored by PROMISE, where women arrested for prostitution in San Francisco can attend PROMISE as an alternative to incarceration through a Pre-Trial Diversion program (http://www.sirius.com/~promise/program.html). PROMISE is modeled on addiction recovery peer-counseling and offers services and support to women who have chosen to get out of prostitution (or as an option to incarceration). It seems that the FASP movement is reconsidering decriminalization in favor of depenalization.

The uncertainty of FASP members about decriminalization is not surprising to PR proponents who questioned their commitment to decriminalize women in 1993 (Jenness, 1993, p. 80). PR activists support broad decriminalization of prostitution, which includes elimination of all laws against buying, selling, or managing prostitution.

Opposition to Legalization

Both PR and FASP proponents object to the state-regulated legalization of prostitution, as in Nevada and Northern Europe (see Table 1). Barry cites evidence that illegal trafficking in women and children has increased everywhere legalized prostitution exists (Barry, 1995, p. 101; Raymond, 1997, p. 5).

The PR movement wants decriminalization yet opposes state-regulated legalization, because often women must be registered and assigned to a brothel—thus losing autonomy and freedom of movement (Scambler & Scambler, 1997, p. 186). State regulated brothels such as those in Germany and Nevada often allow prostitutes no choice in clientele, no right of refusal, and no right to a fair share of earnings. They also entail forced isolation and forced overwork. Legalized brothel prostitution is under the control of the brothel owner, not the individual prostitute. Laws that allow prostitution are not written from a woman-centered perspective. PR members want to participate in writing new laws about prostitution so that these new laws will give women more control over their work and sexuality (Scambler & Scambler, 1997, p. 186; Pheterson, 1989, p. 108; St. James, 1996).

Differences

The differences between these two groups are instructive for understanding their underlying views of the agency of prostitutes. The FASP members' structuralist perspective claims that it is essentially through sex that male dominated society oppresses women. Sex is the primary vehicle of women's oppression and all other discrimination derives from it. Women are almost exclusively sexually victimized, exploited, and objectified by men. Prostitution is not a job but sexual exploitation and victimization carried out by economically dominant men, solely for their pleasure. A liability of the FASP argument is their failure to explain the consent of some to engage in prostitution but consent is irrelevant in this perspective since women's choices are constrined by stronger structural forces.

The PR group counters FASP's arguments that sex is the primary vehicle of women's oppression. PR proponents do not focus on the sexual victimization and objectification of women. Sexism in sex work is like sexism in the rest of society. Prostitution is not inherently a worse job than other jobs. Women can know and like their sexuality without false consciousness. In fact, for some in PR, prostitution is considered another type of sexuality. Although they agree that women are discriminated against, they view patriarchy as generalized throughout society, but not originating from sex. For PR, women *choose* sex work either as a form of work or a type of sexuality. The PR movement can be distinguished from the FASP movement along at least seven dimensions, as shown in Table 2. Each of these characteristics will be taken up in turn.

Speak in the Interest of...

Proponents of FASP attempt to speak for the collective condition of all women because they view structural conditions such as male domination and economic oppression as shaping all women's lives (Table 2; MacKinnon, 1989; Barry, 1995). As empirical evidence of male domination, they note that sexual objectification and sexual violence are done primarily to girls and women. Women have been systematically subjected to men's violence and sexuality. Consequently, women have a common condition of sexual

TABLE 2
Differences Between Feminists Against Systems of Prostitution and the Prostitutes Rights Movements

	Feminists Against Systems of Prostitution (FASP)	Prostitutes Rights (PR)
Speak in the Interest of...	Speak for the collective condition of all women. Women have a common condition of subordination to men and male sexuality. Women are not all the same, but they are united under patriarchal oppression.	Speak for women (and men) who choose sex work, who want to engage in their work without threat of arrest or police harassment.
Views of the Other Group	FASP members question whether the PR group has much membership. Imply that the PR movement could be operated in the interest of the sex industry, if not the leaders of the industry themselves.	FASP are MacKinnon influenced academics who see prostitution as sexual exploitation and victimization. They have created a harsh legal climate for sex workers.
Focus of Analysis— Sexuality	Focus on the power of men over women in society. Male dominance is sexual. Prostitution exists due to male demand. Prostitution is the model of female sexuality.	Focus on prostitution as one among many sexual identities. Missionary, paid, s/m, lesbian, fetishes, etc., are types of sexuality. Sex should be judged by quality and respect, not acceptability.
Focus of Analysis— Choice	Consent to prostitution is irrelevant to the sex industry that provides female bodies to a male market. Consent to objectification is a condition of oppression. "Socially normal decision making" is impaired judgement in a system of male dominance.	Individuals choose the best job among gendered work. Sexism in prostitution. is equivalent to sexism in the rest of society. Prostitution is consensual sexual activity of adults. Sex work is a choice of work as well as a form of sexual identity.
Men	Men collectively are the problem. Individual men may or may not oppress women, but as a whole the patriarchal-capitalist system of male domination is the cause of prostitution.	Pimps, johns, tricks are inflammatory words that dehumanize men. Managers, go-betweens, clients, and dates are preferable. Men are not the problem; the laws are.

TABLE 2 (continued)

	Feminists Against Systems of Prostitution (FASP)	Prostitutes Rights (PR)
Poverty and Prostitution	Due to feminization of poverty, women could not have chosen prostitution. There is no "choice" under economic duress. Women's poverty is sexualized within patriarchal society.	Structure of society impoverishes women, but poor women should not be denied the income from prostitution due to independence, income, and hours, it can be a good job.
Product for Sale	Prostitution commodifies the whole person. It reduces a woman to her body's sexual function. As a commodity, women become alienated. They detach from their bodies, damaging their "self."	Sex work is no more violating than other women's work. A sexual service is for sale. The body is not sacred and need not be protected from intrusion.
Goals of the Movement	Goals are to eliminate prostitution and create a new state that more realistically takes women's experiences into account. Short of that, women in prostitution should not be further punished because of their poverty and exploitation. "Depenalizing" women in prostitution is under discussion. Traffickers, buyers, and organizers of the sex industry should be criminalized.	Laws oppress sex workers most. Some are forced into prostitution, but existing laws against kidnapping, extortion, child abuse, rape, etc., could protect them if prostitution were decriminalized. Eliminate all laws against Prostitution. Regulate it as a service industry without red light districts. Decriminalize buyers, sellers, and managers. Introduce no new laws to protect prostitutes, as they restrict sex worker rights.

inferiority to men (MacKinnon, 1989, p. 243). FASP proponents recognize that women are not the same, but they see a unity of condition among women, a unity due to patriarchal oppression (MacKinnon, 1987). In the FASP view, women are exchanged as indistinguishable objects for men's sexual pleasure. Objectification is a primary process of women's subordination. The state institutionalizes male power over women through writing the male body and point of view into law (MacKinnon, 1987; 1989, p. 169). Prostitution implies to all men that all women can be bought as sexual objects for a price (Barry, 1995, pp. 47–48; Lopez-Jones, 1987, p. 273). This implication victimizes all women, justifies the sale of any woman, and reduces all women to sex, according to the Coalition Against Trafficking in Women (http://www. uri.edu/artsci/wms/hughes/catw/empower.htm).

PR proponents speak only for women (and men) who choose sex work as an occupation. They speak for those who want to engage in sex work without threat of arrest or police harassment. They do not try to speak for all women. Sex work, they argue, is no different than any other service job or gendered occupation.

Views of the Other Group

Due to their underlying theoretical differences, PR and FASP view each other with suspicion (Table 2). FASP members' ability to understand the agency-oriented approach of the PR group is limited by their more structuralist perspective. PR proponents fail to appreciate FASP's structural arguments because they view prostitution as an individual issue. Both seem puzzled by the inability of the other group to understand their reasoning.

Typical of the rancorous debate, Giobbe questioned whether COYOTE[2] and the National Task Force on Prostitution, which were operated by Priscilla Alexander in the early 1990s, have any membership. Giobbe implies that these entities espouse Alexander's philosophy only (Giobbe, 1990, pp. 68–71). Some in FASP also questions whether the PR movement is not operated by the sex industry leaders themselves rather than by women prostitutes. Raymond states, "Although claiming to be a prostitutes' rights organization, COYOTE works more for the rights of the customers and the industry than for the rights of women to leave prostitution" (1997, p. 3). For FASP members, women who would participate in groups such as COYOTE have a "false consciousness" because they do not recognize that they participate in their own exploitation. MacKinnon criticizes the PR type of view as relativistic. MacKinnon states that "Concrete positions of power and powerlessness are transformed into mere relative value judgments about which reasonable people can form different but equally valid preferences. Women's experience of abuse becomes a 'point of view'" (1990, p. 12).

The PR camp is likewise dubious of FASP, claiming that FASP proponents are all academics. Margo St. James, founder of COYOTE, says of Kathleen Barry, "Although she gives lip service to decriminalization, she finds it impossible to grant (sex work) a professional status equal to her own" (cited in Jenness, 1993, p. 80). Proponents of PR criticize FASP for claiming that women do not know themselves. Additionally, sex workers do not feel heard by FASP members. St. James says that FASP arguments, "[have] nothing at all to do with reality and they're totally forgetting the people and not listening to them. And when they say working prostitutes are brainwashed [into prostitution]. I mean they totally belittle and take a super-patronizing attitude" (cited in Jenness, 1993, p. 79). PR activists also argue that the FASP perspective helps create a harsh legal climate for sex workers and prostitution (Almodovar, 1996).

Focus of Analysis

The focus of the FASP perspective is men's power over women in society and in sex (see Table 2). MacKinnon, articulating the FASP perspective, says that "Male dominance is sexual. Meaning: men in particular, if not men alone, sexualize hierarchy" (1989, p. 127). MacKinnon, Barry, and other FASP proponents argue that women do not know their true sexual selves because what is considered sex has been socially constructed by men and socially forced upon women. Male sexuality defines both male and female sexuality (MacKinnon, 1989, p. 113; Barry, 1995, p. 22). Media images, pornography, and male dominance over the sexual experience preclude a woman from knowing her own sexuality. Pornography, rape, and prostitution institutionalize male sexual supremacy and female sexual submission (Bell, 1994, p. 81). As a result of these dynamics and conditions, women respond to the social conditions that are created by men (MacKinnon, 1989, p. 128).

The PR group denies that male sexuality defines female sexuality. Sex work is one of many sexual styles or identities (Rubin, 1993). Rubin argues that FASP's "brainwash theory" of female sexuality explains erotic diversity by assuming that some sexual acts, like prostitution, are so disgusting that no one would willingly perform them. According to this theory, anyone who engages in deviant sex, like prostitution, must be forced or fooled (Rubin, 1993, p. 40). In a PR perspective, erotic diversity includes straight-missionary sex, paid sex, sadomasochism, gay and lesbian sex, swinging, fetishes, and so on. PR seeks a democratic view of sexuality in which sexual acts are judged not by their acceptability, but by "the way partners treat one another, the level of mutual consideration, the presence or absence of coercion, and the quantity and quality of the pleasures they provide" (Rubin, 1993, p. 18). Paid sex is an option among several sexuality choices; as sex work is a choice among other gendered work. PR members argue that individuals choose the best job from an array of jobs that are often both gender differentiated and unequally paid.

According to the FASP perspective, sexuality in prostitution exists because of male customer demand and suits male customer expectations (Barry, 1995, p. 38–39). MacKinnon has no concept that a prostitute could have sexual agency and could exercise sexual control in her commercial sexual encounters, according to Bell (1994, pp. 82–83). Fundamentally, men define what sex is, of which they are the subjects, and women, especially prostitutes, are the objects. Prostitution is the model of female sexual subordination in society; it informs all other sexual relations. Kathleen Barry's title, *The Prostitution of Sexuality* (1995), reflects this claim.

PR statements of consent and choice contradict claims that men or male-dominated society control prostitutes. PR activists say that prostitutes are not sexually submissive but negotiate a service for a fee. To FASP members, some women think they consent to prostitution when there are structural forces that compel women into the sex industry (Barry, 1995, p. 39). Poor, young, minority, uneducated, inner-city girls and women often do not have an array of job opportunities as PR depicts. The idea that these women have many choices deflects attention from the men who cruise the streets and recruit girls and women from bus stops and schools. In impoverished areas, male market demand lures female bodies into the sex trade.

PR members view the societal structures from a different perspective and criticize FASP for failing to recognize the equivalence of the sexism in prostitution to sexism in the rest of society. Rubin argues that sexism exists within the family, religion, education, child-rearing, the media, the state, psychiatry, and employment. Prostitution is not the source of male prejudice that infects these institutions and creates female subordination (Rubin, 1993, p. 37). They think that FASP members should worry about the sexism in these institutions and not oppose the consensual sexual activity of adults. In fact, horrible victimization of the young, the infirm, and undocumented migrants takes place without sex. PR stresses that there are many forms of subordination in society, whereas FASP argues that the primary source of victimization stems first from male dominance and later from institutions like capitalism and the state. The theoretical disputes between FASP and PR are not isolated. They are related to larger themes in feminist thought and debate, and these include discussions of sexual politics and so-called "victim feminism" (see Riophe, 1993, 1994; Segal, 1994a, 1994b, 1997; Segal & McIntosh, 1993; Vance, 1993).

Men

The PR perspective views words such as pimps, johns, and tricks as inflammatory because they dehumanize and vilify men (Table 2; Alexander, 1987, p. 187). Instead of the terms pimps or madams, PR prefers managers and go-betweens. PR thinks of prostitute-pimp relationships as employee-employer relationships. Instead of referring to johns or tricks, they refer to dates (Alexander, 1987, p. 187). Abuses take place, they agree; immigrants and young sex workers are particularly at high risk for abuse; they should be protected using existing laws. Men are not the problem. Laws that prosecute people who engage in consensual sexual activity are the primary problem.

Men are a problem for FASP. Individual men may or may not oppress women but, as a whole, the patriarchal-capitalist system of male domination of women is the primary problem and cause of prostitution (Barry, 1995, p.47). Without the economic, political, and physical superiority of men, prostitution would not exist.

Poverty and Prostitution

FASP proponents argue that because of the feminization of poverty, women who engage in prostitution have not freely chosen it (see Table 2). The "choice" to use your body as an object for a stranger is non-existent when one operates under economic duress. The only way to protect women is to eliminate poverty and, subsequently, prostitution. Women's poverty is sexualized in a society that rewards men and impoverishes women (MacKinnon, 1989, p. 127; Barry, 1979, pp. 9–10). She may be right. Both PR and FASP proponents argue for more social services, alcohol and drug abuse counseling, job training, and child and medical care for sex workers. FASP members stress that the additional service of helping women leave prostitution should accompany other social services.

PR proponents agree that some structures impoverish women, but they argue that poor women should not be denied the often superior income that comes from practicing sex work. Poor women work in low paying jobs such as house cleaning and child care. If a woman can earn more by sex work, she should be able to. For those who choose it, sex work can be a good job because it provides independence, good hours, and higher income. PR members are critical of aid groups that "rescue" women from prostitution by teaching them sewing and domestic service skills (Madra, 1998).

Product for Sale

The PR perspective claims that sex workers provide a sexual service in exchange for money rather than seeing sex work as the commodification of the whole person (Table 2; Jenness, 1993, pp. 67–68). PR proponents do not privilege the body as sacred and in need of protection from intrusion. For some, sex work is part of an alternative lifestyle choice (Rubin 1993, p. 17). In the FASP view, in contrast, prostitution reduces a woman to her sexual function (Barry, 1995, p. 22). The woman *becomes* a commodity that is bought and sold by and for men. FASP proponents privilege the "self" they view as alienated from its true nature, choices, and desires by the practice of prostitution (Barry, 1995, p. 28). Barry believes that a prostitute's distancing and detachment from her body and her actions during the sexual act of prostitution is damaging to her personal wholeness and mental integrity (Barry, 1995, p. 35).

Goals of the Movement

Eliminating laws against prostitution is the primary goal of the PR movement (see Table 2). They view the actions of police officials and agencies, including fines, imprisonment, harassment, and blackmail as more dangerous to women than violent clients (Almodovar, 1998; Velisek, 1997; Pheterson, 1989). They acknowledge that some women and children are forced into prostitution, but PR proponents stress that existing laws can, if fully enforced, protect people from perpetrating crimes against prostitutes (Pheterson 1989). Laws against kidnapping, extortion, racketeering, theft, rape, battery, and child abuse can be used to protect sex workers of any age. It is inconceivable to PR members that women who are *forced* into prostitution are arrested and, if they are immigrants, deported. Since prostitution is illegal, sex workers are often treated as if they had no rights, even when they are subjected to violence.

The PR movement wants to eliminate all laws that prohibit prostitution. They want to decriminalize the activities of prostitutes, their clients, and their business managers and go-betweens. They want prostitution regulated like any other service industry—a situation that would free prostitutes from red light districts or brothel constraints (Pheterson, 1989, pp. 104–108). They oppose new laws that would restrict prostitution, including, specifically, laws to protect sex workers. Protectionist laws restrict sex workers' rights and freedom of movement, they argue (Lopez-Jones, 1987, p. 274).

FASP proponents want to end prostitution and all sexual exploitation, which includes sexual harassment, rape, incest, battering, and pornography. Short of ending prostitution, some in the FASP movement want to depenalize women in prostitution rather than decriminalize it (Baldwin, 1992, p. 79; http://www.uri.edu/artsci/wms/huges/catw/repsr.htm). FASP proponents have not defined "depenalize" yet, as mentioned above. It seems that many within FASP do not want women punished because of their poverty and sexual exploitation. FASP proponents want to prohibit men from buying sex from women and children and to criminalize traffickers and organizers of the sex industry. Such people make their living from the suffering of women. FASP seeks to prevent men from using women as sexual objects more than it seeks to decriminalize prostitution (Barry, 1995, p. 298; Raymond, 1997, p. 6).

Discussion and Conclusion

The key word for the PR side, I would argue, is *choice*. The focus of their analysis is the *individual woman*, a point whose significance becomes more evident below. PR advocates focus on the rights and ability of individual women to "choose" sex work, to choose to make a living by exchanging sex for money. Women make such a choice in less than an ideal world, PR advocates acknowledge, because sex work is defined by the state as illegal. Furthermore, many members of society look down on their activity as distasteful, filthy, even sinful. PR proponents acknowledge constraints on the ability of women to freely choose and practice sex work as an occupation. They focus on the constraints that stem from cultural biases against sexuality, unjust laws, and the failure of legal officials in enforcing the laws that would be helpful if used.

PR advocates do not concentrate on the gender order nor do they analyze sex workers' conditions and exploitation relative to gender. They are able to include male sex workers within their analysis and to insist that (other) men are not the enemy but are merely customers who seek a service. Although gender inequality is acknowledged, PR members do not view men as actors in a societal system of gender inequality whose primary dynamic is the subordination of women to men's collective benefit.

The key word for the FASP side is *coercion*. The primary focus of analysis for FASP is the *institution of prostitution*, not choices made by individual women or girls. In focusing on prostitution as an institution, FASP proponents analyze the history of gender relations, including women's coercion to exchange sex for protection, safety, or other resources—including their lives—besides money. The gender order is central to FASP analysis of prostitution and to its "resolution." Historical and current structures, beliefs, and practices prevent women and girls from making "free choices" of many kinds, including whether to exchange sex for money. Prostitution is an extreme form of sexual coercion to which all women and girls are subjected in ongoing ways. (For example, high school girls are pressured to have sex with dates who spend large sums of money on them.) Thus, choice is tricky. When women's options are so extensively constrained, to frame women as "freely choosing among them" is to ignore the primary conditions in which they live.

FASP believes the state has a role in women's sexual subordination. In the FASP view, the state is a creation of men; men produced it with men's lives and interests in mind (MacKinnon, 1989; Pateman, 1988). Therefore, any laws that men made about women reflect men's experiences and representations of women, not women's experiences and representations of themselves. Being subject to such laws is alienating for women because the laws do not reflect women's standpoints (Hartsock, 1998; Smith, 1989; Collins, 1990; Harding, 1991). A new state, with new laws, must be envisioned and created before things can change. Short of creating a new state, reformed laws that more realistically take women's experiences and standpoints into account can help individual prostitutes but they will not dismantle the institution of prostitution. While PR members seek legal reform in the manner of decriminalization, FASP attempts to fundamentally change the state. The underlying goal of both FASP and PR is to increase the agency of prostitutes.

Choice versus coercion: The line between them is fuzzy. When is a decision a "true choice"? If conditions require one to choose from among a range of lesser and greater "evils," accepting one over another may be capitulation or survival, not a genuinely free choice. Debates about these issues will continue. The difference in levels of analysis—individual versus institutional—helps explain the incommensurability of language that blurs the distinction between choice and coercion. In the meantime, my analysis suggests that the PR and FASP perspectives share some common ground. Their mutual concern for the welfare of prostitutes and their vision of a changed state provide goals and arenas for concerted action.

Notes

The author expresses her special thanks to Patricia Yancy Martin for her tremendous efforts editing and focusing this paper. Thanks are also due Margaret Baldwin, Coral Velisek, Norma Jean Almodovar, Margo St. James, and the anonymous reviewers for their comments.

1. Some information included in the article was obtained through interviews and personal communications, including Almodovar (1996, 1998), St. James (1996), and Velisek (1997).
2. COYOTE = Call Off Your Old Tired Ethics, founded by Margo St. James.

References

Alexander, J., & Geisen, B. (1987). From reduction to linkage: The long view of the micro-macro link. In Alexander, J., Geisen, B., Munch, R., & Smelser, N. (Eds.), *The micro-macro link*. Berkeley: University of California Press.

Alexander, P. (1987). Prostitution: A difficult issue for feminists. In Delacoste, F., & Alexander, P. (Eds.), *Sex work*. Pittsburgh: Cleis Press.

Baldwin, M. A. (1992). Split at the root: Prostitution and feminist discourses of law reform. *Yale Journal of Law and Feminism* 5, 47–119.

Baldwin, M. A. (1997). Public women and the feminist state. *Harvard Women's Law Journal* 20, 47–162.

Barry, K. (1979). *Female sexual slavery*. New York: Basic Books.

Barry, K. (1995). *The prostitution of sexuality*. New York: New York University Press.

Bell, S. (1994). *Reading, writing, and rewriting the prostitute body*. Bloomington: Indiana University Press.

Collins, P. H. (1992). *Black feminist thought: Knowledge, consciousness, and the politics of empowerment.* Boston: Unwin Hyman.

Dworkin, A. (1981). *Pornography: Men possessing women.* London: Women's Press.

Ferree, M. M., & Hess, B. (1994). *Controversy and coalition.* New York: Twayne Publishers.

Giobbe, E. (1990). Confronting liberal lies about prostitution. In Leidholdt, D., & Raymond, J. G. (Eds.), *The sexual liberals and the attack on feminism.* New York: Pergamon Press.

Harding, S. G. (1991). *Whose science? Whose knowledge?: Thinking from women's lives.* Ithaca, NY: Cornell University Press.

Hartsock, N. (1998). *The feminist standpoint revisited and other essays.* Boulder: Westview Press.

Hays, S. (1994). Structure and agency and the sticky problem of culture. *Sociological Theory,* 12(1), 57–72.

Jenness, V. (1993). *Making it work: The prostitutes rights movement in perspective.* New York: Aldine de Gruyter.

Langum, D. (1994). *Crossing over the line: Legislating morality and the Mann Act.* Chicago: The University of Chicago Press.

Lopez-Jones, N. (1987). Workers: Introducing the English Collective of Prostitutes. In Delacoste, F., & Alexander, P. (Eds.), *Sex work.* Pittsburgh: Cleis Press.

MacKinnon, C. (1989). *Toward a feminist theory of the state.* Cambridge: Harvard University Press.

MacKinnon, C. (1987). *Feminism unmodified: Discourses on life and law.* Cambridge: Harvard University Press.

Madra, E. (1998). Cambodia's prostitutes seek new life. *Reuters,* February 25.

March, J. G., & Olsen, J. P. (1989). *Rediscovering institutions: The organizational basis of politics.* New York: Free Press.

Martin, P. Y. (1997). Gender, accounts, and rape processing work. *Social Problems,* 44, 464–482.

Mayhew, B. (1980). Structuralism versus individualism: Part 1, Shadow boxing in the dark. *Social Forces,* 59(2), 335–375.

Mayhew, B. (1981). Structuralism versus individualism: Part 2, Ideological and other obfuscations. *Social Forces,* 59(3), 627–648.

Nagle, J. (1997). *Whores and other feminists.* New York: Routledge.

Pateman, C. (1989). *The disorder of women: Democracy, feminism and political theory.* Cambridge: Polity.

Perry, R. W., & Sanchez, L. (1998). Transactions in the flesh: Toward an ethnography of embodied sexual reason. *Studies in Law, Politics and Society* (in press).

Pheterson, G. (1989). *A vindication of the rights of whores.* Seattle: Seal Press.

Pudlow, J. (1997). Former madam settles sex suit with lobbyist. *Tallahassee Democrat,* September 10, B1.

Raymond, J. G. (1997). Prostitution as violence against women: NGO stonewalling in Beijing and elsewhere. *Women's Studies International Forum,* 20(1), 1–9.

Riophe, K. (1993). *The morning after: Sex, fear, and feminism*. Boston : Little Brown and Co.

Riophe, K. (1994). Date rape's other victim. *New York Times*, June 13, s. 6, p. 26.

Rubin, G. S. (1993). Thinking sex: Notes for a radical theory of the politics of sexuality. In Kauffman, L. S. (Ed.), *American feminist thought at century's end: A reader*. Cambridge, MA: Blackwell.

Sanchez, L. (1998a). Spatial practices and bodily maneuvers: Negotiating at the margins of a local sexual economy. *PoLAR: Political and Legal Anthropology Review*, 21(2), 47–62.

Sanchez, L. (1998b). Boundaries of legitimacy: Sex, violence, citizenship and community in a local sexual economy. *Law and Social Inquiry* (in press).

Sanchez, L. (1998c). Sex-law and the paradox of agency in the everyday practices of women in the 'Evergreen' sex trade. In Henry, S., & Milovanovic, D. (Eds.), *Constitutive criminology at work: Agency and resistance in the constitution of crime and punishment* (in press).

Scambler, G., & Scambler, A. (1997). *Rethinking prostitution*. New York: Routledge.

Segal, L. (1994a). *Straight sex: Rethinking the politics of pleasure*. Berkeley: University of California Press.

Segal, L. (1994b). Let's be straight with one another. *New Statesman and Society,* 7(320), 16–17.

Segal, L. (Ed.) (1997). *New sexual agendas*. New York: New York University Press.

Segal, L., & McIntosh, M. (Eds.) (1993). *Sex exposed: Sexuality and the pornography debate*. New Brunswick, NJ: Rutgers University Press.

Shrage, L. (1989). Should feminists oppose prostitution? *Ethics,* 99(2), 347–361.

Shrage, L. (1994). *Moral dilemmas of feminism: Prostitution, adultery and abortion*. London: Routledge.

Scott, V. (1987). C-49: A new way of oppression. In Bell, L. (Ed.), *Good girls/ Bad girls*. Seattle: Seal Press.

Smith, D. (1989). *The everyday world as problematic: A feminist sociology*. Amherst, MA: Northeastern University Press.

Vance, C. S. (Ed.) (1993). *Pleasure and danger: Exploring female sexuality*. New York: Harper Collins.

Wynter, S. (1987). WHISPER: Women Hurt in Systems of Prostitution Engaged in Revolt. In Delacoste, F., & Alexander, P. (Eds.), *Sex work*. Pittsburgh: Cleis Press.

Zatz, N. D. (1997). Sex work/Sex act: Law, labor, and desire in constructions of prostitution. *Signs,* 22(2), 277–308.

POLE WORK: AUTOETHNOGRAPHY OF A STRIP CLUB

Merri Lisa Johnson
153½ Crary Avenue, Binghamton, NY 13905

My life story draws its shape from the perpetual motion of dressing and undressing; the pull of my wrists on the elastic waistband of a slip worn at the request of my great-grandmother for whom it was necessary that I mask my parting legs as I walked in and out of church; the awkward angling of elbows required to zip and unzip the back of my schoolteacher-gray dress; insistent fingers jabbing bobby-pins through a tulle veil on my wedding day; and most recently, the nervous clicking of fetish-high heels against a strip club stage as they step out of bridal white panties. I have worn many versions of female sexuality, both good and bad, passive and flagrant. In fact, I choose to exist in the space among various states of undress, my body the border across which covering and dis-covering gender identity takes place. I am a seam, a mobile hem-line drifting below and above the knees of girlhood. In refusing to be one kind of girl or another, passing instead among borderlands, I hold open the ideological frameworks that define womanhood in such varying social domains as strip clubs and universities. By remaining ever in motion, dressing and undressing, I am able to maintain contact with my body and control its presentation; and in the space between clasping and unclasping, the impossibility of female sexual agency is suspended. Unstill in the undressing, I resist what tries to pin me down.

I choose motion. As the defining characteristic of my experiences as a woman, I choose motion because of its evocative and dominant presence in contemporary feminist theory. Such formulations proliferate: Julia Kristeva's *sujet-en-process*, Judith

Butler's gender performativity, Carole Boyce Davies's migratory subjectivities, Chela Sandoval's differential consciousness or gear metaphor, Maria Lugones's playful world-traveling, not to mention the myriad aesthetic strategies of women artists and authors who render women's bodies mobile and subjectivities multiple. The trope of motion resonates because it is clear that we, as women, need to get a move on. These ideas share a sense that survival of the spirit depends on not staying in one place too long, slipping from social grasps, taking up space here and then there, deploying our bodies in specific ways in specific places as a mode of asserting agency and escaping restraint. In this way, reworking what it means to have a woman's body becomes possible.

The benefits for me of being an academic feminist stripper have a lot to do with the place of motion in the lives of women. Standing in the middle of a river in Argentina recently, I thought about Iris Marion Young's article, "Throwing Like a Girl: A Phenomenology of Feminine Body Comportment, Motility, and Spatiality" (Young, 1989). In that outdoor setting, I found myself hesitating at the top of steep banks, wondering at my footing on slick rocks, living out the lack of trust in my physical capacities, Young describes as typical in moving like a girl; my body a fragile encumbrance, the space around me constricted. This sensation of incapability is something I do not feel in the strip club, a realization that begins to explain why such a typically non-feminist site seems feminist to me. When I enter the stage, while I occupy and interpret it, I achieve a freedom and control of motion that I do not possess in other places. It is a kind of school in which I unlearn the lessons of girlhood that held me teetering in and around the waters of the Rio Quilquehue. It is a place where moving like a girl no longer denotes uncertainty, incompletion, inadequacy. Indeed, I strip because I need space to move, and before this job, I did not really know I could. My initial fears were not about taking my clothes off; they were about dancing, moving around on stage. I remember a particular evening after about two months as a stripper when I suddenly stopped feeling the earth wobble beneath me. This new sense of inhabiting my body comfortably comes from breaking manacles I didn't even know I was wearing. They were given to me, like Christmas presents, Barbie-pink.

Growing up, I found that certain places restrict the motion of women's bodies, their sexuality, their selves. The church, my grandma's house, school—all said, "Sit in the chair and be good now." But in the semi-darkness of a strip-club, I don't have to. I sketch conceptual and physical paths of desire in the air, and across my body, as intricate as capillaries, as various as women. One criticism of the sex industry is its objectification of women, but I love its emphasis on bodies. I have been looking all my life for a place to be my whole self, a place to wholly be. In some ways, the university has provided this through feminist theory, women who challenged me to a psychic strip-tease: to be erotic (Audre Lorde), to dance with myself (Alice Walker), to be impolite (Nancy Mairs). Yet the shortage of literally embodied activisms is numbing. The strip club picks up where they leave off. I writhe on stage, living out my excesses, refining my ideas through the language of dance. Although the reduction of women to bodies, or worse, to body parts, is a real concern in every cultural arena, strip club included, such reduction is not the only possible result of an emphasis on the physical. On the contrary, this focal point is ostensibly shared with most feminism (e.g., the personal is political, *lecriture feminine*, embodied activisms); however, for most academic feminisms the "body" is textualized in a very non-sensate way. For this reason, the sex industry's focus on the body has the capacity to expand feminist praxis by countering the all-too-Cartesian preference for minds and transcendence of bodies in scholarship. Moving hips and bare stomachs provide a wonderful counter-force in my life to the cerebral university and the buttoned up throats of conservative womanhood. Through these motions, I live out the break with tyrannies I have read about in other feminist essays; these motions are the start of doing my own work.

The particular setting of my sexual activism is no accident. There is a history behind it: I always wanted to be a stripper, even when I was eight, playing in my room in my mother's hand-me-down negligee, a deep silky plum, studying my body, biding my time. I showed my Wonder Woman underwear to little boys at school and prayed for breasts at night. I begged to shave my legs, fascinated by mother's tough stubble grazing my fingertips with the surprising danger of chestnut hulls. I claimed my sexuality like a winning lottery ticket. Just as I crossed over into adolescence, my parents got a divorce, and I ended up living in a Mayberry—one red light, four churches. I bought dime-store smut novels, and my grandma threw them out, scolding me and ripping out the page on which I had inscribed my name. Our preacher, a young guy, spoke convincingly on the perils of physical pleasures. I highlighted all the sections on sex I could find through the concordance of my Bible. I struggled, tried to save myself, repented for the force of my body on my mind, mortified at my capacity for the obscene thought: I knelt to be baptized, looked forward into the crotch of my preacher and thought guiltily, "There is his penis." I got married at nineteen, even though I was a college student and not a factory worker. At least I did it right, grandma said. Well, almost right—he was my fourth. We hung cross-stitched Bible verses on our walls: "Whither thou goest." My photo album from that time records a girl more than devoted to this boy she had chosen. I have a series of pictures that reveal the submersion of my self into his: he meets the camera's lens head-on, my doe-eyes turned on him, in love and riveted. Over and over again, the 4 x 6 world of these photos shows me in this self-appointed secondary role. I wanted, for a brief time, to be good, and good meant being at his side, offspring of his rib. This is the story I was told, the story I was committed to learning by heart. The marriage ended, and "being good" ended up meaning "being lost to myself." I floundered. By no accident, the beginnings of my own self-reconstitution are marked by an upsurge of sexuality that overflowed the floodplains of marriage and Mayberry, when on June 14, 1994—what would have been my second wedding anniversary—I performed my first set as a stripper in my wedding night lingerie, white and demure amidst the thudding beat of night music. And in removing the cultural veil, I broke with its power to define me; I slipped out from under it and began to become something else.

I have been in graduate school for the entire four years since that experience, studying contemporary literature, postmodernity, and feminist theory; I have done a lot of thinking about what it means to be female, to be fragmented, and to survive. In postmodern studies, the fragmented individual has become a truism, but some feminist postmodernisms have begun to articulate the possibility of agency within fragmentation, that is, the ability to gather up one's various parts and keep moving. My sense of personal fragmentation hinges on the split of mind from body that still dominates the university where I study and teach, as well as the sex industry where I dance. The separation of sexuality and scholarship in both these places feels uncomfortable, and at times I think I cannot stand the incompatibility of my selves. But there is nowhere else to go. There is no place where my parts will fit seamlessly together. However, there is a way of "going anyway"— ways of going—within these difficult contexts. In addition to the lessons of physical motion, I also experiment with conceptual movements that similarly create new relationships between mind and body, and in so doing, I assert some control over what it means to be like a girl. I play with various femalenesses, with stereotypes and their undersides, and with the capacity of my body to express a personalized grammar of desire, while working through the links and ruptures between me and social constructions of Woman. "Going anyway" is a matter of engaging in various forms of play that resist, comment on, and circumvent the ways our lines and roles as women are already written and our parts divided up; that is, through playful postmodern slippage along the axes of identity, I find my way to a transforming energy through which my different parts can work together even though they do not exactly fit seamlessly.

The dimension of masquerade inherent in the strip club provides a trap door through which to escape reality, or the fixedness of the day-world. There, it is possible to be a different person each day, with a different history, a different look, a different name. This freedom of identity loosens the traps of one's own consciousness and the force of externally constructed views and slottings. Change and play become integral components of selfhood. I bought a couple of wigs recently, one long and blonde, one short and black. One customer, in his blithering drunken drawl, let me know that he preferred me without them, said he liked all kinds of women, as long as they were natural. I thought, "Boy, are you in the wrong place." While many of the dancers contribute to the illusion of reality in the strip club, I enjoy shattering it and exposing the artifice of sexuality and the construction of beauty there and everywhere. As I walked away from him, I thought about how nothing I do there is about what he conceives as natural, that the club is a space where essentialist views of womanhood and beauty are more often contested than not. I put on a show that works to clarify for myself what girl is, what sexy is, and how I want to play that out on my body. In this night space, where magic and transformation constitute reality, I find room to reconsider these issues consistently through the use of costumes, make-up, stage names, and conscious and transitory shifts of persona.

What a woman's body looks like when reiterating patriarchal scripts and what it looks like when resisting them is a complicated prospect. Picture me, exiting the dressing room in a child's tutu, my waist and hips encased in white netting, my long adult legs taking forever to reach the floor from underneath this little girl costume. I am smoking a cigarette and drinking whiskey. What is this strange apparition? For my music, I choose Courtney Love's *Doll Parts*. She starts quiet: "I am / doll eyes / doll mouth / doll legs." My arms arch upward in a circle, holding the space of the world around me, like a ballerina. I turn gracefully in the small circle, literalizing the fetish of male desire for little girl sexuality, all shaven, fresh, and tender. Is this me? Am I doll parts? The chorus introduces the contestatory punk rock noise and riot girl lyrics: "Yeah they really want you, they really want you, they really do / yeah they really want you, they really want you, but I do, too." My knees bend to a squat, and I thrust my hands under the tutu, clutching the insides of my thighs. I lie on my back and reveal the forbidden crotch beneath a nice girl skirt. Her voice grates over the syllables like salty wounds until the last phrase, which she whispers smooth as licking. And I sing with her, this reclamation of self, this "I am." Yeah, they really want me, but I do, too. I am this space that is quiet and loud, pretty and harsh. It crosses my mind as I leave the stage that maybe my customers would have preferred something a little less theatrical, a little less abrasive, but that set was for me.

Stripping is often an inside joke among the dancers, a way of poking fun at the obviously inadequate structure of desire that undergirds the strip club, one in which women are perceived as subservient, as servicers, when many of us clearly understand ourselves as desiring subjects. The method of satirical masquerade I employ through my tutu act exposes the limitations of conventional sexuality and opens up a space of critique in which women's desires and agency can exist. Barbie (angry Barbie, S & M Barbie, as I like to call her) stands by the bar, and I flit to her. She shares my appreciation of performance and, after countless boring customer jokes about her Ken, she knows well the absurdity of male-centered sexual logic. I bend over in front of her, and with her hands solidly around my hips, she simulates fucking me. Through the manipulation of imagery, we invert the position of the looked-at by claiming the space of the stage and club as places to act up and stereotypical gender roles as matter to be played upon, not unlike the musical movement of which Courtney Love was a part, in which "performance recuperates to-be-looked-at-ness as something that constitutes, rather than erodes or impedes, female subjectivity" (Gottlieb, 1994, p. 268).

Although at moments, this work verges on the carnivalesque, it takes more subtle forms as well. For example, my stage show often demonstrates the hologram of the beautiful and abused body, of the orgasmic and pained moment. Through various archings, stretches and constrictions, one slides right through what is graceful and what is awkward and back, revealing the two kinds of women's bodies as a matter of stance, lighting, timing (Bell, 1994). Hanging in the seam of such contortions exposes the constructedness of beauty and allows me to take back the full range of positions available rather than limping about in what airbrushed magazines deem pretty; I am bringing art back into the artifice of women's sexuality and asking where the line is between porn, prom, and plain, and asserting the important difference between active and passive engagements with these social roles. Further, the continuous motion of this show, the body rolls and writhings, marks the transitory nature of beauty and the potential for change (of self-presentation, location, social position) to be found in the strategic and playful deployment of our bodies.

One of the first questions that concerned me as an academic feminist who strips was how I could put myself on stage for men to look at and scrutinize. What I have learned is that the work and fun and self-expression we dancers engage in is not about the men seated around the stage. They are like fixtures in the landscape of our battles—battles with our bodies (think of the self-denigrating comments heard in the dressing rooms, the countless mirrors surrounding the stage reflecting us back at ourselves, our eyes meeting our own, sometimes shining with the execution of a successful illusion, other times dark and opaque with failure, self-consciousness, or fatigue), battles with the living ghosts of our grandmothers (the question, "does your family know what you're doing?," never fails to make me cringe), and battles with the straight-jackets of our culture (heed the bumper sticker: "good girls go to heaven; bad girls go everywhere"—what is a good girl, anyway?). We merely borrow men's eyes to complete the scene of our grand larceny, the thieving of new personas and a corner of cultural space in which to enact them.

Perhaps one of the most instructive images at the nexus of stripping and feminism is the idea of pole work. Contemporary feminist theory devotes much time to unsettling poles such as good and bad, madonna and whore, white and black, center and margin. This disruption of either-or thought structures is indeed an enabling device in my efforts at straddling the stripper-scholar and mind-body hyphens. That I can be both is an exciting prospect. The motion across that traditional division of roles and parts is as inspiriting as the feeling of lifting my stiletto heels from the stage floor as I swing around a pole as comfortably as I sit here at my desk. When I climb the pole at the strip club or dance around it, I enact the kind of assault launched by feminist theory on conceptual poles that makes possible this reclamation of my physical and sexual selves. Pole work is about wrapping oneself around what would separate. It is about pulling oneself up, holding on; it is about inversions, illusions, and bruises. Watching dancers defy the rules of gravity along with the rules of propriety as they spin and soar, hang from the delicate curve of an ankle, is for me a lesson in my own capacity for motion, both physically and figuratively, as we etch new patterns for girl subjectivities with the movements of our feet and hips and wrists. In the repeated motions of dressing and undressing, what we will not do is be still.

References

Bell, S. (1994). *Reading, writing, and rewriting the prostitute body.* Bloomington: Indiana University Press.

Gottlieb, J., & Wald, G. (1994). Smells like teen spirit: Riot grrrls, revolution, and women in independent rock. In Ross, A., & Rose, T. (Eds.), *Microphone friends: Youth music and youth culture.* New York: Routledge.

Young, I. M. (1989). Throwing like a girl: A phenomenology of feminine body comportment, motility, and spatiality. In Allen, J., & Young, I. M. (Eds.), *The thinking muse: Feminism and modern French philosophy.* Bloomington: Indiana University Press.

HONORING DESIRE

Daphne Patai
Department of Spanish and Portuguese
University of Massachusetts, Amherst, MA 01003

Real Live Nude Girl: Chronicles of Sex-Positive Culture, by Carol Queen (San Francisco: Cleis Press, 1997, 212 pp.)

Carol Queen is a Recovering Shy Person, as she tells us in "Exhibitionism and the (Formerly) Shy," one of twenty-five brief and fascinating essays gathered in this book. Having recognized early on that she had "a sexually adventurous soul" but a "rather mousy erotic personality" (p. 62), she reinvented herself into a performance artist, bisexual activist, sexologist, and major agitator for a "sex-positive culture." This is no mean achievement, and a measure of her success is the confident and even joyful tone of her writing.

Something of the fearless and challenging approach that Carol Queen takes to sex can be gleaned from the first line of an essay entitled "Dykes and Whores: Girls Gone Bad." Queen writes: "I was a dyke long before I became a whore, but first I was a slut" (p. 177). Slut, dyke, and whore, Queen is above all a true anarcho-hedonist, ever wary of efforts (whether from fundamentalist Christians or fundamentalist feminists—whose similarities she notes even while acknowledging their political divergences) to regulate and tame sex, ever critical of a culture that she believes "vilifies sexually free women" ("Fucking with Madonna," p. 112).

In "Through a Glass Smudgily: Reflections of a Peep-Show Queen," she argues that "peep shows are probably the most democratic, open sexual space there is" (p. 56). About the men who visit her booth, she says: "I love them, too, because it makes it safer to be who I am, a decidedly kinky woman who'd rather masturbate for an audience than alone, who stays a peep-show queen not so much for the money as for the sex and the stories. Maybe my patrons don't know it, but I'm on the other side of the glass for a lot of the same reasons they are" (p. 57).

Queen, who believes that sex is "sacred and healing" (p. 202), is tireless in her efforts to promote a sex-positive climate that would begin to undo the ravages wrought by what she characterizes as our sex-negative culture. In fighting this good fight, she also contributes important concepts and terminology to the sex debates. One of the most interesting of these is "absexual," a word suggested by her partner, Robert, a physician. Queen uses the term to refer to anti-porn censors as well as vigilantes such as Andrea Dworkin whose mind, or psyche, is such that they hold the sex that fascinates them at arm's length, pretending thereby to turn away from it. This posture is not asexual, for these critics display an intense involvement with sex—Dworkin's writings, in particular, serving as an instance of the very pornography Dworkin claims to detest. Queen comments: "Crusading against other people's sexual behaviors and images lets [anti-sex activists] wallow in a very safe form of sexual obsession" ("Dirty Pictures, Heavy Breathing, Moral Outrage and the New Absexuality," p. 33).

Having discovered early in her life (by contrasting her parents' marriage and the gay movement) that "sexual honesty" is crucial to happiness, Queen never looked back. Her childhood training served her well as a source of energy for her still-evolving critique of our sex-negative attitudes. The first piece in her collection of old and new essays, "Dear Mom: A Letter

about Whoring," conveys Queen's characteristic stance: sympathy toward and pity for fellow humans, especially those whose lives are tormented by sexual secrets and prohibitions. Why was her mother able to accept her relationships with other women? Because, Queen realizes, loving another woman meant—so her mother thought—being free of "all that sex stuff" (p. 4); on the other hand, she could never have tolerated the knowledge that her daughter was a whore (and died at just about the time Queen was contemplating telling her). Being a whore, however, quickly altered the view of male sexuality Queen originally derived from her mother: men are all alike, want only one thing, and giving it to them is unpleasant. This notion evaporated as soon as she turned her very first trick, who, Queen realized with surprise, "had a complex, fantasy-based, non-intercourse-oriented, emotional sexuality" (p. 4).

One doesn't have to be into Queen's own taste for exhibitionism and sex games to sense the appeal of her approach and its extraordinary moral superiority to the anti-life and anti-sex vision promoted by many who call themselves feminists. Perhaps I was touched by Queen's writing because I have spent much of the past year immersed in the hate literature produced by heterophobic feminists. Queen's work is, by comparison, a breath of fresh air. She doesn't hesitate to challenge feminist orthodoxies that attempt to dictate acceptable sexual practices to women, nor is she gentle with male ideologues such as John Stoltenberg (whose workshop on "What Makes Pornography Sexy" Queen dissects in an essay entitled "Pornography and the Sensitive New Age Guy"). The feminist movement that attracted her, she explains, promised to support her right to do what she liked with her body, "and that definitely included my clit, cunt, and brain, thank you very much" (p. 137). But arriving at the point where she was ready to object to the feminist anti-porn line was hard work. As anti-porn at one point in her life as Stoltenberg and Dworkin, Queen tells us, she had for years, like other feminists, "sniffed that porn 'insulted either my politics, my intelligence or my sense of the erotic.'" Those judgments, she says, resulted from "trying to take my politics to bed with me, like all good dykes were supposed to do back then" (p. 142). "One of the most important gifts of feminism," she writes, "has been to expose all the lies we're told about how the sexes feel and behave; why perpetuate this sex difference by naming pornography a male evil? The least we can do is turn it into an evil that both sexes can share!" (p. 146). In another essay, Queen explains that her difficulty coming to terms with the fact that she liked sexual submission resulted not from a sense that this was kinky, but that it was "unfeminist." Submission to a man, she writes, rather than to a woman, was "*really* perverse" ("On Being a Female Submissive [And Doing What You Damn Well Please]," p. 175). With undeniable authority, Queen writes: "politics don't make a cunt wet" (p. 175).

While studying pornography as part of her graduate work in sexology, Queen discovered that the purpose of porn is "to produce and enhance sexual feeling" (p. 142). It was the exposure to porn that forced Queen to recognize her own "fear of cocks" (p. 102), as she writes in an essay entitled "The Four-Foot Phallus." Hers is a far less academic description of heterophobia than my usual definition: fear of and antagonism toward the Other, especially to men and to heterosexuality.

Unlike feminists who see the power of the phallus everywhere, Queen argues that heterosexuals do not have much in the way of a sex-positive culture available to them and, indeed, that this is one of the causes of antagonism to gay culture, which many straight people see as more liberated, more exciting, and more fun. She celebrates diversity in all of its forms (including sexual styles) and defines "queer" as follows: "The queer in all of us clamors for pleasure and change, will not be tamed or regulated, wants a say in the creation of a new reality" ("The Queer in Me," p. 14).

Queen's exuberant, thoughtful, and often touching essays cannot help but invite comparison with Andrea Dworkin's hate-filled caricatures of male sexuality and heterosexual activity in particular. But Queen is right to call attention to what she and Dworkin have in common: an utter fascination with sex. The problem is that Dworkin's preoccupation drives her to male-bashing fanaticism, while Queen's leads to a sympathetic recognition of the vulnerabilities (even) of men and the sexual power (even) of women.

Some of the most effective writing in these essays is Queen's descriptions of the male clients who visited her peep-show booth. Dworkin would, of course, want us to believe that Queen must be oppressed (rather than having found a creative venue for her own exhibitionism and sexuality) and that her involvement in the sex trade degrades her. But reading Queen's work quickly discredits that judgment. Here is a smart, tough, and talented woman—much more in touch with her life and the life around her than is Dworkin. How telling, then, that Andrea Dworkin is famous far and wide, while Queen's is not a name generally recognized. This rather suggests that Queen, not Dworkin, is right in her appraisal of our culture and its values.

Interestingly, given that she is a celebrator of polymorphous perversity, Queen does not hesitate to label lesbians as sexually "deviant" ("Dykes and Whores: Girls Gone Bad," p. 179). In fact, she is critical of women who understand their lesbianism strictly in terms of feminism, as she also is of "political lesbians" who "really didn't want to stick their fingers anywhere" ("Bisexual Perverts among the Leather Lesbians," p. 25). She is particularly hard on the intolerance expressed on all sides toward bisexuals, and on feminist dogma that prevents many lesbian feminists from making common cause with other sexual deviants. It is a justified argument, far removed from the mainstream feminist critiques that, over the past few decades, have done a pretty good job—at least in academic and countercultural circles—of constructing heterosexuality as itself deviant and incompatible with feminism.

Queen respects both nature and culture, sees mental and physical differences as a source of pleasure and fascination, and provides astute analyses of the politics of sex and the joys of transgression. Above all, as a bisexual who has tried just about everything, she has no difficulty accepting other people's sexual choices, whatever they happen to be. "Honoring desire," is how she puts it, and it is her fundamental ethic (p. 147). Experience has cured her of the "starry-eyed baby-dykedom's assurance that with women, everything would be wonderful" ("Bisexual Perverts among the Leather Lesbians," p. 25). She emerged an equal-opportunity free-thinker, no more tolerant of lesbian orthodoxies than of conventional homophobia. She even respects plain old heterosexuals, and this sets her miles apart from the sex police so prominent in feminist circles today. In an essay against male circumcision and impromptu penis-removal à la Lorena Bobbitt (an act of violence celebrated and laughed over by many feminists), Queen reveals that it took her years to begin to wonder why "if feminists excoriated men for being insufficiently respectful of and devoted to female plumbing, it was perfectly okay for women to trash tender male bits" ("Body Modification: Blood and Knives," p. 85).

Other essays in the book deal with such subjects as heterosexual men's enjoyment of dildos ("In Praise of Strap-Ons"); the overriding importance of accepting sexual diversity ("Don't Fence Me In"); spanking ("Over a Knee, Willingly: Personal Reflections on Being Spanked"); and Queen's occasional gigs as a subject on whom doctors can practice giving pelvic exams ("Just Put Your Feet in These Stirrups"). The titles alone provide a provocative indication of the range of subjects Queen addresses. Some others are: "Inside the Safe Sex Clubs," "Why I Love Butch Women," and "Healing and Holy Acts: Sacred Whoredom," a moving essay in which Queen explores the spiritual and sexual connections arising out of prostitution when it is rooted in acceptance and a kind of love.

Queen's vision is certainly not that of the average social reformer, but it is a far saner one than the alternative presented to us by the better-known feminist "theorists," with their debased view of heterosexual intercourse as indistinguishable from rape and their denunciation of butch-femme sex games as corrupt carry-overs from patriarchy. Queen is serious about promoting a sex-positive culture, and her writing has a strong utopian undertone, a vision of a sexually open and pleasure-loving society in which people won't have to pay for the sex they want and need. Until we get there, she argues for the freedom of both men and women to serve as prostitutes and clients, thus providing a much-needed balance to sex work (p. 204). Meanwhile, Queen knows that erotic power is real and that feminist analyses that miss this point and portray women as perpetual victims are part of our problem, not the solution to it. Above all, her writing promotes tolerance and sympathy for all human beings, and this—despite all the rhetoric—is an attitude in short supply these days.

TRAFFICKING IN MYTHS?

Jo Doezema
School of Social Sciences, University of Sussex
Brighton BN1 9QN, United Kingdom

Trafficking in Women, Forced Labour and Slavery-Like Practices in Marriage, Domestic Labour and Prostitution, by M. Wijers and L. Lap-Chew (STV, Utrecht, 1997, 226 pp.)

Since the mid-1980s, the issue of trafficking in women has been high on the international agenda. The stereotypical picture of the "victim of trafficking" runs pretty much as follows: an extremely poor, very young, "third world" woman is kidnapped or lured from her village with promises of a lucrative, respectable job overseas. But, according to this scenario, what awaits her is a horror—a life of misery and degradation when she finds out that the job is prostitution. Rape, beatings, confinement, disease and even death are standard elements of this stereotypical story. To what extent is this picture born out by Wijers and Lap-Chew's report *Trafficking in Women, Forced Labour and Slavery-Like Practices in Marriage, Domestic Labour and Prostitution*? Wijers and Lap-Chew's report,

grounded in the view of prostitution as work, goes a long way towards debunking many current myths about trafficking in women. Significantly, the report expands the scope of trafficking to include trafficking for domestic work and marriage. This is contrary to the more common international approach, reflected in much national legislation, that equates prostitution with trafficking and trafficking with prostitution. The authors stress that it is not the nature of the activity itself but the conditions under which it is performed that should be the focus of anti-trafficking and anti-slavery activism.

The distinction, explicit in the title, between trafficking, forced labor, and slavery-like practices is crucial to the development of Wijers and Lap-Chew's analysis. As they point out, a lack of agreement about what precisely "trafficking" means has led to conflicting and contradictory national and international legislation. Accordingly, they re-define the term, splitting what is commonly known as "trafficking"

165

into two parts: the recruitment process (i.e., "trafficking") and the working conditions themselves (i.e., "forced labor and slavery-like practices"). The act of defining "trafficking in women" is not merely a technical one; it is overtly political. Unlike other definitions of trafficking, this one also condemns unlawful working conditions for those who were not "tricked," "lured," or "kidnapped" into prostitution, and represents a recognition of prostitution as work.

For years now, some of the hottest debates about prostitution center around whether or not a person can "choose" to be involved in sex work. By drafting the above definition, the authors come down firmly on the side of prostitution as a profession. However, unlike other recent publications on trafficking (for example, *Human Rights Watch Global Report on Women's Human Rights*, New York, Human Rights Watch, 1995), this report avoids situating "choice" as an option solely for Western prostitutes. An essential element of the trafficking stereotype is the passive, un-emancipated, Third World woman as "victim." In contrast, a key theme throughout the work is the agency of women who are involved in abusive recruitment or work situations. Far from being passive victims, these women are shown as actively attempting to change their lives.

Another big myth-buster is the finding that, for sex work and do-mestic work, neither kidnapping nor deception about the nature of the work are common. That is, most women who migrate for work in the sex industry as well as for domestic work know what kind of work they will be doing: "The fact that most deception is not about the nature of the work indicated that a substantial number of women do know that they are recruited for prostitution and consent to the work itself, but clearly do not know that they will end up in slavery-like conditions" (p. 198). This is in contrast to trafficking for marriage, in which kidnapping or deception about the purpose of migration are frequent occurrences.

Importantly, the distinction made in Wijers and Lap-Chew's definition between recruitment and work conditions allows the problems faced by some sex workers to be understood as "forced labor in prostitution," rather than the much more commonly used "forced prostitution." As it is usually understood, "forced prostitution" refers only to the initial decision to become a prostitute: "Force defined in this way excludes those women who agree to work as prostitutes, but who are subject to force in the course of their work or who are promised other working conditions than those in which they find themselves" (p. 30).

The authors are unequivocal in calling for the decriminalization of prostitution. The fourth chapter of the report is dedicated to an exploration of the various state policies regarding prostitution and the extent to which these contribute to trafficking. This examination is especially illuminating for the light it sheds on the morality underlying prostitution and trafficking laws. Women who defy conventional moral codes are denied customary legal protection; in Germany, for example, "trafficking" is considered a less serious crime for a person who is "not far from prostitution" (p. 126). It becomes obvious that the purpose of most national legislation on prostitution and trafficking is intended to protect "innocent" (read: non-prostitute) women and to punish "guilty" (read: prostitute) ones.

The authors also avoid simplistic notions of "poverty" as the cause of migration and trafficking for sex work, domestic work, and marriage. In chapter three, the authors place trafficking and forced labor firmly in the context of a gendered labor market, traditional female roles, and the feminization of migration. Unfortunately, in this section, some myths begin to slip back into the analysis. For example, while the link between (sex) tourism and trafficking is stated, the link is merely asserted, not analyzed. This reflects a more general problem throughout the report. Too often, examples and quotes taken from the literature or from respondents reflect a much less "positive" or "progressive"

view of prostitution than that of the authors themselves. Statements like "Kenya, with its flourishing tourism industry, has not escaped the global racket of trafficking in women for purposes of prostitution. Regarding the situation of trafficking it has already been noted that young women from Uganda are lured into Kenya to serve as prostitutes for the millions of tourists who constantly flock into Kenya" (Butegwa, quoted on p. 53) reproduce stereotypes.

This illustrates the difficulties in the continued conceptualization of women subject to abusive recruitment or work practices as "trafficking in women." While the authors' definition makes the crucial distinction between the type of work and working conditions and firmly situates prostitution as work, it is doubtful that the widespread confusion will be swept away by this definition. Given the emotive content of "trafficking" and the potent images of defiled innocence associated with it, it is unlikely that organizations who reject all sex work, and governments intent on curbing (illegal) migration, will be willing to adopt the new definition. Indeed, many sex workers (and others) have voiced the opinion that due to the confusions of meaning and negative associations of "trafficking," the word should be scrapped altogether. (This was evident in discussions, both formal and informal, at the "NoTraf" conference in Noordwijkerhout, Netherlands, April 1997.)

And therein lie the potentially contradictory implications of this report. On the one hand, it has great potential for destroying myths around trafficking, not least because it comes from an "anti-trafficking" rather than a "sex workers rights" position. Arguments that originated in the sex worker rights movement may be more palatable to policy makers when coming from the mouths of "anti-traffickers." If this gives sex workers' arguments for the recognition of prostitution as work, for decriminalization, and for the condemnation of sex worker human rights abuses an added legitimacy in the eyes of policy-makers, this is a good thing. On the other hand, continuing to speak of a worldwide epidemic of "trafficking" has in itself the potential to reinforce the very myths that this report contests.

ON RADICAL SEX WORK: SERVICES, SYMBOLS, AND FEMINIST QUESTIONS

Leslie Cole
Department of Sociology, University of Southern California
Los Angeles, CA 90089

Live Sex Acts: Women Performing Erotic Labor, by W. Chapkis (Routledge, 1997, 248pp.)

Shouldn't sex work be grouped among other service industry occupations? It is slightly ironic when influential sociologists, Barbara Reskin and Irene Padavic (*Women and Men at Work*, 1994), point out that through continued economic restructuring and de-industrialization, 81 percent of all jobs in the year 2005 will be in service industries (pp. 165–166). From data obtained through the United States Bureau of Labor Statistics, Reskin and Padavic highlight service-related occupations with the largest projected job growth for 1990–2005. Among the occupations listed, the majority have been, and will continue to be, female dominated, which includes registered nurses and nurses' aids, clerks and receptionists, waitresses and cashiers. It is disturbing that de-skilling and downsizing contribute to and problematize the nature of the workplace and contemporary labor market. But perhaps it is more disconcerting to realize that "official" lists and statistics, coupled with leading sociological research, reinforce the validity and legitimacy of certain service jobs and occupations while never mentioning the existence of others. In *Live Sex Acts: Women Performing Erotic Labor*, Wendy Chapkis has written a provocative and engaging cultural ethnography about a misrepresented and marginalized category of labor and the female "service" workers who perform that labor. Under the umbrella of erotic labor and sex work, Chapkis presents the variations among the occupational subdivisions that range from adult film actresses, call girls, street prostitutes, and performance artists, to phone sex operators, sensual massage practitioners, and tantra therapists.

Chapkis describes the historical dimensions of prostitution and sex work and discusses its cultural symbolism within the political debates, legislation, and policy surrounding it. Chapkis asserts that "when erotic labor is viewed as work, it is transformed from a simple act of affirmation of man's command over woman, and instead is revealed to be an arena of struggle, where the meaning and terms of the sexual exchange are vulnerable to cultural and political contestation" (p. 57). Throughout the text, she provides original transcriptions from interviews and conversations from those who work as erotic laborers and performers, law enforcement agents and sex-worker advocacy organizers. Through comparative research conducted in the United States and the Netherlands, she also illustrates the differences regarding prohibition, regulation, and decriminalization measures.

Structurally, the book is divided into three sections: "Sex Wars," "Working It," and "Strategic Responses." Motivated by her own course of feminist inquiry, Section I details the vitriol of the varying feminist positions surrounding the meanings and interpretations of sex and commercial commodification that is juxtaposed with the historical development and cultural meanings of "sexual slavery" and trafficking. In Section II, Chapkis focuses on the workers themselves and offers insight into "the emotional labor of sex," while also providing explanations on how workers locate themselves with regard to differences in the positional hi-

erarchy of the operative sex/class system. Ultimately, the final section provides insight into improving public tolerance through decriminalization of the profession. Among strategies that support legalization, regulation, and licensing, the importance of sex worker self-advocacy as an innovative and empowering forum for possible resolution is also discussed.

Overall, Wendy Chapkis's new book is as cleverly crafted as her previous, *Beauty Secrets: Women and the Politics of Appearance* (1986). She has presented an impressive body of intricately nuanced and detailed, socio-cultural research that stimulates both emotional and intellectual reactions in the reader.

Feminist Conflicts

There are always contested meanings surrounding the ideological perspectives on gender, sex, and sexuality. Most confusing (and perhaps aptly so) are the pronouncements and deliberations of the feminist positions toward the "meaning of sex," as Chapkis presents them in the opening chapters: "When I began writing this book, my ambitious attempt was not only to pose a challenge to the enduring divisions between 'good girls' and 'bad girls,' but also to help heal the schism within feminism that had developed around the subject of commercial sex" (p. 1). The hotly contested terrain of the feminist "sex wars" has evolved out of the radical politics and activism of Second Wave feminism. Chapkis presents the Radical Feminist positions that historically have encompassed both the pro-"positive" sex feminism of Gloria Steinem, Kathlen Barry, and Carol Pateman and the anti-sex feminism of Catharine MacKinnon and Andrea Dworkin. Chapkis is critical of the perspectives held by some anti-sex feminists who decry that "the very meaning of sex is male domination.... Not only is sex synonymous with male supremacy and female objectification, but woman is synonymous with whore" (pp. 17–19). Under the anti-sex feminist framework, Chapkis argues that "the prostitute becomes the symbol of women's abject powerlessness" (p. 19).

Chapkis contrasts these "classic" standpoints with an examination of some of the contemporary feminist perspectives. In this sense, contemporary feminist sexual politics further complicates the discussion but broadens and enlivens the dialogue. Under the contemporary guise, Chapkis contrasts the perspectives held by Sexual Libertarians like Camille Paglia with Sex Radical feminists like Pat Califia and Rebecca Kaplan. Focusing on the perspectives of Sex Radical feminists, Chapkis stresses how they "position their analyses as a terrain of struggle, not a fixed field of gender and power relations...feminist Sex Radicals understand sex to be

a cultural tactic which can be used both to destabilize male power as well as to reinforce it" (p. 29). Thus, the cultural symbolism of the prostitute "instead can be understood as a place of agency where the sex worker makes active use of the existing sexual order" (p. 30). Utilizing traditional terms of oppression like "whore," "dyke," "slut," etc., for one's own appropriation poses a threat to patriarchal control over women's sexuality and "a symbolic challenge to confining notions of proper womanhood and conventional sexuality" (p. 30).

Women behind Theories

Where much feminist and sociological research employs deconstructive practices to examine how the structures of inequality and institutions of power are represented at the macro level, it is always refreshing to hear the voices of the persons who "act in" or "live within" the drama of the theoretical domain. Importantly, Chapkis demonstrates that she can successfully interweave the theoretical perspectives of feminist Sex Radical theorists in support of the body of her empirical research on women who are living their lives as Sex Radical workers and performers. Exemplar is Section II, "Working It," which elucidates the full flavor of Chapkis's book as it uncovers and brings to consciousness the once hidden meanings behind sex war and erotic labor.

Particularly intriguing is the transcript of a 1993 conversation between Vision and Annie Sprinkle, sex workers whose contrasting lifestyles converged when they formed the "Sluts and Goddesses Workshop." Vision, who approaches her style of sex work as "sacred" prostitution, infuses it with Goddess Energy, thus recontextualizing it as tantra practice. Sprinkle enjoys being the "down-and-dirty" whore when working with street clients but channels her creativity into avant-garde sex-related performance art. About the workshop, Sprinkle reflects on how the two groups of women came together:

> It was amazing, that kind of integration, tearing down our prejudices toward each other. When I made up the name "Sluts and Goddesses" I thought it was kind of funny, but now I am becoming more and more convinced of the power of that symbology, those archetypes. It allows you to give a persona to those different parts of yourself and its about embracing both. (p. 90)

This evokes a kind of living feminism, an elation that is reminiscent of the inspiring qualities attributed to second wave consciousness raising. However, it is important to note that it is not taking place within the confines of academic discourse and rhetoric.

Sex "Service" Work: Advocacy and Organization

In examining the myriad styles and occupational subtleties that exist in the world of erotic labor and sex work, Chapkis's study affirms that it is a place where many women freely choose to pursue their economic livelihood. As with many employment situations, problems may stem from the social location of the worker and the conditions of the work itself; for example, sex workers who are self-employed as "call girls" may experience a more desirable situation than those who work through a third party (pimp, brothel, agency). Alternately, the experiences of women who work indoors are comparatively different from those who work on the street. While sex work is paid labor, it is often exploited labor. And, like many other service-oriented jobs performed by women, Chapkis points out that a worker's position in other social hierarchies like race, age, and physical appearance can also be of significant influence (p. 105).

The fields of sex work and prostitution have historically carried the stigma of deviant and criminal associations; hence advocacy, legislation, and policy making on its behalf have been extremely limited. Therefore, "sex worker self-advocacy strategies are directed not only at transforming the social conditions under which their work takes place but also at improving the status of those performing erotic labor through a transformation in the cultural meanings attached to prostitution" (p. 192). Reclaiming, redefining, and reconstructing the image of prostitution and erotic labor is significant: "Professionalizing the trade is a necessary step toward its legitimization" (p. 193). Here Chapkis professes that "by taking prostitution off the streets and out of the hands of 'unskilled labor,' it presumably could be repositioned as a middle-class, professional activity, and thereby achieve social respectability" (p. 193).

Ultimately, one comes to realize as Chapkis reiterates: "There is no such thing as The Prostitute, there are only competing versions of prostitution" (p. 211). Similarly one could add that there is no such thing

as The Feminist and no exact feminist theory that can fully articulate the truth for and about all women. Amidst the smorgasbord of conflicting theories and competing ideologies, Chapkis offers a strategic conclusion by suggesting a "hybrid perspective" that draws on combining the strengths of Radical Feminism, the innovative and creative subversion techniques of feminist Sex Radicals, and the activism of prostitutes' rights groups. Thus grounding a feminist prostitution politics on a hybrid perspective fuels the desire to achieve her goals of an organized and empowered workforce where prostitutes are guaranteed full workers' rights and benefits and where consensual sexual activity is effectively decriminalized.

SEXUAL REVOLUTION AND OTHER FUTURE BUSINESS

Wendy Chapkis
Departments of Sociology and Women's Studies
University of Southern Maine, Gorham, ME 04038

New Sexual Agendas, **edited by Lynne Segal (New York University Press, 1997, 278 pp.)**

In the early 1990s, the queer political action group, "The Lesbian Avengers," distributed a pamphlet on "The Homosexual Agenda for America," echoing an important slogan of the religious right. On the inside, that agenda was spelled out: "Respect, dignity, and liberty and justice for all."

Lynne Segal's anthology, *New Sexual Agendas*, pulls the same punch. The agendas advanced are no more or less radical than, in Segal's words, a renewed commitment to "diversity, mutuality, and respect" (p. xviii). Underlying these "new affirmations" is the ongoing project to unseat "the heterosexual male as the uniquely empowered sexual agent" (p. xviii). While this is not exactly what I would call a "new agenda," it certainly remains unfinished business. The contributors' strategies for achieving this

goal range from community-based, context specific, educational campaigns, to subversive resignification of sexual practices and identities, to efforts to achieve greater structural equality between and among the sexes.

The essays in this volume grew out of a 1995 British conference organized "to tackle some of the urgent practical and conceptual challenges in the sexual arena" (p. xi). Focus within an already diffuse mandate was further complicated by the diversity of participants. Contributors are primarily British but also include American, Dutch, and Australian academics and are located in a wide variety of disciplines including sociology, psychology, politics, history, literature, women's studies, and media studies, as well as clinical and applied fields.

This broadly cast net, combined with the challenges of turning conference proceedings into a coherent anthology, has resulted in an uneven but interesting collection. Some of the contributions are stellar, but others would have benefited from additional work. Some essays, for example, are overly long, belaboring an interesting point (Jill Lewis's discussion of "Sex Talk and Daily Life" comes to mind), while others are too short to fully develop a provocative premise (such as Mandy Merck's reflections on Leo Bersani and "Death Camp"). At least one of the essays feels dated for an American audience, perhaps reflecting different developments in the United States and Britain; in "Gay and Lesbian Standpoints," Mary McIntosh argues that "so far there is no sign of a bisexual way of life emerging, but people seem to live out bisexual inclinations in very varied ways, usually inserting themselves more or less comfortably into existing heterosexual or homosexual institutions" (p. 209). This certainly is no reflection of the vibrant and self-defining bisexual community developing in the United States.

More serious than minor mismatches between the British and American experience is the "in-process" feel to some of the contributions, likely a product of their origin as conference talks. For instance, Ine Vanwesenbeeck's essay on women's power and powerlessness in heterosexual encounters is strongest when she is describing her very fine published research on Dutch prostitution; the essay is far less

successful when she attempts to apply those findings to her very preliminary research on young, heterosexual (non-working) women. This is particularly frustrating because the issue she raises of negotiated power within heterosexuality is so interesting and important.

Fortunately, one of the finest essays in the volume, "Feminist Sexual Politics and the Heterosexual Predicament" by editor Lynne Segal, covers some of the same territory. There Segal offers an introduction to ideas central to her recent book, *Straight Sex*, in which she argues for the radical potential of women's heterosexual desires and practices. Segal very persuasively argues against the position advanced by some feminists that heterosexuality is inevitably an expression of women's subordination. Segal does this not only by "queering" straight sex, but also by provocatively insisting that "all sexualities, including lesbian and gay ones, are 'hetero' in one way or another" (p. 87).

Another strong and related essay is Jane Ussher's "The Case of the Lesbian Phallus." Ussher examines both the material and discursive construction of bodily experience and sexed identities by looking at representations of the phallus in heterosexual pornography, in diagnoses of male "erectile disorders," and in practices of "gender-fuck" among lesbians. She argues that each of these offers evidence of "the power of the penis at a symbolic and material level" (p. 166) while also providing opportunities to challenge the understanding of that power as a pre-given, natural fact. For example, "the fact that women can 'do' masculinity...draws attention to the fact that in other contexts, women are 'doing' femininity; it is not a biological given, but a discursively constructed gendered position" (p.167).

Leonore Tiefer picks up this examination of phallic power and its relationship to the unreliable penis in her essay on public management of male impotence. From her perspective as a clinical sexologist, she describes the limitations of the medical mode of sexuality. She points out that "ironically, both the contraceptive revolution and the medicalization of sexuality have only reinforced a limited script for heterosexual life—arousal, intercourse, performance, false universals, technical focus, mind-body dualism" (p. 112). A nice companion to Tiefer is the essay by Lesley Hall, "Heroes and Villains," which offers a critical appraisal of the ambivalent legacy of early British sexology. Hall exposes the limitations of the sexological perspective, which both opened the possibility of understanding sexual diversity as natural and benign while simultaneously reinforcing notions that some identities are more "natural" than others, some practices more "pathological" and "less healthy"

than others. One of the more provocative essays in the volume, "Sexual Values Revisited" by Jeffrey Weeks, attempts to articulate a strategy for resisting both the medical and moral model of sex without succumbing to sexual libertarianism. Weeks proposes an "ethics of relationship" to replace a "morality of acts": "It is not so much what you do but how you do it that should concern us" (p. 44). To this end, Weeks outlines several principles that should underlie sexual interactions including "care," "responsibility," "respect," and "knowledge." Weeks's essay is an explicit attempt to reposition the left in relation to sexual "values" rhetoric currently dominated by the moral right.

Martin Durham, in his essay, "Conservative Agendas and Government Policy," suggests that right-wing rhetoric focusing on "family values" is, in any case, disingenuous and serves as a smoke screen for more material concerns like government budgets and taxation. Durham argues that the so-called "pro-family" agenda of the right in both Britain and the U.S. is most centrally about fiscal issues, not moral issues: "Economic and social conservatives cannot agree that campaigning against homosexuality or abortion is crucial, but they can coalesce around defunding and discouraging sexual relationships that call on the state for aid" (p. 100). This, according to Durham, lies behind the right's assault on single-parent families, which is "about saving the government a significant portion of welfare expenditures" (p. 100). Durham's thesis, that despite anti-gay and anti-abortion rhetoric, the teenage mother/welfare queen is a more central concern for conservatives, is a provocative one, but not entirely convincing. Poor, single mothers receiving AFDC payments, for example, account for less than 1 percent of the U.S. federal budget. The ideological threat to patriarchy of families without fathers, and sexually self-determining women, is also central here.

Robert Connell points out in his excellent essay on "Sexual Revolution" that social and economic structures are indeed central to practices of sexuality and to strategies for liberation. Structural inequalities, Connell argues, currently work to reduce sexual liberation to "liberation of sexuality" or "liberation of people via sexuality" rather than allowing for true "democratization of sexual social relations" (p. 73). Sex within the current social order is not a "free for all"; women, for example, continue to carry primary responsibilities for children as well as for contraception; women's economic inequality reinforces their dependence on a male wage and thus on marriage. As Connell suggests, any "revolution" that does not also challenge such disparities is inadequate. Sexual revolution, properly understood, is deeply threatening to the established order because it requires "the pursuit of justice in the whole sphere of social life, ending the patterns of oppression and domination that are found across this sphere" (p. 73).

Not all who challenge the strictures of the existing sexual order see their struggles in such comprehensive terms. Indeed, as Anna Marie Smith points out in her very interesting essay, "Good Homosexual and the Dangerous Queer," accomodation and assimilation are the expected price for sexual minorities to be "granted" civil rights. Smith's essay provides compelling evidence of how the privatization of public space works to pit the good homo against the dangerous one, offering "acceptance" into the social order only to those who "assimilate into an unchanged heterosexist society" and abandon "any claim to a collective right to occupy public space" (p. 223). As a whole, *New Sexual Agendas* refuses to relinquish an inch of that territory and provides an incitement to rethink the price of admission.

A TRIADIC PERSPECTIVE

Nina Hartley
1442 A Walnut Street #242, Berkeley, CA 94709

Three in Love, **by Barbara Foster, Michael Foster and Letha Hadady (Harper Collins, 1997, 427 pp.)**

I found the book *Three in Love* to be fun, informative, well researched, and accessible. It especially has value for lay readers (those who are not practicing an alternative love/life style and have no plans to do so).

As the junior member of a long-standing triad, I was compelled to buy the book for the title alone. I was delighted to learn about another triad of multi-year duration whose members were informing the world about triads and speaking from the knowledge of their own experience. One of the few books ever written on the subject, it looks at triads as positive, even common, as opposed to sick "love triangles" or twisted expressions of self-loathing.

Three in Love is an important addition to the growing collection of material devoted to alternative sexuality. It deftly combines extensive research with pertinent social history, accurate psychological insights, and cultural commentary. While I was already aware of many of the subjects and their historical importance (Engels, Lenin, Hemingway, de Beauvoir, Sartre, Nietzsche, to name just a few), I had no idea of the central place of the menage in their lives nor of its influence on their work and, subsequently, the profound effect of menages on our culture.

That our ideas of ourselves frequently come from, or are shaped by, popular culture (books, film, theater, art) is not a new concept. However, the revelation that the dynamics of the triad (real or imagined) had such an influence on the content of much of that popular culture is astounding and exciting to contemplate. For example, deconstructing the meanings and subtext of classic films is, for me, made more relevant if I know that a performer lived in a menage or was bi-sexual.

We often think of "the past" as more puritanical, more closed-off, with fewer options for women. Yet, in their time, the existence of many of these menages were common, if not public, knowledge. The negative social consequences reported seem, overall, actually quite minimal even when taking into account the social/economic class of the players.

The strongest individuals in many of the triads were women— fierce, avant-garde, intellectual, sexual and political mavericks who were willing to take the consequences of living for themselves. The men, as well, were sexually diverse, often living erotic and domestic lives that were at odds with what society permitted.

The authors take pains to differentiate between a true menage (typified by mutual consent) and the jealousy-based "love triangle" (marked by deceit and guilt). The latter, with all its traditional morality played out, is the staple of fiction. In life, however, it becomes apparent that people have, in fact, always striven to create the family structure they need. Indeed, this is the book's strong point for me. The matter-of-fact, seamless detailing of the emotional nuances, particular to multiple intimacy, is handled with great insight. The book's description of how love and desire work in the real world is very helpful for those who seek to understand how we triads can "do this," and it

rings true for someone like me who is actually "doing it." What menagers have done is to acknowledge and accept the ever-changing dynamics of love and desire as they seek to fulfill their needs openly. Indeed, menagers often relish the moral, intellectual and philosophical struggle necessary to battle hypocrisy and make a new world for themselves because of the dominant culture's repression of primal needs that can only be met in an unhealthy manner, unless the individual is brave or desperate enough to fly in the face of convention and is willing to suffer any consequences.

Those looking for a social manifesto, a diatribe against the existing order or a theoretical blueprint for mating styles will be disappointed here. The scope of this book takes the reader from the garden of Eden to the present day, pointing out significant, documented menages along the way and how they relate to our times. Filled with telling detail about the daily life of triads, these anecdotes are the most engaging part of the book. I have always thought that my way of living is "normal" (at least for me). After reading *Three in Love*, I know that it is, if not the norm, at least much more common than I previously thought.

SEX: FREEDOM AND RESPONSIBILITY

Cathy Young
477 Clubhouse Drive, Middletown, NJ 07748

Promiscuities: The Secret Struggle for Womanhood, by Naomi Wolf (Random House, 1997, 286 pp.) and *Last Night in Paradise: Sex and Morals at Century's End*, by Katie Roiphe (Little, Brown & Co., 1997, 208 pp.)

In the past thirty years, American sexual mores have undergone an often dizzying transformation. For women, and teenage girls in particular, the old norms of premarital chastity have given way to a confusing patchwork of old and new rules. Recently, the effects of the sexual revolution have been complicated by feminism's turn from liberation to repression, by the growth of conservatism, and by the AIDS epidemic.

The post-1960s landscape of sexual adventure, confusion, and danger is chronicled in two books by two young women who have grown up with this legacy. *Promiscuities: The Secret Struggle for Womanhood* is the third book by Naomi Wolf, who made her debut in 1991 with *The Beauty Myth*—a radical indictment of women's alleged oppression by patriarchal culture—and then struck a more moderate note in *Fire With Fire*.

This volume combines elements of a confessional coming-of-age story, a generational portrait, and a feminist treatise on sexuality and womanhood. Of these different aspects, the memoir works best.

There is poignancy in Wolf's vivid description of growing up at the epicenter of the 1960s counter-culture, in a world where adult authority was collapsing, where the lines between "moms" and "sexy girls" were suddenly blurred, and children often felt like "an obstacle to our parents' self-realization." She describes well the world of childhood with its eager, fancy-filled curiosity about sex. And her (surprisingly tame) tales of her girlhood romances, despite a penchant for self-importance and lush prose, have their moving moments. Unfortunately, when it comes to cultural analysis, *Promiscuities* falters and stumbles on its own contradictions.

While Wolf promises to counter the perception of the teenage girl "as a victim of culture and sexuality [rather] than as a sexual and cultural creator," she herself often falls into the victim trap: "We needed boys more than they needed us," she plaintively asserts, never considering that boys might have a different view. The penchant for the language of victimhood is especially evident in her account of dynamics between nubile girls and older men—a simplistic scheme of nasty predators versus scared prey, with the briefest acknowledgment that, for some girls, adult male sexual attention was "great fun."

More disturbingly, young women dealing with male authority figures appear to be equated with girls. Describing an episode from her college days when a worshipped professor made a pass at her, the acclaimed author in her early thirties writes, "I am still afraid of him." Rather pathetic, if true. One of the Big Ideas in *Promiscuities* is that women are at least as lustful as men and are probably "the more carnal sex." Yet, invoking a hodgepodge of historical and anthropological evidence, Wolf evades the hard questions.

No one disputes that women have a robust capacity for sexual pleasure; indeed, as Wolf makes clear, about the only time this was disputed was in Europe in the nineteenth century. But are men and women equally interested in sex for its own sake, or is women's sexuality more dependent on a context of affection and long-term relation-

ships—as many evolutionary psychologists (whose work is very selectively cited by Wolf) argue? About this, Wolf says nothing. Often, in fact, she does not seem to understand the implications of what she reports. As an example of respect for female sexuality in other cultures, she mentions that the Zuni Indians considered it unseemly for a man to "enjoy a woman's body without giving her a gift in return." But such a custom, which treats sex as a favor men receive from women, hardly gibes with what Wolf claims is a near-universal belief that women want and enjoy sex more than do men. That female desire has been "better understood" in non-Western cultures is a leitmotif in *Promiscuities*. But, dwelling on the erotic texts of ancient India and China with their vision of women's sexuality as a sacred force, Wolf is oblivious to the irony of women's actual status in those societies; there men had concubines while women were held to a strict standard of monogamy that condemned remarriage for widows.

If Wolf's observations about other cultures are myopic, she also appears to harbor serious misconceptions about things closer to home. Consider her claim that the expression of female sexual desire is still taboo in our society; nearly a half-century after the Kinsey report and more than two decades after Erica Jong's *Fear of Flying* and Nancy Friday's first collection of women's sexual fantasies; in a culture where a new breed of female pop music stars celebrates the aggressively sexual woman who pursues her pleasure, and where women's magazines are full of tips on how to have more and better sex.

Wolf is on more solid ground when she argues that sexual liberation has not fully dismantled the double standard attached to boys' and girls' sexuality, embodied in the "slut" label. Her argument, however, is undercut by hyperbole. The story of "Tia," the glamour girl who disappeared from summer camp after learning that she was pregnant, is followed by a historical overview of penalties suffered by loose women—punctuated with reminders of Tia, "dead" to her friends from camp and rumored to have gotten fat (which is right up there with being garroted). Nor does Wolf notice the paradox in her quest to reclaim the "slut"; she complains that women are stigmatized for promiscuity, *and* that sexual access to a woman is not regarded as "precious" or "special."

This desire to have it both ways is also evident when Wolf laments that our lack of rituals to "incorporate girls into womanhood" leaves them to rely on sex to "become women"; she is oblivious not only to the parallel predicament of boys but to the fact that rites of passage exist in societies where each individual's destiny is rigidly circumscribed by the group. (Wolf proposes a warm and fuzzy version of an initiation ritual—wilderness retreats during which adult women teach girls about "self-defense, contraception, sexual pleasure, and parenting.") She wants the benefits of personal freedom and the security of communal life, the excitement of risk and the comfort of being shielded from adverse consequences.

In *Last Night in Paradise: Sex and Morals at the Century's End*, Katie Roiphe turns a more ironic eye to the anxieties of sexual liberation. Perhaps because Roiphe is a few years younger than Wolf, the AIDS epidemic—which makes only a brief appearance in *Promiscuities*—casts its shadow over all of Roiphe's narrative, starting with the story of her own sister who became infected (through heroin use, though, not sex).

One of Roiphe's central points—that the cultural response to AIDS was not just about the fear of the fatal virus but about "disillusionment with the sexual revolution"—is hardly original. Still, she makes the case well, pointing out the oft-forgotten fact that AIDS had a precursor of sorts, herpes, also described as a death blow to the sexual revolution. Many in the media, and in the culture at large, saw the scary new diseases both as the wages of sin and as instruments of a return to virtue. It is almost as though, if the AIDS epidemic did not exist, we would have to invent it and, in a way, we did, vastly exaggerating the risk of heterosexual transmission.

Roiphe's own sentiments about the sexual revolution and the counter-revolution are full of ambivalence. She is put off by the prematurely wise caution of young people raised to believe that, as one girl says, "It's just not worth risking your whole life for one hour of hoopla." She finds it sad that sexual adventure—the chance encounter with a stranger on a train—now seems all but impossible. Yet Roiphe understands, and to some extent shares, the permissiveness fatigue and the yearning for limits.

Reflecting on safe-sex TV spots which remind us that "You are sleeping with everyone your partner has slept with" and their imagery—rows of identical beds with identical couples, a couple whose bed suddenly fills with his and her past lovers—Roiphe notes that the messages speak to anxieties about more than health. "The identical beds seem to tell us, *You think you're special, but you're not.*" We fear that "the fast and fluid nature of modern relationships reduces us all to notches on each other's belts," that our affections are "random and interchangeable."

Generally avoiding true confessions, she mentions experiences that gave her this chilly feeling, such as the "endless repeating men in towels" emerging from the bathroom of an apartment she shared with three other women in college and the realization that one of the men had been there before, only he disappeared into a different bedroom. Roiphe also recalls leaving a man's apartment after a one-night stand, looking rumpled and wondering what the doorman would think; when the doorman barely gave her a glance, she suddenly felt disappointed because "no one cared." This may seem narcissistic, but there is a larger point. The knowledge that what we do in our personal lives is of no concern to anyone can be not only liberating but dismal: "[A]long with the freedom…comes a certain sense of pointlessness."

Yet when Roiphe looks at the pro-abstinence movement, which attempts to reattach moral significance to sex, she has little sympathy: the simplistic prohibition on all sex before marriage becomes an excuse to avoid moral choice, to dodge adult experience and responsibility. Does Roiphe, then, want sexual liberation or not? Is she merely confused?

I think there is a logic to her position, even though she does a rather poor job of explaining the apparent contradictions. The casual sex for which she waxes nostalgic is really not so casual; it may be an encounter between strangers, but there is still something special about, some meaning beyond physical pleasure—adventure, the "thrill of unexpected intimacy," the sense of recklessness, wildness, freedom. What she finds depressing is a climate in which there is nothing reckless, crazy, or wild about casual sex, and the choice of partners has no more significance than the choice of Chinese or Italian food. Interestingly, Wolf strikes the same chord when she wishes that her loss of virginity had been less matter-of-fact, fraught with more mystery, abandon, even danger.

But that does not keep Wolf from championing demystified, matter-of-fact sex education, while Roiphe is both amused and repelled by a class in which masturbation is discussed as matter-of-factly as algebra. Astutely, Roiphe notes that the purpose is not learning but "talking about masturbation in the classroom," making it "an officially acceptable, school-sanctioned activity." She does not want masturbation to be stigmatized; she just wants it to be left alone, untouched by official authority. "There is a certain kind of knowledge that we have to grope our way toward on our own," she says, in a perhaps infelicitous choice of words.

As a survey of the landscape of sexual issues in the nineties, *Last Night in Paradise* is haphazard. Sometimes it reads more like a series of essays than a book with an internally consistent structure. Some of these essayistic chapters offer fascinating insights into the cultural phenomena of our age: the response to basketball star Magic Johnson's announcement that he was infected with HIV, the presentation of Alison Gertz (white, affluent, ruined by a night of passion with the wrong man) as the paradigmatic AIDS victim, the sanitized portrayal of gay life in the movie *Philadelphia*.

Unfortunately, the book's power is lessened by its lack of a clear central point, the kind that gave Roiphe's first book *The Morning After*—a critique of the feminist crusade against date rape and sexual harassment—its appeal. There is often a thin line between ambiguity and muddle, and Roiphe is not always on the right side of it.

Another problem is Roiphe's penchant for generalizations. Only in passing does she concede that many Americans always remained relatively unaffected by the sexual revolution; the stigma may have been lifted from premarital sex, but college girls who had different boys drifting in and out of their bedrooms every weekend were never typical. She also probably exaggerates the effects of the anti-sexual revolution backlash: are we really to believe that teenage girls no longer lust after male pinups? Nonetheless, the merit of *Last Night in Paradise* lies in the moral complexity Roiphe brings to her topic, a complexity most evident by contrast with *Promiscuities*.

Unlike Wolf, Roiphe does not try to eat all her cake and have it too, or propose rose-colored solutions to difficult problems. Rather, she knows that there are no definite solutions to many of these problems, and that each generation will have to grapple with them in its own imperfect way.

WHAT CAN WE SAY ABOUT SEXUAL HARASSMENT?

Roberto Refinetti
504 Lake Colony Drive, Vestavia Hills, AL 35242

Confronting Sexual Harassment: What Schools and Colleges Can Do, by Judith B. Brandenburg (Teachers College Press, 1997, 174 pp.)

Judith Berman Brandenburg, the author of *Confronting Sexual Harassment*, is Professor of Psychology and Education at Teachers College, Columbia University. Her position as an educator at an institution dedicated to forming teachers may account for her repeated assertion that "the main hope for preventing sexual harassment is education." Unfortunately, very little evidence is presented in support of the idea that education is indeed the major avenue to the prevention of sexual harassment. As a matter of fact, the book fails in clearly defining sexual harassment, in demonstrating that it is an important social problem, or in presenting strategies for its prevention.

The author seems concerned about being perceived as a fair and evenhanded person. Thus, after asserting that stringent rules and policies against sexual harassment must be instituted, she warns the reader in the Introduction that "when these rules or policies encroach on freedom of speech and academic freedom, they do a disservice to our institutions of learning." Yet, the rest of the book then says otherwise. As a matter of fact, in the Introduction we can already detect the strong effect of her ideological preferences. Consider the following passage: "When a teacher has an intimate relationship with a student, other students may hesitate to approach that teacher about academic matters, either out of discomfort or because they are concerned that they might be harassed themselves." Certainly, the issue of students' perceptions of faculty-student relationships is an important consideration in discussions of sexual harassment, but the phrasing of the sentence preempts any discussion by equating teacher-student intimate relationship with harassment (the students are supposedly concerned that they *too* will be harassed). Obviously, this attitude disregards completely the complex issue of consensual relationships (which was featured in the 1997 volume of *Sexuality & Culture*).

The first chapter is dedicated to "Defining the Problem and Its Scope." Very sensibly, the author asserts that "the book defines sexual harassment according to the EEOC (1980)." EEOC (1980) refers to the guidelines published in 1980 by the Equal Employment Opportunity Commission. These guidelines embody "sexual harassment law," in the sense that they have been often utilized in court decisions. The guidelines are very clear about quid pro quo harassment but very vague about "hostile environment" harassment, and one would expect the book to help clarify the notion of hostile environment. Instead, it throws at the reader all sorts of speculations. It is true that clear cases of sexual harassment are listed (such as "a supervisor threatens to cut an employee's hours if she does not have a sexual relationship with him"), yet, in the list of examples of sexual harassment, one can find the case of "a school counselor discouraging girls from applying to engineering programs." Is *this* sexual harassment? *If* it is true that girls and boys are equally apt at skills required in an engineering program, and *if* an engineering program can be shown to be a better professional choice for this student than, say, a law program, *then* one could claim that the counselor is not helping the girl but dis-

criminating against her. This could then be used to claim the existence of discrimination on the basis of gender. However, while sexual harassment is illegal in the United Sates only to the extent that it leads to discrimination based on gender, not all discrimination based on gender is sexual harassment!

The second chapter, "Legal Responsibilities of Educational Institutions," is very informative and clearly makes the point that educational institutions are legally responsible for preventing sexual harassment on- and off-campus, and that the courts have held institutions responsible for employees found guilty of sexual harassment. Unfortunately, chapter 3, "Origins of Sexual Harassment," erodes the trustworthiness of the preceding chapter. Here, carefully selected social "science" studies are cited in support of the view that sexual harassment "is predicated on sociocultural views and sex-role stereotypes that males are active, dominant, and entitled to power, while females are passive, nurturing, submissive, and powerless." If this is true, one must conclude that sexual harassment is something that powerful men do to defenseless women. One must, therefore, totally ignore the valuable discussion of peer harassment, same-sex harassment, and counterpower harassment that was presented in chapter 2.

Chapter 4, "Creating Policies and Grievance Procedures," provides advice from an individual who has been involved in the process of creating policies for sexual harassment for some twenty years. However, aside from the scare of a few law suits here and there, the reader will wonder how important it is to create such policies if "only a limited number of K-12 school systems have sexual harassment policies" and, at the college level, "critics suggest that the notion of 'hostile environment' is too vague and object to schools taking any responsibility in this area."

The last two chapters are dedicated to the theme of educating faculty, students, and the public in general to avoid sexual harassment. Much advice is given here but, fortunately, the reader is warned early on that while many educational programs on sexual harassment have been developed, "there is as yet little research on the effectiveness of such programs." Thus, after being presented with the facts that we do not know what sexual harassment is and that we do not know how to handle it, we are now told that we don't know if we know how to prevent sexual harassment. Maybe, then, we should not write a book about it. Or, if we do write a book on *Confronting Sexual Harassment*, we should acknowledge our limitations and not give it a subtitle, "What Schools and Colleges Can Do."

Finally, although the book falls short of its goal, it does contain a very helpful set of three Appendices. Appendix A lists and briefly describes current state, local, and institutional policies and grievance procedures on sexual harassment. Appendix B provides a list of educational resources on sexual harassment, including organizations, publications, programs, and curricular materials. Appendix C lists federal organizations whose mission is of relevance to the issue of sexual harassment.

FEMINISM, SEXUAL HARASSMENT, AND THE ATYPICAL CASE

Valerie Jenness[1]
School of Social Ecology, University of California Irvine, CA 92697

***Feminist Accused of Sexual Harassment*, by Jane Gallop (Duke University Press, 1997, 101 pp.)**

When I first read *Feminist Accused of Sexual Harassment*, the media was consumed by reports of sexual harassment: Paula Jones's accusations of sexual misconduct against President Clinton, the military's highest ranking enlisted man's defense against four women's allegations of sexual misconduct, and *Court TV*'s gavel-to-gavel coverage of the so-called "Seinfeld Viewer Firing" case. Despite the diverse contexts, facts (contested and agreed upon), and adjudication procedures that surround these cases, they nonetheless share commonalities that render them stereotypical sexual harassment cases. In each case, a woman is accusing a man of sexual harassment, the act deemed sexual harassment involves sex or a (real or imagined) request for sex, it is a *he* who is denying the acts and the attendant allegations of sexual ha-

rassment and, in the end, one party will be deemed more believable than the other and the other party's reputation will be tarnished. In contrast, the case of Jane Gallop, a Distinguished Professor of English and Comparative Literature at the University of Wisconsin at Milwaukee, represents the antithesis of the stereotypical case—the exceptional case. Here the exceptional case is clearly defined in the first paragraph of the book. Gallop explains:

I am a feminist professor who was accused by two students of sexual harassment. This book is centered on that fact: the title is modeled after the style of tabloid headlines because of the way this fact lends itself to sensationalism. While any accusation of sexual harassment seems to promise a juicy scandal, this particular accusation is more sensational due to the newsworthy anomaly of a feminist being so accused. While sexual harassment is customarily a feminist issue, feminists usually appear on the accusers' side. For a feminist to be accused is a dramatic reversal. What kind of feminist would be accused of sexual harassment? (p. 2)

As "the accused," Gallop is a *she*, a feminist professor and, most importantly, an unapologetic defendant alleged to have engaged in sexual harassment with one of her female students without having requested or had sex with the accuser. As in research where the exceptional case provides the opportunity to redirect theory and redefine research agendas, the Jane Gallop case, as reported in this book and discussed in *The Chronicle of Higher Education*, *Lingua Franca*, *The New York Review of Books* and, most recently, the *Women's Review of Books*, provides the opportunity to rethink the content, consequences, and future of sexual harassment policies in higher education.

Although *Feminist Accused of Sexual Harassment* can be, indeed has been, read as Jane Gallop's self-aggrandizing attempt to exonerate herself from publicly scrutinized foul-play, it is more useful to read it as a rethinking of the ways in which feminist inspired and implemented social control policies, in this case sexual harassment policies that have been institutionalized on college and university campuses across the U.S., can be appropriated and used in non- or anti-feminist

ways. As Gallop, "a feminist theorist of sexuality" who considers it her "business to understand sexual harassment" (p. 7), explains: "My purpose is not simply to tell my story but rather to use that story to understand what's going on with sexual harassment. This spectacle taught me a thing or two, and I'd like to try and explain what I've learned" (p. 7).

To set the stage for the "lessons learned," Gallop offers her account of the events that led up to and followed two student's accusations of sexual harassment. In April of 1991, Gallop attended the First Annual Graduate Student Gay and Lesbian Conference. It was here that two events occurred that proved central to charges of sexual harassment against Gallop. Gallop describes the first event:

I figured it was precisely the combination of the two [graduate student and gay conference] that made the conference the event it was. I wanted to express my admiration for this fortuitous conjunction, my sense of how grad students and queer studies were, in fact, a perfect match. Everyone seemed so clever and sassy; I wanted to rise to the occasion. So, in the heat of the moment, in the process of phrasing a question for one of the speakers (a really good looking woman from out of town), I came out with the statement:

"graduate students are my sexual preference." The statement was meant to be a joke. We were at the first ever Graduate Student Gay and Lesbian Conference, a conference distinguished by a unique conjecture of identities—one institutional, the other sexual. The joke was playing with these two identities, trying loosely to suggest that "graduate student" was somehow like "gay and lesbian." The two categories worked so well together at this conference that it seemed fun to imagine the more intimate connections. Of course, with any joke, deeper truth lay behind the wordplay. The truth behind the joke was my real passion for graduate students. Of all my professional interactions, working with graduate students is what matters most to me, what provides me with the most satisfaction, and what continues to give me the impetus to teach and research as well as I can. I get more intellectually from interactions with graduate students than I do from undergraduates or from colleagues. So graduate students are my "preference." I termed the preference "sexual" to make a facetious connection with gay and lesbian. But in calling it "sexual" I also meant something more serious. At heart a Freudian, I believe that our professional impulses are sublimated sexual drives. The pleasure I get from working with graduate students, the intensity of my wish that certain promising graduate students will choose to work with me, and the satisfaction I get from seeing the imprint of my teaching in their work all strongly suggest a sexual analogy. I was trying too hard to be clever; no one got the joke. It was certainly not the first time I had embarrassed myself in a professional forum by telling a joke that flopped. But my bad jokes had never had such serious repercussions. Both accusations of sexual harassment take my sexual preference statement as a point of departure. The students claimed that the statement completely altered their perception of my behavior: it made them think I was trying to sleep with them. Both complainants and many fellow students took my statement as a public announcement that I fucked graduate students. And, based on this newly revealed "truth" about me, they reinterpreted all my behavior that previously had not troubled them. (pp. 86–89)

The interpretation of Gallop's behavior was especially problematic when, later in the evening, at the same conference, participants of the conference witnessed Gallop kiss a graduate student with whom she worked. This kiss, which occurred late in the evening and after much dancing and drinking, was the second event that proved relevant to accusations of sexual harassment against Gallop. As Gallop explains,

> I don't really know who started it. I know it surprised me and seemed to occur simultaneously to both of us, as if spontaneously generated out of the moment. In any case, whichever of us actually initiated this torrid kiss, both of us were clearly into it. It was a performance. By that I don't mean that I wasn't really kissing her or that I didn't find it sexy. What I mean is that we didn't just happen to be seen kissing, but we kissed like that because we knew we were being watched. And it was precisely the knowledge of being watched that made it sexy.... The kiss was brazen and public—and thus particularly appropriate for a conference distinguished by its intellectual and sexual daring. This was a performance tailor-made for the First Annual Graduate Student Gay and Lesbian Conference, whose title, after all, was "Flaunting It." I was, admittedly, trying to be outrageous. (pp. 91–92)

This "outrageous" act was subsequently interpreted as sexual harassment by one of two students who, a year and a half later, filed charges with the university against Gallop. In her complaint, the student alleged that she was upset by the kiss but was too afraid to tell Gallop. From Gallop's point of view, however, "if she were upset, she showed no sign of it at the time. Whatever her real feelings might have been, those who witnessed it saw her a willing and even eager participant. And she was well aware of how it looked" (p. 93).

After an investigation that included interviewing witnesses and reviewing the evidence, university officials did not find Gallop guilty of sexual harassment. According to Gallop, "the university found no evidence of compromised professional judgments, or of discrimination, unwanted sexual attention, or any sort of harassment; it found that I wasn't even having sex with students" (p. 35). She was, however, deemed guilty of failing to "respect the boundary between the sexual and the intellectual, between the professional and the personal" (p. 35); more to the point, she was deemed guilty of engaging in an "amorous relationship" with a student. Uncontested by Gallop, who acknowledges that her relationship with the complainant included "flirtatious banter" and "frank discussions" (p.33), this finding constituted a clear violation of the university policy that specified "consenting amorous relationships between instructor and student are unacceptable" (p. 95).

It is this policy (as well as others that are in place at many of the nation's most prestigious institutions of higher education—including, most recently, Yale University) that receives most of Gallops's attention in *Feminist Accused of Sexual Harassment*. Indeed, the most compelling parts of the book are those wherein she raises questions about how, "in the climate of the nineties, our engagement in a consensual sexual relationship (albeit one that lasted no more than a minute and didn't go below the neck) could actually function as proof of harassment" (p. 93). To address this question, Gallop offers a discussion of the changing parameters of that which constitutes sexual harassment and how those changes marginalize the importance of gender as a line of stratification and deny feminist pedagogy as an effective approach to teaching.

She begins her now controversial analysis by reminding the reader of the early connection between feminism and sexual harassment:

> Feminism has a special relation to sexual harassment. One could say in fact that feminism invented harassment. Not, of course, the behavior itself, which presumably has gone on as long as men have held power over women. But, until feminism named it, the behavior had no official existence. In the mid-seventies, feminism got women to compare notes on their difficulties in the workplace; it came

out that women employees all too frequently had to cope with this sort of thing. Feminism named this behavior sexual harassment and proceeded to make it illegal. (pp. 8–9)

She reminds us that, quite appropriately, "sexual harassment is criminal not because it is sex, but because it is discrimination" (p. 10). Further, and again quite appropriately, it is a feminist issue because it systematically and overwhelmingly disadvantages women.

Taking the way in which feminism and gender are implicated in the historical development of sexual harassment as a commendable and embraceable given, Gallop then warns against what she sees as the "rampant expansion of the concept of sexual harassment" (p. 8). In particular, she warns against what she sees as a problematic shift in the operationalization of sexual harassment, from a purposively feminist-informed and gendered conceptualization to an increasingly popular and utilized gender-neutral one, at precisely the moment when "the nation finally rallies against it" (p. 27). The result is a conceptualization that has "no necessary link to either gender or discrimination" (p. 27):

> When it is possible to conceive of sexual harassment without discrimination, then sexual harassment becomes a crime of

sexuality rather than of discrimination. There is, in fact, a recent national trend toward findings of sexual harassment where there is no discrimination. This represents a significant departure from the feminist formulation of harassment. (p. 11)

Troubled by this departure, Gallop warns that, as sexual harassment has moved away from its original feminist frame, it is increasingly used as a tool to further disadvantage and harm women. She argues that "under the guise of sexual harassment we find ourselves once again vilifying women who presume to be sexual and powerful like men" and that "as outrage at sexual harassment becomes popular, a role-reversal fantasy allows a wide audience to embrace the feminist issue of sexual harassment and at the same time turn it against a liberated woman" (p. 26). Throughout the book, Gallop paints a picture of sexual harassment as a policy akin to a useable weapon, one that can be used to address sex discrimination in the workplace as well as to target "outrageous" women in the workplace.

This point of departure and reversal—when sexual harassment is separated from gender and discrimination and thus available to be used against women—is of great concern for Gallop. Once separated from the related issues of sex discrimination and gender, harassment can be easily linked to various versions of "undesirable sexuality." That is, this separation paves the way for (outrageous) women to be differentially targeted for crimes of sexuality. Of course, crimes of sexuality are as diverse as modern sexualities, but Gallop is most interested in crimes of sexuality related to teaching. As she says about her case,

The university officer who investigated the charges against me was convinced that I had not in fact discriminated—not against women, not against men, not on the basis of sexual orientation, and not on any basis whatsoever. She believed that my pedagogical practices had been, as she put it, applied in a consistent manner. Yet she nonetheless thought I probably was guilty of sexual harassment. (p. 10)

But why? Gallop surmises, "I was construed as a sexual harasser because I sexualize the atmosphere in which I work" (p. 10). Throughout the book, Gallop makes no apologies for sexualizing the workplace in particular and the educational experience more generally. Indeed, very early in the book, Gallop makes clear that "it is because of the sort of feminist I am that I do not respect the line between the intellectual and the sexual" (p. 12).

At the center of Gallop's book is a sustained discussion of how contemporary efforts to regulate sexuality, especially women's sexuality, in higher education are problematic from a feminist point of view. In perhaps the most controversial chapter of her book, "Consensual Amorous Relationships," Gallop argues that sexualizing the workplace, especially the academic environment, is not necessarily an undesirable thing. Unlike other feminists and academic administrators who remain committed to desexualizing that which occurs between professor and student, she does not assume that sexualizing the learning process is automatically or necessarily disadvantageous to women. Many pages of the book are devoted to detailing the many events in her life—both as a graduate student and as a professor—that sex, knowledge, and the desire to learn were intimately infused without negative consequences for her or the recipients of her affection and desire. She revels in detailing her sexual encounters with faculty when she was a graduate student, as well as her sexual encounters with graduate students as a faculty member. In each case, she is careful to point out,

> The stories I have just told portray human relations. In these affairs, my motivations as well as the motivations of the students are profoundly—sometimes sadly, sometimes sweetly—human. They span the usual range

of reasons why people make contact: loneliness, sympathy, rebounding from a recently failed relationship, and, of course, admiration.... In every instance, it was the student who made the first move; it was always the student who initiated the sexual activity. This certainly runs counter to the cliché of the lecherous professor putting the moves on innocent young things.... I am still convinced that desire is good and that when mutual desire makes itself felt, it is a very fine thing indeed. (p. 49)

Although Gallop notes that she no longer has sex with students, "I still embrace such relations in principle" (p. 15). Accordingly, she questions policies to the contrary.

> University administrators who piously intone against teacher-student sex, citing the student's impossibility to freely grant consent, would be shocked if they knew their position was based in a [feminist] critique of the institution of marriage. And I don't think you could get them to agree to policies likewise prohibiting heterosexuality on the grounds that the power differential means a woman's consent is always to some extent coerced. (pp. 37–38)

In many ways, the experiences Gallop reports throughout her book, as well as her vehement opposition to university policies that prevent consensual, amorous relationships between faculty and students, seem to evoke the most controversy. It is her effort to initiate the acceptance of what I will call a "positive understanding of the erotics of teaching" and what Gallop simply refers to as "the erotics of pedagogy" (p. 89), that presents the greatest challenge to recent trends in policy around sexual harassment and dominant feminist conceptualizations of sexual harassment. Acknowledging that many "quid pro quo" forms of sexual harassment occur and that not all faculty-student relationships are as enjoyable and empowering as the ones she experienced, Gallop nonetheless remains committed to ensuring that women, including female students who find themselves attracted to faculty, are not denied the choice of when to be sexual, how to be sexual, and with whom to be sexual:

> As a feminist I am well aware of the many ways women are often compelled to sexual relations with men by forces that have nothing to do with our desire. And I see that students might be in a similar position with relation to teachers. But, as a feminist, I do not think the solution is to deny women or students the right to consent. Denying women the right to consent reinforces our status as objects

rather than desiring objects. That is why I believe the question of whether sexual advances are wanted is absolutely critical. Prohibition of consensual teacher-student relations is based on the assumption that when a student says yes she really means no. I cannot help but think that this proceeds from the same logic according to which when a woman says no she really means yes. The first assumption is protectionist; the second is the very logic of harassment. What harassment and protectionism have in common is precisely a refusal to credit women's desires. Common to both is the assumption that women do not know what we want, that someone else, in a position of greater knowledge and power, knows better. (pp. 38–39)

For Gallop, to deny women the ability to consent is not only an inappropriate intrusion into students' lives, it is infantalizing and dehumanizing as well. With regard to the latter, she argues that "it is ironic that relations between teachers and students have been banned as part of the fight against sexual harassment. We fight against sexual harassment because it's dehumanizing, but the ban on consensual relations is dehumanizing too" (p. 50).

Finally, Gallop argues that bans against consensual relationships and other efforts to desexualize higher education are antithetical to good teaching. With reference to her case, for example, she explains:

> As upsetting as it was to have someone I worked so hard to help turn against me and accuse me of a loathsome crime, I am much more disturbed by the implications of the university's determination. Seeing a relation between a student enamored of a teacher's work, a student who wanted to be like that teacher, and the teacher who responded deeply to the student's desire to work with her, who wanted profoundly to help her do what she desired, the university deemed such a connection, passionate and involving so many personal hopes and dreams, an amorous relation. And indeed it was. (pp. 55–56)

With the help of many examples and the clever turn of phrases, Gallop argues that, at its best, "the pedagogical relation between a student and teacher is, in fact, a consensual amorous relationship" (p. 57). Moreover, "by moving from the restricted field of romantic love to the exceedingly wide field of relationships that are either social, personal, or involve intense feelings, what was originally a policy about sexual relations could become a policy restricting and chilling pedagogical relations" (p. 57).

In the end, Gallop is advocating a "pro sex" position commensurate with her "power feminism" orientation to gender inequality in higher education, one that emphasizes choice over constraint and the pursuit of sexual pleasure over preemptive strikes (in the form of regulation) against potential—but as yet unrealized—victimization.

Unlike many others, I find much of what Gallop has to say about contemporary feminism, pedagogy, and sexual harassment compelling. However, since being asked to review this book, I have engaged in many conversations with many friends and colleagues who, in the main, express a great deal of interest in "what really happened" with Gallop, but little appreciation for Gallop's arguments about feminism, pedagogy, and the social control of sexuality. As a graduate student currently embroiled in a sexual harassment case recently exclaimed: "Gallop is weird! The comments she makes are outrageous." If "outrageous" implies controversial, left of center, and evoking, I am in agreement. Notably, more than one feminist statement has been outrageous at time one and worthy of consideration and institutionalization as policy at time two; indeed, feminism has survived and been successful as a movement because this is true! In the case of sexual harassment, I suspect that, as universities continue to find themselves immersed in legal and political controversy surrounding the content and implementation of sexual harassment policy and as an increasing number of feminists find themselves dissatisfied with the way in which the content and implementation of sexual harassment is appropriated and differentially deployed within the context of patriarchal institutions, some of Gallop's "wake up" calls will be heard. Of course, this could just be wishful thinking on my part.

In the end, those who read *Feminist Accused of Sexual Harassment* as nothing more than a "she said" version of a nationally known and famous atypical case of sexual harassment in a university setting will find it disappointing and, perhaps, infuriating. In contrast, those who read the book as a provoking treatise on sexual harassment as a feminist invention designed to combat discrimination, but increasingly appropriated and used as a weapon in less than feminist battles, will be challenged to at least entertain alternative views on what is still taboo—the sexualization of the teaching relationship. As Gallop explains in a chapter entitled "Object of Intellectual Inquiry": "I felt that the anti-harassment movement had monopolized the conversation on teacher-student sex, and I wanted there to be an open discussion of the topic rather than just moral certainty and silence" (p. 76). Because she accomplishes this goal, feminist discussions about the intricacies of sex, sexuality, and social control can be richer insofar as feminism is more alert to the limits of sexual regulation and worried about its indiscriminate expansion.

Notes

1. I write this review as someone who shares many, although not all, of Jane Gallop's sensitivities and subjectivities. Like Gallop, I took my first job after graduate school at a "medium sized state university in a dinky little town where there wasn't really anything but the university" (p. 43), where "it seemed like everyone in town was either under twenty-two or married," and "it didn't look like there would be much in the way of romantic possibilities" (p. 44). Also like Gallop, I am a feminist who became involved with a graduate student from outside of my department, endured the wrath of a "brash young seducer" (p. 47), was accused, but not found guilty, of sexual harassment, and am "pretty sensitive about the issue" (p. 31).

SEXUAL TURMOIL DOWN UNDER

Roberto Hugh Potter
Department of Sociology, Social Work, and Criminology
Morehead State University, Morehead, KY 40351

The First Stone: Some Questions about Sex and Power, by Helen Garner (The Free Press, 1997, 256 pp.)

If you have ever had a fear of being accused of sexual harassment, you *won't want* to read this book. If you have ever had a fear of being accused of sexual harassment, *you'd better* read this book. The bewildering world of what constitutes sexual harassment, what it means to be a "real" feminist, and how academic tradition and institutional image come together in the lives of individuals are presented in a manner that stirs emotions and thought on all levels. Lurking in the margins throughout is the relationship between sexuality and power, and whether the conjunction between the two is as important as it seems to have become, at least in the academic mind. This is not journalistic fluff. Rather, it is a cool analysis of a real-life situation and the ramifications it had on the individuals and institutions drawn into the maelstrom of a sexual misconduct charge, including the author.

The Facts in Question

The events that led Ms. Garner to produce this work occurred at the University of Melbourne; Melbourne Uni is one of the "sandstone unis" in Australia. These are roughly equivalent to our Ivy League, though they would surely strive for "Oxbridge" status. The two incidents occurred on the same night, following a formal party in one of the "colleges." For those of you who may have never experienced a "college" atmosphere in the United Kingdom or Australia, I can best describe them as being something between a dormitory and a fraternity or sorority house with tradition.

Of course, some of the colleges at the sandstone unis are much more than that; they are mini-unis within their own doors. Colleges, while part of the university property, are often operated by religious or other organizational bodies. Ormond College, where this alleged incident took place, in addition to being a residential hall on the campus of Melbourne Uni, is also a seminary for the Uniting Church (an amalgamation of Methodist and Presbyterian congregations).

Unlike U.S. dormitories, occupancy of many Australian colleges is not simply on a space available basis. Rather, one has to apply to live in the college, be interviewed, and accepted into the college. Most of the colleges with which I am familiar are co-educational. By this I do not mean the often encountered U.S. form of co-ed, with alternating floors or separate facilities for men and women. Rather, the co-ed dorms in Australia tend to be completely so—men and women sharing bathrooms, as well as all other parts of the facility.

The college is often one's point of affiliation, rather than the university to which it is attached. Colleges on particular campuses have varying degrees of prestige. Ormond College was (and is) one of the most prestigious at the University of Melbourne and in Australia in general. Colleges such as Ormond have a hierarchical structure similar to the unis at which they exist. The head of the college, sometimes called the "master," "principal," or "director," combines administrative duties with academic rank. At my old uni, for example, college principals hold the academic rank (and salary) of Associate Professor (slightly higher rank than in the U.S.

system—just short of demi-god status), though they have no necessary affiliation with any particular department nor teaching responsibilities. Their primary task is to manage the delivery of services at the college level and provide academic and pastoral service to the college residents. Thus, a college principal (and other members of the college staff from associate principals to tutors) combine levels of authority with care-giving. Some would still argue that they act *in loco parentis*, even though almost all uni students are of legal adult age.

Colleges often combine the "high table," senior and junior commons rooms and other traditions of the Oxbridge universities. Many of the functions are "black tie" and include invited guests and speeches. The night of the incidents alleged in *The First Stone* involved the informal party following just such a formal occasion. During the party, two female students allege that the Master of the college (Dr. "Colin Shepherd") groped them (squeezing breasts and/or buttocks, or "bum" in Aussie). One incident allegedly occurred in the Master's office, the other while he danced with a different young lady. Neither of the young women verbally rebuked the Master at the time, according to their sworn testimony, although neither allowed the events to proceed further, and one expressed her distress over the event to friends that evening. The issue of response or lack thereof is one of the continuing themes throughout the book.

The exact chronology of events is a bit vague in Ms. Garner's telling of the story. While a chart of some sort laying out the events might be instructive, I believe the more disjointed telling of the story helps to convey the confusion surrounding the incidents. By jumping from various actors directly involved in the story with their recollections of knowledge and action, to outside observers and their perceptions, to Ms. Garner's own thoughts and feelings, the reader may well sense the frustration of those involved and of the author herself.

Suffice to say here that it was months after the alleged incidents occurred that Dr. Shepherd learned of the exact nature of the charges against him, only shortly thereafter to be officially charged with criminal indecent assault by the Victorian Police. Two trials resulted, the first ending in Dr. Shepherd's conviction and the second, an appeal, in which the charges were found not to be proven beyond a reasonable doubt. As a result of the acrimony surrounding the incident, Dr. Shepherd "resigned" his position as Master of Ormond College. The last best information I had from former colleagues in Australia was that he was still unemployed. The fate of the two complainants (both law students, an undergraduate degree in Australia), who never agreed to speak directly with Ms. Garner, is unknown.

Ms. Garner admits that it was what she perceived as the heavy-handed response of a criminal charge for groping that drew her to the case. As a member of the "second wave" feminist community in Australia, Helen Garner has strong feminist credentials. Ms. Garner was a moving force in the Victorian Women's Electoral Lobby and abortion law reform groups in the 1960s and 1970s. She has remained a steadfast commentator on women's issues in Australia over the years. Yet, it struck her as "a bit over the top" to bring criminal charges for what she perceived to be rude behavior. As she sought to gather more material on the situation surrounding the Ormond affair, she was dismayed by the reactions she encountered from younger women who self-identified as feminists. The afterword, available in the U.S. edition of this book, documents some of the response to the book, especially from feminist critics.

There are so many themes that may be explored in *The First Stone* that it is difficult to justify focusing on only a few. Without wishing to venture too close to post-modernist territory, it appears to be the subtextual constructions placed on Ms. Garner's words that make reactions to the book so varied and visceral. However, there are three themes that I think are core to the work. The first involves a historical snapshot of what was occurring on Australian university campuses regarding student-faculty romantic relationships in the early 1990s (Bacchi, 1992). The others have to do with the notions of power, institutions, and group prestige, especially the role of feminism on university campuses (Faust, 1994; Roiphe, 1993).

It Couldn't Happen Here, Could It?

A faculty member at a prestigious university is forced to resign his position because of developments surrounding allegations of sexual impropriety of which he was unaware and, when informed, strongly denied having committed. It just couldn't happen here, right? After all, we have due process ("natural justice") and other rules in place to avoid this. Reading *The First Stone* will alert one to the reality that sexual harassment is unlike any other accusation in the current academic environment. If the criminal charges had not been filed, it is quite possible that the outcome of this chain of events still might have been exactly the same for those involved.

The First Stone is about more than simply the incidents around which the text revolves. Throughout are the themes of how feminism has changed over the past thirty years and the author's concerns

with where those developments have taken women, particularly young women. The theme of the university as a battleground on which the program of some feminists take root and attempt to spread beyond with little regard for the realities of the non-academic sphere is also present. Finally, the concerns over personal responsibility and the abdication of such by members of various factions is visited again and again.

Ms. Garner illustrates these themes through the impact the events in question had on the lives of individuals involved directly and peripherally. As I read the book, the individuals fade into the background as almost hapless pawns maneuvered by the forces of various groups whose purposes are sometimes clear, oftentimes not so. That may be my bias as a reader trained in sociology, or it may be that many of the groups whose representatives Ms. Garner interviewed base their world view on status relations, rather than individuals. Status politics, as Gusfield (1963) noted, is about achieving or retaining "respect" for a particular group in a social setting. As Ms. Garner makes clear in her book, the individuals who get sacrificed do not matter to the group that wins.

The First Stone is not an academic work about sexual harassment or campus politics. It is a wonderfully written exploration of these issues and broader issues about the role of sex and power in the development of the feminist movement. I admit reading *The First Stone* again was depressing at times because of the damage I knew had been wrought in real lives. There is also the knowledge that similar events have ruined careers and lives in the U.S. (faculty, staff, and students), where we believe we have more protection against such unfounded charges. However, as *The First Stone* demonstrates, when the interests of groups and organizations collide over power and prestige, the individuals whose lives are affected generally find themselves overpowered. It can and does happen more than we want to believe in institutions that claim to be among the most tolerant environments in our societies. C.Wright Mills (1959) wrote that sociology is to some extent the study of the intersection of history and human biography. In *The First Stone*, Helen Garner has provided a documentary comment on just one such instance in the lives of several people. We are all living in that same space.

References

Bacchi, C. (1992). Sex on campus: Where does "consent" end and harassment begin?, *The Australian Universities' Review*, 35 (1), 23–36.

Faust, B. (1994). *Backlash? Balderdash! Where feminism is going right*. Sydney: University of New South Wales Press.

Gusfield, J.R. (1963). *Symbolic crusade: Status politics and the American temperance movement*. Urbana: University of Illinois Press.

Mills, C.W. (1959). *The sociological imagination*. New York: Oxford University Press.

Roiphe, K. (1993). *The morning after: Sex, fear, and feminism on campus*. Boston: Little, Brown, and Company.

READ JUDGE POSNER

Joseph S. Fulda
701 West 177ᵗʰ Street #21, New York, NY 10033

Privacy and the Politics of Intimate Life, by Patricia Boling (Cornell University Press, 1996, 192 pp.)

In the first chapter of *Privacy and the Politics of Intimate Life*, "Why the Personal Is Not Always Political," author Patricia Boling offers this view of the scope of her book:

> I explore these two positions— the skeptical feminist critique of privacy, and the legal-liberal defense of privacy as a value— with a view to discovering what is insightful and valuable, as well as flawed or problematic, in each. By using feminist theory and legal theory to interrogate each other, we can see more clearly what each approach has contributed to thinking about private and public, as well as the questions that have gone unanswered and the problems that remain unresolved. Exploring these complementary, even antagonistic, approaches is a crucial first step toward developing a more adequate approach to thinking about public issues rooted in intimate-life venues and practices and the relationship between private, public, and political life. (pp. 3–4)

This interrogation, she adds a few pages later, is "not to be dismissive of the theoretical[1] insights that have revolutionized the way we think about public and private distinctions. Instead, I write as a sympathetic critic, nurtured and taught by theorists whose work has broken crucial theoretical and political ground." Put another way, this is a book by a feminist addressed to other feminists, making the case that "the personal is the political" is an overstatement (but not a misstatement) and the attacks on privacy as a core value overwrought (but not misdirected).

As a feminist-to-feminist communiqué, this book succeeds in its limited aims. Of Catharine MacKinnon, for example, she writes that her contributions are "original and important" but also "shot through with sweeping generalizations and harsh overstatements," are "frequently insightful" but also appear "doctrinaire, dictatorial, and condescending" and seem "reductive." (Boling is usually not courageous enough, or is perhaps too respectful, to use any form of the verb "to be" in a criticism of MacKinnon; deficiencies in the latter's writing usually seem or appear.) But, and much more importantly, Boling herself endorses sweeping generalizations and harsh overstatements and is herself reductive in her thinking (although her tone is anything but doctrinaire); the difference is that Boling's radical views are brought in as asides in a seemingly placid inquiry.

Five quotations should be sufficient to indicate what we mean by Boling's "quiet radicalism":

Privacy has played an ideological function, masking oppressive relations within the family, and obscuring the way state power has supported patriarchal relationships in intimate life. (p. 13)

For women, intimate life is where they are most oppressed and unfree, most vulnerable to male sexual predations. (p. 13)

Addressing the various forms that oppression takes in private life—economic exploitation, racism, sexism, homophobia—is crucial for invigorating political life, for making citizens out of private sufferers. (p. 59)

A dialogue with Arendt can be productive because working through her objections to treating household matters as public issues can help us find the right approach or vocabulary for politicizing them. (p. 61)

Once we pose the problem in terms of finding appropriately political language and sensibilities with which to address issues housed in private life rather than walling-off private life concerns from politics, several tightly latched intellectual doors swing open. (p. 74)

These five examples—all drawn from Part I of the book, "Theoretical Considerations," comprising Chapters 1–3—are representative of Boling's attempt to make privacy palatable to feminists and feminism palatable to those who value privacy. In the former objective, she may have succeeded—her feminist audience will have to decide; but in the latter objective, she has not succeeded, for almost nothing she says about privacy per se or privacy theory is original, in any sense of that word; there are no new arguments. The two exceptions are her very fine linguistic analysis of "private," "public," and "political," which does genuinely both reveal and clarify ambiguities, subtleties, and complexities in these conceptual complexes and her correct dismissal of Judith Jarvis Thomson's critique of privacy as purely derivative as essentially irrelevant. But she goes no further with these conceptual complexes and their ambiguities, subtleties, and complexities than to affirm *both* the feminist view and the liberal-legal view, adding to neither of them in the process. Moreover, her paragraph on Thomson, while insightful as far as it goes, would have been better if it had pointed out that the liberty and property interests from which privacy may be said to derive can also in their turn be seen as derivative of privacy, thus making it clear that the concepts of liberty, property, and privacy are inextricably intertwined, a unitary whole.

This brings us to the larger question of whether this book has *anything* to say to those outside the small cadre of willing-to-be-tamed feminists at whom this book is, by her own candid admission in the preface, directed. Certainly, a serious book on whether or not the personal is or ought to be political[2] and to what extent and when and how, even if not strikingly original, would be a useful contribution to social thought. But this book does not even mention the father of that subject—Plato. Nor does it mention Marx or Mill, whose views on these matters cannot possibly be ignored. Indeed, no major political thinker other than Hannah Arendt is even discussed. And this in a treatise by a professor of political science! The intellectual world as described by Boling begins somewhere in the 1950s, with citations of largely

ephemeral works that have neither stood, nor will stand, the test of time. Many of the recent works that she criticizes and then uses to contradistinguish her own views are so obviously trivial and limited in scope as to lend themselves to very easy dismemberment, and hence a very easy book is born—a reply is far easier to write than a study or an exposition.

The absence of history and context is just as visible in the discussion of privacy as in the discussion of the politics of intimate life. Although Warren and Brandeis's seminal *Harvard Law Review* article is footnoted as "often credited with originating the idea of a right to privacy" (p. 175), neither it nor its concerns are discussed. No serious discussion of privacy before *Griswold v. Connecticut* is undertaken. Moreover, the *most* important decision on privacy, *Katz v. United States* 389 U.S. 347 (1967), is never mentioned or referred to even by indirection, probably because, as a Fourth Amendment case, Boling did not consider it germane to a discussion of privacy in intimate life. However, since the decision handed down the expectations theory of privacy (the government is barred from unreasonably intruding on one's privacy if there was a subjective expectation of privacy and society is prepared to accept that expectation as reasonable), laid down in Justice Harlan's concurrence, how could it not be relevant?

The good news is that there is an exceptional book, concerned with the history of ideas from antiquity to both modern feminism and modern sociobiology, that delves into the connections between intimate life and privacy, that beautifully deals with the legal and philosophical issues involved in both privacy (to some extent) per se and (especially) in intimate contexts, and that covers virtually all the case law and issues Boling covers in Part II—including an extensive, brilliant discussion of homosexuality and the law. It is *Sex and Reason*[3] by Richard Posner, Chief Judge of the Seventh Circuit and Senior Lecturer at the University of Chicago Law School. Read *that* book (not cited in the book under review) and learn and enjoy.

Notes

1. Boling uses the word "theoretical" almost exclusively to refer to feminist theory; likewise "theorist" almost always refers to feminist writers; legal and philosophical arguments, in contrast, are typically referred to as "analysis" or "philosophy."
2. Her concluding sentence on this matter, and indeed of the book, is: "Political engagement depends on our discovering how our private lives are connected to politics; the task is to learn to translate private need into political claim" (p. 160), a statist call if ever there was one.
3. Posner, R.A. (1992). *Sex and Reason*. Cambridge: Harvard University Press.

IN THE COMPANY OF MEN BEHAVING BADLY

Warren Farrell
103 North Highway 101, Box 220, Encinitas, CA 92024

In the Company of Men, directed by Neil LaBute (Sony Pictures, 1997)

The credits are rolling, and my stomach is churning. Not a single woman exiting *In the Company of Men* was speaking with even a tinge of warmth toward her male partner. Women in all-female contingents are laying into men-as-bastards in voices easy to hear—in a disturbing manner no one would do with the commonly berated minorities.

I seek some female perspectives. I find myself unable to approach any woman—each seems surrounded with an energy field saying, "You are man...stay back."

In the lobby, I notice two women whose energy seems softer. They stop to read the movie review. I read with them. As they finish, I gently ask what they thought of the movie. Their bodies shudder in disgust; they mumble, "Men." Then they look up, eyes registering and, without embarrassment, they turn their backs and leave.

I am shaken. I decide to walk it off. After a light bite, I wander into a bookstore. There are the two women. My first thought—"Maybe now is a better time"—is canceled by a deeper fear: "Stalker." I leave. I feel like a black man at the turn-of-the-century deep south approaching the wrong restroom.

The film packs its wallop by portraying two men filled with hatred toward women ("Women...they're meat, gristle, hatred—they're all the same"), each hurt by a woman. They conspire revenge.

So far, it is *The First Wives' Club*, but in the company of men. But then the screw turns. *The First Wives' Club* drew half of all the opening weekend female moviegoers in America to cheer the "vaporization" of the husbands-as-bastards. But *In the Company of Men*, draws no cheers as the two men plot to hurt a woman. They fear a woman being hurt.

The male characters' *In the Company of Men* target is Christine, the personification of vulnerability: deaf, innocent, beautiful, young, and female. Her deafness has made men neglect her romantically, so the men plot to separately but simultaneously court her, send her flowers, confess love, then coldly drop her and laugh as she "reaches for the sleeping pills."

Christine's sweetness courts the audience and...uh, oh...even the men. We watch even Chad, the ringleader who has thus far come across as the worst of Iago and Manson, soften, weaken, fall in love.

Christine returns Chad's love. And then Chad grabs her face, mockingly tells her it's all a game, he just wanted to hurt her. He haughtily exits the bedroom. The audience realizes that it, like Christine, has been sucked in by Chad's pretenses of love.

Women in the audience, who have just heard virtually every loving assurance a man ever gave them and now see they were duped, cannot help but recall their most blistering pangs of rejection. It is the actual feeling of having been sucked in (once again) that emotionally seals their feelings of identity with Christine as victim and Chad as Evil personified (or is it Man personified?).

It is still possible, though, for someone, somewhere, to have the slightest compassion for Chad—after all, he was hurt. But then he admits his womanfriend had never left him as he had claimed. In fact, we meet her. She is loving, trusting, unsuspecting. She naively feels she knows Chad. She is Everywoman. Meet Everyman.

So, what is the point? When a man says he has been hurt, be suspicious. His pleas for compassion are the bait and you are just the fish. Proof? Men love fishing. Motivation? It gives them a thrill to exercise their power. In the film's words, he does it because he can. Because he has power. That is it. Don't even listen to men.

Can we portray men this way, assuming that men do have the money and the power, and that so many of society's problems are caused by men? Let's see. Didn't Nazis feel that Jews had the money and the power and that so many of society's problems were caused by Jews?

Pretend for a moment that this film was called *In the Company of Jews* and made its debut in Nazi Germany. Suppose Christine was the innocent Aryan, and Jews were being portrayed as plotting to psychologically rape her. Would we now be considering it a classic example of Nazi hatred?

Yet, with the title featuring men, not Jews, the public relations people initially expected to promote the film as *a men's film*. Were the film portraying Jews rather than men, wouldn't even a Nazi have been conscious enough not to give a second thought to promoting the film to the Jewish community? It is the unconsciousness of our anti-male sexism that makes it so dangerous. So unconscious that, when men hate women, we call it misogyny; when women hate men, we don't have a word for it.

Do these attitudes in reality make us more receptive to disposing of men? Yes. Would we ever *require* only women to register for the draft? Or only blacks? Or only Jews? Then, why only men? While violence kills three times as many men as women, we have only a Violence Against Women Act. In 1920, American men died one year sooner than women; today, they die seven years sooner. Yet, we have only an Office of Women's Health, not men's. Objectifying a group always makes us callous to its deaths.

It is not just those men we hate who suffer these consequences. When we call it "progressive" to care more about saving whales than saving males, we are considering it progressive to feel callous toward our sons. It is hard to say this. My stomach is still churning.

HEY, I'M A FEMENIST!
A MALE PROFESSOR WEIGHS
IN WITH FEMINIST PEDAGOGY

John C. Hampsey
English Department, California Polytechnic State University
San Luis Obispo, CA 93407

It seems that in recent years whenever men and women "mix it up" over feminism and feminist pedagogy the result is often contentious, divisive, and patronizing. In terms of the classroom, the question of whether a male professor can de-politicize feminism enough to effectively teach from that perspective is very real, as is the corollary question of whether it is "legitimate" for him to do so. The larger issue, of course, is whether any sort of "cross over" is legitimate. For instance, can a white male professor teach a course on ethnic literature?

A few months ago, after an energetic class examining the black female novelist Zora Neale Hurston, three students (two female, one male) came up and told me that they had decided I was a feminist. Well, I thought, wouldn't my friends have a laugh at this. The students were not kidding either. They had that buoyant self-satisfied look that appears when one has finally figured something out. It was week seven of my course on the Modern Novel, and as far as they were concerned, I was a feminist, and that was that.

The course had opened with Joseph Conrad's *Heart of Darkness*, followed by William Faulkner's *The Sound and the Fury*. But by week five we had switched genders and read Virginia Woolf's *To the Lighthouse*, followed by Zora Neale Hurston's *Their Eyes Were Watching God*. Narrative technique is one of the focal points in the course, and both Woolf and Hurston offer splendid variations upon the formalist tradition claimed by Conrad and Faulkner.

By the end of the day, my shock at the students' comment had worn off, but not my sense of intrigue. Had I taught Woolf and Hurston so well that my students would naturally draw such a conclusion? Or had something gone very wrong? As a male professor I had assumed that I was hopelessly trapped, by my very gender, in the masculinist tradition. Yet, could I still be a feminist?

Great progress had been made, I was sure, from my early teaching days (early 1980s), when lack of self-confidence caused me to tremble if ever I set foot upon the feminist literary terrain. Back then, I would have been insulted by a gender-specific term like "feminist" being applied to me. But now, it was not so much the term that bothered me, as the labeling itself. My students' supercilious use of the word "feminist" was simply an enactment of the need we all have to define people (as liberal, racist, fascist, etc.), to stick people on the wall as trophies to our success at "knowing" the world. We triumph by doing to others what we despise having done to ourselves. Literary history is filled with examples, such as Jean-Paul Sartre, who hated being called an existentialist.

The case with my students seemed especially ironic since, a few years earlier, when teaching an upper division course on Classical Greece, a colleague responded: "Ah, I knew it. You're a classicist!"

Thus, it follows that when I end my Modern Novel course with works by Pynchon and Calvino, students will probably deem me an "absurdist." But what about when I taught Conrad and Faulkner at the beginning of the course? Was I nothing then? Just a teacher?

Certainly feminist criticism has reached a point where it is no longer considered a "radical" approach carried out by an emboldened and enlightened few. In fact, it has reached a point where the feminist province itself is no longer a "Women's Room." Men have been slipping into the territory, sometimes unnoticed and under cover, many times to the dismay of ardent and puritanical feminists who urgently shoo them away.

A few years ago at the University of California-Santa Barbara, Richard Rorty, the renowned American philosopher, delivered a paper entitled "Feminism, Ideology, and Deconstruction." Afterwards, he was attacked by feminists in the audience for presuming to redefine feminism. Would the feminists have reacted so if Rorty were a woman?

Men never so much as said, "Hey, I want in, too." Rather, the encroachment began with certain male scholars being granted special passes enabling them to waltz right over the ramparts of feminist discourse. Consciousness-raising efforts by feminists in the seventies had been successful to a certain extent, particularly within the walls of academe. Many male professors found themselves moving through training exercises, from emotional sympathy with the feminist cause, to intellectual recognition of its importance, to a high degree of dogmatic understanding and expression. (Ironically, all this progress led to some confusion among the feminists.)

I, myself, stumbled through these training exercises. At Boston University in the mid-eighties, a female colleague once wondered why I wasn't doing a segment on feminist ethics in my Humanities 202 (History of Ethics) course. I did not have an answer for her, so I made something up like, "I don't have room in my syllabus." In truth, back then I felt that my gender denied me the legitimacy to teach feminist ethics. Moreover, I did not know very much about feminist ethics since I had concluded it was "out of bounds." The result: my students would graduate without knowing anything about this profound addition to contemporary intellectual culture. Fortunately, my colleague's arguments won out the following year, and I taught, with some dread and anxiety, a week-long segment on "feminist ethics."

This experience led me to question whether feminism was qualitatively different from other "isms." For instance, do you have to be a marxist to teach marxism, an existentialist to teach existentialism? Most importantly, do you have to be a humanist to teach humanism? To a degree, I think the answer is yes. Even when playing devil's advocate, the professor should always feel a part of what he or she teaches, a part of the so-called "truths" that are often cavalierly thrown out there.

At present, feminist criticism is no longer a marginalized discourse domiciled in an outbuilding on the academic terrain. In the last decade it has finally earned respectable housing on the main campus. The battle of the genders, not as intense as heretofore, has been absorbed into a larger battle softly raging between the right and left. From the right's perspective, feminists are not as threatening as the engulfing group of gays, marxists, deconstructionists, or culture critics with whom they associate. Perhaps the right, in regard to feminism, has merely acquiesced to the facts that are no longer in their favor: the English profession is more female dominated, at conferences and in publication; the Modern Language Association consistently reports more women receiving doctorates than men.

Yet the bothersome question remains: should I have felt displaced when students declared me a feminist? Can a male actually practice feminist criticism? (The question makes me think of Spike Lee's assertion that only a black man could properly direct a film about Malcolm X.)

And the question itself causes men to feel cheated. After years spent learning to view culture from the perspective of women (who have been largely left out of literary history), years spent analyzing the role of women in every book they teach, male professors no longer want to be messengers of feminist lore, no longer want to be told by feminists, "listen to what we say, but don't try and make it up yourself." (It is, of course, somewhat ironic that the territorial feminists are the ones who feel threatened and the masculists the ones who feel unsatisfied.)

An ancillary problem for feminist scholars is the issue of "theory," which they fought to keep out of feminist criticism. Theory itself has long been considered by feminists as a historical male fetish (never mind non-theoretical critics such as Dryden, Johnson, and Arnold). Feminist dread of men hoisting an umbrella theory over their feminist camp has caused a leading feminist critic, Elaine Showalter, to assert (at an MLA convention several years ago) that feminist criticism is indeed in crisis. Showalter admitted that she does not know where the answer lies. (When pushed, she confessed her desire to abandon criticism altogether in favor of writing fiction, perhaps a novel, she said, modelled on the splendid academic satires of British writer and scholar David Lodge.)

If literary feminism is in crisis, renegade anti-feminist scholars such as Camille Paglia have only complicated the problem and furthered the divisions, the result being that feminist academics cannot agree on any unified political dogma. Meanwhile, any continued effort to segregate themselves will undoubtedly result in new labels, such as using the term "femenist" to describe male practitioners of feminism.

In the classroom, of course, male professors are free to teach from any perspective they wish, without the threat of feminists bursting in to admonish, "Watch what you're saying there, Mister!" But this does not mean that students will understand the professor's political intent. For instance, when I recently tried to argue (in a Contemporary Political Novel class) a feminist perspective on *Waiting for the Barbarians*, a novel by the acclaimed South African writer J. M. Coetzee, students were clearly confused. After all, the novel was not only written by a male, it was about politics and state terrorism. What did this have to do with feminism?

Yet, Coetzee's little masterpiece includes, for instance, a climactic scene in which the protagonist, an aged magistrate of an outpost on the fringes of the Empire, is hung by his arms from a tree while wearing only a woman's smock. Through his cathartic experience, the magistrate gradually understands that his guilt regarding the exploitation of the so-called Barbarians (the indigenous desert-folk) is no different than his guilt regarding his personal exploitation of women (particularly with a blinded Barbarian girl). Thus, his hanging from the tree unites the book's political and sexual arguments.

The truth is, one doesn't need a book by a woman in order to teach feminist issues. Almost any book will do. Great works in the patriarchal tradition—Homer and Chaucer, for instance—can produce profound feministic insights. Moreover, the ability to interpret through a feminist lens should be a capacity all professors share; utilizing feminist interpretive skills should go hand in hand with other pedagogical skills.

The fundamental truth behind any feminism/masculism debate is that men and women need to behave differently to each other than they have in the past. As William Blake argued in his poetic chastisement of Milton (for Milton's misunderstanding of women), the key is imagination. We have to imagine other possibilities for the opposite gender, as well as for our own. In this sense, feminism is not so much a gender-specific word as it is an opposing philosophy to masculinism, or to the unquestioned belief in male hegemony simply because it has existed for as long as anyone can remember.

For such imaginative regeneration to take place within the halls of academe, literary feminism can no longer be limited to women. Male colleagues must be trusted to teach these ideas, despite the fact that they obviously lack the "experience" of being female.

Meanwhile, as I teach my British Romanticism courses, including samples from practically unheard-of women poets such as Jane Taylor and Charlotte Smith, I expect it will just be a matter of time before some student exclaims: "Hey, you're a feminist!"

I look forward to the day when such proclamations are no longer necessary.

Journal's Mission

Sexuality & Culture is a forum for the discussion and analysis of ethical, cultural, psychological, social, and political issues related to sexual relationships and sexual behavior. These issues include—but are not limited to: sexual consent and sexual responsibility; sexual harassment and freedom of speech and association; sexual privacy; censorship and pornography; impact of film/literature on sexual relationships; and university and governmental regulation of intimate relationships, such as interracial relationships and student-professor relationships.

Open discussion of material published in the journal is encouraged. Comments may be submitted via electronic mail to *case@csulb.edu* and will be posted on the journal's web site (http://www.csulb.edu/~asc/journal.html) or published in the next issue of the journal.

Submissions

All manuscripts will be reviewed by two or more members of the editorial board or qualified *ad hoc* reviewers. Articles will be accepted in three categories:

- *Theoretical Articles* are articles based on logical argumentation and literature review.
- *Empirical Articles* are articles that describe the results of experiments or surveys on the ethical, cultural, psychological, social, or political implications of sexual behavior.
- *Book Reviews* are critical reviews of published books or videotapes whose contents are pertinent to the journal's mission.

Manuscripts should conform generally to the APA style (*Publication Manual of the American Psychological Association*, Washington, DC, 1994). Briefly, manuscripts should be double spaced and should include a summary of approximately 200 words. Empirical articles should include standard sections (Introduction, Methods, Results, and Discussion). Citations should be in the author-year format (e.g.: Smith, 1998). All cited sources must be listed in alphabetical order at the end of the manuscript (including authors, article title, full journal name, year, volume, and pages). Four copies of the manuscript should be submitted to the Managing Editor:

Dr. Roberto Refinetti
Sexuality & Culture
504 Lake Colony Drive
Birmingham, AL 35242
(*e-mail: refinetti@msn.com*)

Submission of a manuscript implies that the same manuscript is not currently under consideration by another journal. After the manuscript is accepted for publication, authors will be requested to provide an electronic copy of the final manuscript either as a disk file or as an e-mail transmission. Copyright will be transferred to the publisher.

Subscriptions

Sexuality & Culture is published by Transaction Publishers, 35 Berrue Circle, Piscataway, NJ 08854-8042 (*Phone*: 732-445-2280, *Fax*: 732-445-3138). Publication frequency is one issue per year (*Volume 2* in 1998). Issues may be purchased separately or by subscription at $24.95 per issue. Shipping costs are added to orders from outside the United States ($8 surface, $16 air mail).